Dearest Binnie,

with much lov

Elspeth

22nd September 2013

LIFE'S ENCHANTED CUP

"Granny Dot" — as Vicky now refers to her, lived in such a fascinating and changing era. She was Vicky's Great Great Grandmother.

MYSELF, WHEN YOUNG, WITH CECILIA

LIFE'S ENCHANTED CUP

AN AUTOBIOGRAPHY

(1872—1933)

by

MRS. C. S. PEEL, O.B.E.

WITH 11 ILLUSTRATIONS

LONDON
JOHN LANE THE BODLEY HEAD LIMITED

First published in 1933

Printed in Great Britain by Western Printing Services Ltd., Bristol.

TO

CECILIA

Within my earthly temple there's a crowd,
There's one that's humble, one that's proud,
There's one that's broken-hearted for his sins,
And one, who unrepentant, sits and grins,
There's one who loves his neighbour as himself,
And one who cares for naught but fame and pelf—
From much corroding care would I be free,
If once I could determine which is me?

EDWARD SANDFORD MARTIN.

16, MONTPELIER PLACE,
   THE HAMLET OF KNIGHTSBRIDGE,
      LONDON, S.W.7.
March, 1933.

CONTENTS

PAGE

CHAPTER I

The end of the World—An earthquake—When my father was a giant and a bear—Her hair made a tent—A country house in 1872—The Duke and the Duchess—A new little sister—The people who walked on their heads—The sea serpent—The losing and the finding of a seal 3

CHAPTER II

Looking for adventure—I run away again—A painful lesson——Five years old and a partner in sin—My Aunts and their establishment—Visiting the respectable poor—When Income Tax was 3d. in the £—Say ninety-nine—A room of my own—Playing whist in the middle of the night!—A little grey, long-haired, bone-gnawing saint—My Creed at seven years old—We leave Wyesham 14

CHAPTER III

We arrive at Clifton—The navvy who drank soup—She had murdered her baby—The new house—The first bathroom I had ever seen—We go to school—Clean, tidy, ladylike and very plain—Education in the 'seventies—The school concert—Life in a mid-Victorian vicarage—Half a crown a week to give up witchcraft—The village poor 27

CHAPTER IV

The books of my youth—Storing the mind with beauty—Studying "Art"—Admirers—That humiliating ball—My conduct had been "marked"—"It was God's will"—Religion as it was taught to me—We did not powder our noses then—Bustles—On being a nice girl—It was anxious work being "nice" in the days of my youth 39

CHAPTER V

Young girls in the 'eighties—Pinning up improper pages—Tennis parties—Temperance Meetings—The murderous footman—A Sunday school class—My ancestry—Brave Jane Lane—Anne Hyde, Duchess of York—A striking likeness—I visit London—A brave and good woman—We did not walk alone—Out of the brougham stepped a stout, dignified gentleman, the Prince of Wales—The murder in the shocking street—We leave Clifton—A summing up 48

PAGE

CHAPTER VI

I come out—What we wore and how we behaved—"God knows I never wish that time back again," said the Queen—Visiting the rich and great—At Twickenham—How odd to earn money—I become engaged—The *Queen* Newspaper—*Hearth and Home* and *Woman*—"Why do you not learn to write?" asked Arnold Bennett—Women would not trouble to learn their job, said he—Three-quarters of an author's business could be learned—Twelve miles from a s-s-s-shop—Writers of renown —When George Moore's books were terribly shocking—Lady Duff Gordon and Mrs. Elinor Glyn—A wedding outfit—Mothers-in-law and marriage   57

CHAPTER VII

At Dewsbury—Pigs begin to scream—Three widely different worlds—The artistic London world, the manufacturing town world, the country house world—Jacob and John Bright—Down a coal mine—Country Squiredom—The parties of that day—Country houses—The host ate some more rice pudding—Mrs. Town Councillor gave a high tea party—"You do see life in a bar"—"Love don't last, comfort does" said the pretty horse-breaker   71

CHAPTER VIII

Life in Notting Dale—A horrid story—The memory of a brave and kind woman—Happy-go-lucky and sane—We take a flat—Ellen goes mad—Albert Charles Alexander, what chance in life had he?—Alice, a girl like a Persian kitten—We go to Teneriffe—The Dragon tree—Oh! that enchanted time—A Gaiety girl—The *Poulet Marengo* was cooking   .   .   .   83

CHAPTER IX

London in the 'nineties—Dress—Society—Habits and customs —The early days of the motor—Bloomers and bicycles—At Hurlingham and Ranelagh—They ran pell-mell to see an aeroplane—The Season—Mrs. Grundy—Bridge—"You are requested not to sta-r-r-e at the King"—We were more ignorant then—The Oscar Wilde case—The Beardsley Period—An illogical standard of morality—Drawing-rooms and Courts—Her Majesty Queen Victoria—Her Majesty Queen Alexandra—Her Majesty Queen Mary   94

CHAPTER X

We move to Chelsea—A nurse who was too kind—" 10/- a head for House Books "—Edwardian extravagance—The cost of living—" My husband is a disagreeable, greedy man "—

In Paris—Clothes, food and night life—The Empire Promenade—Monte Carlo in the 'nineties—" Can't we meet again? " he asked—£1,000 in his boots—It was a good day, that . . 111

CHAPTER XI

A wonderful " buy "—Brompton Square—Life in the early 'nineties—Prices—When Income Tax was 1/- in the £—The Coronation of King Edward—Unexpected guests—A Suffrage debate—A trio of Women's papers—The Hat Shop—Odd customers—" Dear me and why not ? " said the lady, blandly —Miss Ellen Terry buys a hat—The Merry Widow Model —How the working girl lived—They liked to make expensive hats—Hypnotised by clothes—Writing novels—Fallen girls—But it is hard for men too 123

CHAPTER XII

Operations were different then—Sir William Watson Cheyne —Sir Thomas Parkinson—The Lister technique—It was quiet and comfortable being dead—" Come back, come back," he cried—Wintering in Switzerland—The Children's Commonwealth—They sent themselves to school—God knows what were the memories of that child—The age of consent—Modern Babylon—Oh happy days—The tragedy of Miss Lucy . . 138

CHAPTER XIII

When Edward was King—His death and funeral—The Suffragettes must " pester and be patient "—Lady Constance Lytton—When the ladies appeared the gentlemen sang, shouted, jostled and threw mud—Hence the sheep—In Holloway Prison —Girls' Borstal—She was mad with jealousy and distress— Education—Bridge and Bridge Clubs—The lucky day—A salary of £700—Winning the Derby at 100 to 1—Intuitions— At Monte Carlo and at Aix les Bains 149

CHAPTER XIV

Belgian, French, German and English—" And perhaps they will not be there "—We sell our house—The murder of the Austrian Archduke and Duchess—The Suffragettes try to petition the King—Trouble in Ireland—War looms large—War is declared—People fear for their food—Working parties— Prices—The Moratorium—The grocer lends me £3—Yet another home—The Soldiers' and Sailors' Wives Club—Gentle, mousey looking and middle aged—The *Lusitania* riots—A war party—War songs—National War Savings—War changes our lives—Munition workers—Canteens—Smart to be shabby— Coal shortage—Begging a lump here and there—The knitting mania—Eat, drink and be merry, for to-morrow . . . ? . 162

PAGE

CHAPTER XV

Board of Agriculture or Ministry of Food?—Mrs. Pember Reeves—" Round about a £1 a week "—Furniture suitable to our position—Voluntary food economy—So little sugar, so little fat and that horrible cocoa butter—Some humorous stories —A speaking campaign—How different some men are—The odd ways of Chairmen—" Some of 'em 'ad a bit o' muck ready in their pockets "—" I like to feel a bit between me and them 'planes," said he—The great daylight raid—The airyplanes amused baby very much—A woman's head came rolling towards him—They gathered on the kitchen stairs—The raid night novel —Sheltering in the Tube—Food meetings in theatres—What the children thought about it—Food economy and patent shoes —A desirably dowdy appearance—From Plymouth to New-castle and 176 meetings 182

CHAPTER XVI

Southampton Dockyard—I am sent to France—To the War in a Pulman—Boulogne in War time—In Paris—At the Citroën Works—Perfect organisation—2,700 to *déjeuner*—The Renault Restaurant—Introducing oatmeal porridge—From Paris to the Front—Where the Uhlans came—Tragedy and Comedy—A large pink pig—They looked like pantomime rats —A treeless desert—In the town of Ham—Like a deserted theatre—Stones and dust and weeds and rusted wire—And so back to Paris 204

CHAPTER XVII

The end of voluntary rationing—Tea with Lord Northcliffe —He asks me to go to America with the American Mission— The *Daily Mail* Food Bureau—£20 a week to stick up envelopes —I edit the Woman's Page—The summer and autumn of 1918— The Armistice—A wheezy old gramophone played " God Save the King "—" Have we won the War ? " roared the crowd— " Yes, we've won the War "—One of the grimmest tragedies of Peace—Lord Northcliffe and *The Times*—" They were born in the Ark and they are still in the Ark "—Nagger in Chief—When all the people turned up and nothing happened—The interests of women, *vide* the *Daily Mail*—Writing leaders—The 1920 Husband hunt—There are drawbacks to being a woman—Not a normal woman—Tea at Printing House Square—" I am sorry. I am very sorry," said Lord Northcliffe and tears were running down his face—I walked down Wimpole Street thinking that my day was done—The Insulin treatment for diabetes was dis-covered 218

CONTENTS

CHAPTER XVIII

A wedding with cakes and cream—Mr. and Mrs. Walter Page, Cabbages and Carnations—In a nursing home—Dreams—In Bavaria—What German ladies said about the War—In Germany, Italy and France—The housing question—How some of us live —The baby in the chest of drawers—Why did they not use the bath? Ah! Why!—Women's Pioneer Housing—The Peckham Health Centre—A thrilling experiment—Stowe Palace becomes a Public School—The domestic servant problem—She threatened to shoot me *dead*—In Venice—The tragedy at Domo d'Ossola—I see Sir Henry Wilson murdered—The General Strike—People who make revolutions—" A Hundred Wonderful Years "—" How We Lived Then "—Husband and wife in partnership—" The Stream of Time."   233

CHAPTER XIX

Sixty years of change—Weaving the world together—The downfall of the aristocracy of Birth and Wealth—Education, Insurance and Amenities—Dishonesty—Well-to-do squalor— Bad manners—Changes in the life of the educated classes—Less ceremony—Bed and breakfast houses—Birth control—A new standard of morality—Men in my youth—Women become citizens—How changes come—What lies before us?—How strange are human beings—Reflections—Beautiful places, interesting people and Parties—Why fear old age or death?—Age brings freedom—If I had my life to live over again?   .   .   256

INDEX   ·   275

LIST OF ILLUSTRATIONS

MYSELF WHEN YOUNG, WITH CECILIA   - - *Frontispiece*

FACING PAGE

A FAMILY GROUP IN THE LATE 'SIXTIES   - - - 20

BRAVE JANE LANE - - - - - - - - 52

THE EYES OF HEROD, *by Aubrey Beardsley* - - - 104

A LUCKY "BUY" - - - - - - - - 124

DOROTHY C. PEEL, 1917 - - - - - - 178

THE THREE FOOD CONTROLLERS - - - - - 200

LORD NORTHCLIFFE - - - - - - - 230

LIFE'S ENCHANTED CUP

CHAPTER I

The end of the world—An earthquake—When my father was a giant
and a bear—Her hair made a tent—A country house in 1872—
The Duke and the Duchess—A new little sister—The people
who walked on their heads—The sea serpent—The losing and
the finding of a seal.

M Y first memory is of the end of the world. It
happened in this way. We, that is Carli, Hugh,
Dick, myself and the baby, shepherded by
Manie, our Spanish nurse, and a nursery maid, were
taking our afternoon airing in fields through which flowed
the river Wye, when suddenly the air became still and the
light faded. As a clock stops, so the world stopped. Then
as suddenly as the stillness had begun so it ended. A wild
wind blew, the trees lashed about, a cloud of dust flew up
from the path, the river, now a deep steel colour, was
whipped into waves, a streak of flame lit the darkened sky,
thunder rolled and clashed and there came a hissing fury
of rain.

Manie, who had snatched the baby from the perambulator and with her disengaged hand was alternately
crossing herself and the child, and with her first and little
fingers outstretched making the sign which protects from
the evil eye, shrieked and jabbered in her mother tongue.

"It's the end of the world," blubbered Jane, the nursery
maid, with none of the fear and fury of Manie but with
the dull resignation which was her armour against a life
made up of workhouse, other people's children and head
nurses.

3   B

Carli and Hugh, who were brave people, remained outwardly calm; Dick, who at that period was a bawler, bawled; I, feeling perplexed and frightened, excited and interested, observed; and the baby slept.

Then, when we were wet through, so wet that the rain squelched about in our boots, the wind ceased to blow, the rain stopped, the clouds cleared, the sun shone.

I, Dot, aged nearly four, had seen the end of one world and now a new world had begun.

In the drawing-room before bedtime I told my Mother that I had seen the end of the world and it had made a great noise. "Not the end of the world, my dear, but a thunderstorm."

I had already learned from experience that grown-up people were like that; they flattened everything.

"You see, it could not have been the end of the world because here we all are just as usual," she continued; and added, "And now, Dot dear, it's bedtime."

I did not argue. I knew that I had seen the end of one world and the beginning of a new world. And if I did not see it then, at all events I have lived to see the end of one civilisation and the beginning of another.

. . . . . .

My next memory is of an earthquake.

By this time I was over four years old, and we had come to live at a house called Wyesham in Monmouthshire. Running into the garden one morning I saw the earthquake happen. A piece of the lawn subsided, leaving a hole ever so deep; so deep that had I stood in it there would have been a good six inches of hole beyond the top of my head. I was deliciously frightened and rushed away, shrieking for Dick. Dick came and distrusted the earthquake. "Perhaps it'll get bigger and bigger and deeper and deeper and swallow everything up. You're not to go near it and I shall tell Mummie."

So Mummie was told and she told Paito—the name we called our father—and both came to look. The gardener, Bellingham, a silent man rather like a mole but with a beard of a kind known as a Newgate Fringe, came too. None of them was in the least excited. My mother said, "Not an earthquake, Dot, only a little earth fallen in."

But *I* knew that it was an earthquake. I had heard my elder sister's governess tell her about an earthquake . . . the ground fell in. The ground *had* fallen in, I had seen it fall in. I was willing to admit that my earthquake was not a very large one, but it was large enough to have swallowed me and large enough to frighten Dick. Undoubtedly it was an earthquake.

.   .   .   .   .   .

At this period my father, after a long illness brought on by sunstroke contracted in Canada while serving with his regiment, was Adjutant of the Monmouthshire Volunteers. He was a tall man, six foot two in his socks, and when dressed in a black—or was it a very dark green?—uniform with a wide cross belt of black patent leather, silver badges, and a shako with a tall plume, was a noticeable figure.

I do not remember him in any other clothes and I was convinced that he was a giant, though whether it was a glory or a shame to be a giant, I was not certain. In story books it was shameful to be a giant, yet in real life, everyone touched his hat or curtsied to "the Captain" and seemed very pleased to see him.

But stay, I do remember him not as a giant, but as a bear. When he was a bear he wore what was called a *couvre-pied*, made of yellow and green wool crocheted in

5

LIFE'S ENCHANTED CUP

stripes, crawled about on his hands and knees and growled.
He frightened both Dick and me terribly, though we never
said so. We tried to play at bears with spirit and woke in
the night believing that at last he really had become a bear,
like the Dancing Bear which came shambling up the drive
one day, wearing a large muzzle, and danced a mournful,
grotesque measure in front of the hall door. My mother
kept saying, "Poor thing, poor thing," fed it with bread
and sugar and gave it water to drink, while its brown-faced
brigandish-looking owner sat drinking coffee and eating
bread and meat.

My mother I remember as a dark, handsome, plump
woman, in voluminous mauve muslin, much bunched out
at the back and made with a train. She had a large chignon
and did not need any pads or puffs to bring it to the fashionable dimensions for when sitting at her dressing-table
her hair flowed in a thick curtain to the floor, so enabling
me to play at living in a tent.

I remember, too, that the smooth, parted front hair was
"bandolined" with a stick of some white greasy composition
which smelled nice and tasted nasty.

Although it is manifestly impossible that my father
should have alternated between wearing uniform and a
green and yellow *couvre-pied*, and that my mother should
have dressed exclusively in mauve muslin, those are the
only clothes in which I remember them until after we had
left Wyesham.

The house I can recall in detail. It must have been a
charming little country house and unusual in design. A
straight drive led to a carriage sweep and from the hall
door a wide passage led to the inner hall. This passage
was remarkable because on the right hand side were two
dark, low apertures with rounded ceilings, where bears lived.

6

In the front of these were stored the box which contained the croquet set, baskets, gardening tools, hanks of bass and pails full of eggs in lime water (waterglass was then unknown). The bears slept in the dark depths of these caverns by day and came out at night. Dick knew this and so did I, but no one else knew it or no doubt they would have removed the bears, though after witnessing my mother's kindness to the dancing bear, I doubted that. The bears were quite harmless by day but might be very dangerous at night, for then they *might* climb the stairs though we did not really believe that they would.

At the end of the bears' passage, to the left of the inner hall was an ante-room and a drawing-room, in which was a davenport, that is, a kind of writing-table, my mother's sofa, the home of the *couvre-pied* when it was not being a bear, a piano, a harp, a guitar, a violoncello which my father played well, a gilt wicker stand full of flowering plants, some china (which I now know was Worcester) in a glass-fronted cupboard, and some other china mounted on velvet stands, which hung upon the walls together with water-colour sketches of foreign scenes.

The curtains were of chintz with wide pink and green stripes and a pattern of pink and white oleanders and humming birds. There were books, including a "Sunday book" with fine engravings. One picture of Abraham about to kill with a large knife, a much bound Isaac, while a ram struggled in a thicket, made me hate that book with a smouldering red-feeling hatred.

It was no comfort to be told that in the end it was the ram that was sacrificed, that dear little curly-horned ram which had done no harm to anyone. I verily believe that it was that picture which gave me such a distaste for sacrifices as later made me refuse to remain in the fold of a Faith

7

which—so I understood—approved of the sacrifice of the innocent for the sake of the guilty. A door in which were narrow panels of red and blue glass opened from the drawing-room into the garden, where tall lilies grew. To me they were lily trees, and I loved to walk through an avenue of them, now and then holding up a gentle finger to touch their yellow-dusted anthers.

Lilies and tulips are the only flowers I remember. Of the tulips I do not like to think; they are connected with an atrocious deed. One day having been sent to play in the garden, I picked every one of the tulip buds, fat, pale green buds waiting to unfold.

On the other side of the hall was a short flight of wide, shallow stairs leading to the dining-room, to the baize door behind which were the kitchen premises, and to the front stairs. On the next floor were bedrooms and nurseries and another baize door, through which one reached the servant's rooms (we did not talk about "maids" then) and the back stairs.

Servants in houses such as ours worked harder than they do now and their wages were lower. Our cook earned £20 a year, the house-parlourmaid £18, the nurse £22, while the gardener's daughter was content to sew all day for 2/- and some food. When there was a party a woman from the village came for 1/6 a day and food, to help in the kitchen and pantry.

Our nurse, for Spanish Manie had now returned to her own country whence she had come with Carli and Hugh from Gibraltar, was called Nurse or occasionally Nursie dear. Her ideas differed somewhat from those of my mother, for when Paito and Mummie paid short visits to neighbouring houses, as they did now and again, Nurse would entertain a gentleman friend named Paul whom I loved passionately, almost as passionately as Nurse loved him, I think. Then the day came when Paul went for a soldier and after a long absence returned, wearing a beautiful uniform, his hair brushed up into a "quiff," a hat like a pill box on the side of his head, and a little cane in his hand.

My parents were away and Bellingham was at his dinner so Nurse and Paul lifted me over the locked gate of the kitchen garden and ate fruit which I brought to them and then bribed me with three peppermint lozenges decorated with pink hearts and mottos, to stay quietly in the nursery like a good little girl with the baby, who was having her sleep, and Jenny, the nursery dog. Becoming tired of this occupation, I wandered out, looking into various rooms and at things in them. In one I saw something which surprised me. I thought Nurse and Paul were being very rude. Offended I returned to the nursery and decided to ignore the matter. Nurse also ignored it, as long as she was able, and then departed weeping, poor lass. People did not look upon unmarried mothers with so lenient an eye then as they came to do during the War. They called them by harsh names. I feel sure, however, that my mother, though she might speak severely, did what she could for Nursie, for she was a woman with a pitying heart.

Another and older Nurse appeared, of whom I remember little, and life continued to be full of interesting events.

One afternoon the grandees in excelsis of the neighbourhood, the Duke and Duchess, came to call. We were at tea in the nursery and were allowed to leave the table and look out of the window to see a gentleman with a hooked nose and dyed side whiskers driving four beautiful horses. A lady sat by him, and two grooms, who sat on a back seat, their arms folded, sprang to the ground as the equipage drew up at the front door and stood at the horses' heads. There was a short parley with our awe-stricken parlourmaid; then one of the grooms procured a ladder from the back of the coach. The Duke climbed down it, the Duchess did likewise, the Duke holding his Duchess's skirts decorously round her ankles, and they went into the house. They stayed but a short time, and then returned with my father and mother. There was a tossing of horses' heads, a jangling of bits; one horse ventured to rear and was smacked on his shining shoulder by a scandalised groom. The Duke gathered up the reins, the Duchess smiled at the nursery window, the horses bounded forward, the grooms ran back and climbed into their places, folded their arms and stiffened into immobility. In a moment this exciting vision had passed.

Dukes and Duchesses are useful people. Our servants liked them to visit us; it cast reflected glory upon them. Many years after my mother told me that she had then been battling with a house-parlourmaid who had fixed and peculiar ideas about laying the table. After the coming of their Graces she accepted my mother's criticisms in a meek spirit. Ladies upon whom Duchesses called certainly must know how to lay dinner tables.

Before we came to Wyesham, the baby who had slept throughout the ending of the world had died, but by the time that I was four and a bit, there was another. I was taken to see my mother and the new baby sister. Strange to say, my mother at eleven o'clock in the morning was still in bed and so was the lazy little sister, who turned out to be a bundle of flannel with a red face and blinking kitten-blue eyes. I felt a furious hatred flare up in me. "Slap her, slap her, slap her," I cried, and would have done so myself had I not been restrained by a starched, rustling person, who I was afterwards told was my mamma's nurse.

LIFE'S ENCHANTED CUP

My poor mother, as I learned later, wanted another
baby no more than I did, though when it was there she loved
it, but she did not live long enough to know how good a
citizen she had given to the world.   It was her ninth child
and before and during each confinement she suffered much.

There were now five children alive and it was evident
that my father's health would not permit him to remain in
the Army.   He had been a keen soldier on the threshold
of a successful career, and now it was ended.

The children's education was beginning to cost a considerable sum and would cost more . . . the income would
lessen when his Adjutancy terminated.   No wonder my
father looked anxious and my mother sighed.

Hugh was now at school, Carli went to art, dancing and
music classes in Monmouth and studied with my father.
Master and pupil were mutually devoted and he took great
interest in her vivid, unfolding intelligence.   My mother,
I think, taught Dick and me to read and write and say our
tables, but I have no recollection of this stage of my education.   Nurse's attention was chiefly taken up by the baby
so Dick and I had the run of the garden, shrubbery and
paddock.

We played exciting games.   On Wednesday and Saturday afternoons, Thursday and Sunday being clean clothes
days, we set out to sea in washing-tubs on a shallow muddy
duck pond.   On other days we dug in our garden, our
ambition being to dig a hole so deep that through it we
might pour water on the heads of the people who lived on
the other side of the world.   We imagined that heads
being heavier than feet, they must walk on their heads,
otherwise they would fall off.   Never by any chance did
we garden in our garden.

Sometimes my father and Carli would take us for walks

by the river and there one afternoon, having loitered behind, Dick saw the sea serpent. The Wye was in flood and there was the sea serpent swirling down the stream, sometimes one part of it and sometimes another rearing out of the water, a terrifying sight indeed. Dick, who knew that sea serpents were evil, bellowed. His fright gaining force as he lost control of himself, soon the whole valley rang with his cries. Paito and Carli returned at the run. Dick was incapable of speech. I, terrified, could only point down the river and stammer that Dick had seen the sea-sea-sea-serpent. As usual, we were not allowed to see what we had seen. The sea serpent was the trunk of a tree.

Dick was an imaginative, nervous little boy who suffered tortures, many times of his own invention. A few days after seeing the sea serpent he began to bellow again. This time he had the plague; there were spots under his arms. He would shortly be d-d-d-dead. So ill did the child appear that the doctor was sent for, a kind horsey man who always had a drop at the end of his beaky nose. It was exciting as he counted one's pulse to watch whether the drop would drop before he had finished. The doctor calmed the patients fears and elicited the fact that he had been reading a book about the Plague, and had then proceeded to have the Plague.

Other exciting days were those on which my mother lost and found a seal. This seal, it appears, had belonged to her father, Mr. Robert Peel, then dead, and she valued it greatly. Later I asked Carli what a seal was, and she, forgetting our mother's seal, said, "Oh, a nice sleek thing with flappers and whiskers and lovely bulgy brown eyes." It sounded most attractive. I did hope my mother's seal would be found, but felt puzzled and annoyed that she had been able to keep it so securely hidden that none of us had seen it. We should have enjoyed the seal.

A few Sundays after that, the family set out for church, as all respectable families did in those days. Church itself was dull, but the walk there was exciting because we went through a field and over the river in a ferry boat.

Paito, Mummie, Carli, Hugh, Dick, if he did not have a sufficiently convincing Sunday pain, and I, all washed and combed and clad in our Sunday best, carrying Prayer Books and with collection pennies in our pockets, sat in two pews. We listened to a wheezing harmonium played by Bella Bellingham, to whose rather erratic accompaniment her father—the clerk besides being our gardener—and various other people sang, or at any rate made some sort of noise. On the way home, when nearing the gate in the field which led into the road, my mother suddenly stooped, picked up something, and exclaimed, "Oh, Richard, I have found my seal."

How disappointing life can be, and sometimes is. The seal was a tiny thing not more than three inches long, made of ebony and agate, engraved with a crest on which was a lion holding a shuttle, emblem of her cotton-spinning family's wealth.

CHAPTER II

Looking for adventure—I run away again—A painful lesson—
Five years old and a partner in sin—My aunts and their establishment—Visiting the respectable poor—When Income Tax was
3d. in the £—Say ninety-nine—A room of my own—Playing
whist in the middle of the night!—A little, grey, long-haired,
bone-gnawing saint—My Creed at seven years old—We leave
Wyesham.

A S the months passed, life became less exciting. Dick,
sick with apprehension, went away to a preparatory
school, kept by two spinster ladies at Hereford.
Carli, now a grown-up thirteen, had lately been confirmed and photographed in a white dress with a full
tucked skirt and a veil. Her hair was smoothly parted and
tightly plaited in two braids which were looped up and tied
with a white ribbon. I doubt if this was fashionable; my
mother preferred her daughters to be neat rather than
modish. She was seated on a low chair with a curly
mahogany frame upholstered in wriggly patterned velvet,
against a wooded background with a rustic stile in the
middle distance, and held a Prayer Book in a hand which
was slightly out of focus.

Naturally a person of her consequence could not be
bothered with me, and the new baby, now three, was as
little use to me as I was to Carli. It seemed necessary then
to look for adventure outside the home. To find it I ran
away to a farm about a mile off. I had been there in the pony
carriage with my mother when distributing the Parish
Magazine, and I had liked the farmer's wife very much.

She called me Missie and gave me cake. On this occasion a turkey cock barred the way. He gobbled and looked proud and fierce and I feared and hated him. Just at the right moment, however, the farmer's wife came out, flapped her apron at the turkey which shrank into a mere cowardly fowl, and asked how little Missie came to be all by herself. I explained and she invited me to enter. She gave me milk and cake, let me help to put the eggs away and to skim some cream, and showed me a shell box with looking-glass inside the lid, and set a musical box playing. Time flew and I had decided to live at the farm for the rest of my life when the pony carriage appeared with a stern-looking Mummie in it. The farmer's wife had betrayed me and sent a boy running to acquaint my family of my whereabouts. To bed, supperless. Next time I would run further, I decided.

Choosing an afternoon when everyone seemed occupied, I set off, and, in spite of meeting some large red cows, safely reached the toll gates at the entrance to Monmouth Bridge. There on the right was a shop where bacon and candles, lilac print and string, postage stamps and lollipops were sold. The woman who kept it knew me well and made no bones about selling me a paper screwfull of black and white striped bulls-eyes. "Them's tuppence, my dear." When I admitted that I did not possess any money she smiled a toothless smile and supposed my Mamma would pay for 'em the nex' time she came along. Sucking a bulls-eye, I wondered what next, and decided to visit the field where the Volunteers drilled, which was near by. True, my father might be there, but if so I planned to hide in the hedge so that he should not see me.

Drill, however, was over, but though the Captain had departed, the Colonel had remained. He saw me and told one of the men to pick me up and put me on his horse, laughed a good deal, gave me a shilling and in spite of all protests, trotted me home.

Again to bed supperless, and this time a whipping and a sermon about the iniquity of buying anything for which I could not pay. "But I have a big shilling, and a shilling is very rich; twelve whole pennies." "But you hadn't a shilling when you bought the bulls-eyes. You are a very naughty little girl. You must never buy anything for which you cannot pay. The shilling must be taken to pay for the bulls-eyes, and what is left must be given to some poor person."

That the shilling should be taken to pay for my sweets I could understand, but why was it just of Mummie to take my money and give it away when it was mine? It was not just. I raged inwardly, and would have raged outwardly if I had dared. So I learned that I must never buy what I could not pay for, but that the world in other ways was an unjust world.

That winter I went to a party at Courtfield, the home of a houseful of handsome young men of the Catholic faith. I fell in love with two of them, one being he who afterwards became the famous Father Bernard Vaughan, who preached at Farm Street on the Sins of Society, and who I afterwards met at a luncheon party when he had become a stout elderly gentleman. But what really mattered at the Courtfield party was that I disgraced myself at tea. My partner in sin was a chocolate eclair, a dainty new to me, which when bitten basely spat out custard. The custard dribbled all down my party frock, even on to my new blue ribbed silk sash with fringed ends, which came from Jolly's, of Bath.

I can feel now the sickening horror of that moment. Mummie mopped me rather fiercely. No wonder she was fierce, poor soul, for both frock and sash were new. Not even the appearance of a real live donkey with panniers full of presents quite consoled me. I felt utterly ashamed and convinced that everyone was looking at me and scorning me as a little girl who could not even eat her tea tidily.

Food often played me dreadful tricks, for at my first dinner party I cut off the top of an ice pudding and it went whizzing on to the floor and turned me from a pink and white girl in a white frock into a sort of shameful Mont Blanc of a person who would go through life labelled as the girl who did not know how to help herself to ice pudding.

Then came one of the great delights of our life. Our darling little Aunt Charlotte, our mother's eldest sister appeared in the brougham drawn by a large roan horse with a Roman profile, called Hector, who was driven by a crotchety, grey-faced, grey-whiskered coachman, wearing a cockaded hat and a sand-coloured livery coat with plated, crested buttons.

Aunt Charlotte was tiny and fair, with smoothly-parted hair, a bonnet, exquisite little kid boots, which she bought from a celebrated London bootmaker, and in winter a sealskin coat, in summer a silk jacket trimmed with lace and jet. And always she carried a sweet-smelling green Russian leather bag containing, amongst other things, a boxful of pink and white caraway comfits. And always she wore a rakish-looking eye glass firmly fixed in one of her pretty blue eyes.

Aunt Charlotte loved us all, but especially she loved Dick, because she understood his nervous unhappinesses better than most people. She was our mother's favourite sister and now she had come to luncheon and would stay for an early tea in order that Hector might be well rested for the return journey to Doward, where she lived with another married sister and brother-in-law.

She bore an invitation to us all to a Christmas party, and

a whole fortnight's visit for Dick and me. What joy, what excitement! When would the great day come? Is it the day we go to Doward, nurse? Will it be the day we go to Doward to-morrow, Mummie? At last the great day came, and there was a Christmas tree so tall that the fairy doll on the topmost branch touched the ceiling. Imagine that, it actually touched the ceiling!

Doward House was larger than Wyesham. It contained a hall, a drawing-room, a gun room, a library, a dining-room, an appropriate number of bedrooms, a workroom where we children ate our meals, and a store room.

Aunt Charlotte and Aunt Marianne were considerably older than my mother and, as was the custom of the day, dressed themselves as elderly women. Marianne had married, rather late in life, a kind, ginger-whiskered, sporting little man, younger than herself and a fine steeple-chase rider. Memory shows him to me dressed in cord breeches and gaiters, a black and white check tweed coat, and a square-shaped hard felt hat. Aunt Charlotte loved him, as she loved most people; but I am not sure that Aunt Marianne did. She was a tall, thin woman with a crooked mouth and dark wavy hair and she, like her sister, wore admirable boots. She spent most of the day in the garden, protected from the weather by a loose coat, a mushroom hat, generally tilted over one eye, galoshes and loose wash-leather gloves. She carried an alpenstock and there was always a hank of bass in the pocket of her blue check gardening apron. At most other times she sat retired in her own sitting-room. When going into the world she dressed remarkably well and was, I believe, something of a local personage. This aunt disliked children. Dick hated her and loved her little husband, but I decided to like her and, by dint of ignoring snubs, forced her into something like affection for

18

me, an affection influenced by my passion for her heart's delight, a wild-tempered Welsh pony which I would fearlessly feed. At Doward there was a cook, a between maid, and a housemaid, and a footman in a blue coat with plated buttons and a yellow and blue striped waistcoat.

Aunt Charlotte did the housekeeping and kept "a good table" consisting of excellent joints (the day of imported meat had scarcely dawned), large hams and tongues, Stilton cheese, trifle, meringues, delicious calves foot jelly and raised pork pies and curry made from jealously-guarded recipes.

I was allowed to visit the kitchen premises with her and to give out the stores. The store room was an earthly Paradise with cupboards full of jams and pickles, boxes of maccaroni and preserved fruits, bags full of rice and tapioca, blue-papered cones of sugar, chests of tea, cannisters of coffee, sardines, anchovies, soap, candles, string, brown paper, kitchen paper, stationery for the writing-tables, pens, pencils, boxes containing india-rubber bands, and a large pair of scales.

Stores were issued bi-weekly to the servants, and on a slate my aunt noted the orders which must be given to the trades-people. In this room were also hyacinth glasses, spare flower glasses, a bag of "black" which provided a mourning armband or a pair of bonnet strings or a child's sleeve ties for village families too poverty-stricken to purchase funeral garments. Here too were rolls of old linen, cotton wool and bottles containing household remedies for the sick poor.

Charlotte and Marianne did not visit the poor; they relied on the Vicar, a sad-mannered, elderly bachelor, who wore a badly-brushed top hat and a white tie, to recommend "suitable cases" for assistance. The "suitable cases" presented themselves at the back door, were interviewed by Charlotte in the servant's hall (a dreary room overlooking a shrubbery and furnished with a long table, some forms and one chair, sacred to the cook), and were suitably relieved.

My mother personally visited her "respectable poor," giving them much satisfaction by driving to see them. The sight of her pony carriage with the cockaded Bellingham standing at the pony's head gave a cachet to the visited, just as the visit of a Duke and a Duchess had given a cachet to us. She was a popular visitor because a truly interested one. Only in two ways did she fail. Inspect bad legs and view corpses she would not.

Sometimes I too visited the respectable poor, staring at the children who stared back at me, making friends with pussies and puppies, listening to big pink shells, gazing at daguerreotypes, funeral cards and family Bibles, and always hoping that this time we might visit the house where cats made of snail shells glued to a board covered by a piece of red flannel lived under a glass case, or if not, then that house where there were nine children and a board set up across the door to prevent the young ones from crawling into the road. Most of the cottages were dark because the windows were small, and were veiled with coarse Nottingham lace curtains and filled up with scraggy geraniums and other plants.

But to return to Doward. I knew that my aunts were very rich; they had their brougham, their wagonette and their high cart, used when the groom fetched the fish or the afternoon post by which the newspapers came, as well as Marianne's pony carriage and Uncle Edwin's hack. But it was not these possessions which impressed me. It was the fact that they dug their cheese with a scoop made of silver with a long ivory handle. It was my ambition to dig the

Charlotte   Marianne and Edwin   Susanna   Markey   Richard and Henrietta
            Scobell   holding   and Percy   Lane Bayliff and
                        Carli   Hart Dyke   ᵖenny, the nursery dog

A FAMILY GROUP IN THE LATE SIXTIES

The ladies are in mourning for their mother, Mrs. Robert Peel

cheese, and one day, hearing that Aunt Charlotte was going out to lunch and Uncle Edwin would be sitting on the Bench (whose bench I neither knew nor cared), I approached my Aunt Marianne and told her that I would have my dinner with her and dig the cheese. She looked at me from under her sideways-tilted hat, through her eye-glasses which sat crookedly upon her handsome nose, and replied mildly, "Well, if you must, you must." And so it was.

Dick was furious at being left to dine alone in the work-room, but protested that nothing would induce him to go near that beastly old woman. I was interested on that occasion to see on a tray on the sideboard a collection of jam pots. These were brought to my aunt, who placed in them helpings of roast mutton and vegetables. Paper covers bearing the names of the recipients were twisted over them, and later old men or women or small girls or boys, called for these dinners and took them away. I have since had reason to suppose that that lordly cheese scoop was supported upon an income of about £1,700 a year and that my parents income then amounted to £800 a year. The value of money was very different then and Income Tax but 3d. in the £. A fairly frequent visitor at Doward was a young bachelor who lived near by and imperilled his existence by driving a tandem. He was a plump young man, who wore tight clothes of a sporting cut and shone with soap and water, material plenty and mental satisfaction. I fell in love with him and he, touched by my adoring stares, took me for a drive in a high and shiny dog-cart. Sometimes the leader of his tandem would turn round and take a good stare at us and have to be straightened out by a tiny and agile groom, and sometimes he would rear. The wheeler, old, experienced and conscientious, just did what he ought to do, which I think was fortunate.

Only too soon Dick's holiday ended, and, accompanied by Aunt Charlotte and myself, the miserable child, wearing a suit the coat of which fastened right up under his Eton collar and the knickerbockers of which fell well below his knees, striped stockings, thick boots, dogskin gloves and a mortar board with a tassel, returned to the care of his school mistresses, first eating luncheon at "The Green Dragon," while Hector rested. This meal for Dick was a waste of money, for he was sick on the way back to school. The next day Aunt Charlotte conveyed me home, and Hector rested again.

After that life once more was rather dull. I did not like to run away for the third time, and even if I had it was unpleasant weather in which to run, snow and sleet and bitter winds prevailing.

Then I had a pain, and the pain became inflammation of the lungs. And one day the drop on the end of the Doctor's nose did fall before he had finished with my pulse, and yet another fell while he was listening to my chest and advising me to say "Ninety-nine" several times over. I thought it to be part of the cure; an incantation in fact.

Recovered from my illness, I fell down the back stairs, bumping my head heavily on the stone-flagged passage. Recovered from the bump and sitting pressed against the high nursery fender, the kettle suddenly boiled over and the steam scalded my ear. There seemed to be no end to the afflictions which befell me. They actually caused Aunt Marianne to come to see me and bring me a rabbit called James, which went to live in an empty stall in the stable. When I was able to visit him it was a great comfort to me to watch him twitch his nose, and soon I could twitch mine almost as well. Darling Jenny, our nursery dog, was interested in the rabbit, but when it was explained that it was *my* rabbit and not just *a* rabbit, she treated it with courtesy, until one day, familiarity having bred contempt, the bouncing fellow bounced over her and back again. This she would not endure so she bit one of its legs just hard enough to let it know what she could do in the biting line had she a mind to.

The next event of importance was my elevation to the dignity of a room of my own, a slip of a room opening out of my mother's. By day, I was proud of my room; by night, well—who knew that the bears might not . . . ? One hot summer night I woke, terrified. The terror grew until I felt as if I was going mad. I called. No one came. There was no light in my mother's room. She must be in the drawing-room. Down the stairs, a slip, a bump, a wild rush past the passage where the bear caves were, through the lighted ante-room into an empty lighted drawing-room. The garden door was open. On the terrace sat my father, my mother and a strange lady and gentleman, playing whist. Imagine that, playing whist, out in the garden in the middle of the night! Suddenly there came to me the knowledge that Mummy and Paito were not just our parents who belonged to us, but people who lived a life of their own with which we children had no connection.

Mummie picked me up, I sat on her knee, Paito brought the *couvre-pied* and wrapped it round me. I wriggled, for I was too hot already. The sky looked almost black and the stars shone in it, the air was so still that the candles burned without a flicker, and the baize on the card table and the red of the hearts and diamonds were brilliant in their light. There was a lovely smell, for but a yard or two away bloomed the lily trees.

Then there was a noise of horses, a shining of lights. A

pair-horse brougham was at the door. "Good-bye, good-bye." Then bed, a drink of nice cold water, Mummie's door open, the light shining through.

. . . . . .

It was toward the end of the summer holidays that we learned that we were to leave Wyesham, to go in a train, to live at Clifton "because of education."

There was no money to send the boys to Eton, Harrow or Winchester. At Clifton they could be day boys and get quite as good an education. Carli needed better teachers—she promised to draw well.

Several times I surprised my mother crying. "Char, dear" (her pet name for her sister), "do you think that Marianne would take Phyllis?" (the pony). "I would rather have her shot than that she should fall into bad hands." (I saw huge red hands jagging at our dear Phyllis's mouth, slashing at her with the whip.) "Jenny will go with us." But Jenny did not go. She was found dead in her basket, lying peacefully curled up as if asleep and stayed at Wyesham in a little green grave with a little tombstone at its head, under the walnut tree where she had dug for so many rats and never found one.

Even the boys sniffed and were grumpy, and Carli, great girl though she was, cried. As for me, I howled and howled and howled, for since Dick had gone to school Jenny had been my greatest friend; Jenny who wagged her tail and beamed and wriggled when life was gay, and whined and licked and cuddled close when life was gloomy, and only on rare occasions, when her patience was too far tried, crawled away under the night nursery chest of drawers where no one could reach her.

If ever there was a saint, Jenny was a saint—a little grey, long-haired, bone-gnawing saint.

Looking back I try to remember what mental and spiritual equipment I had to take with me into the new life which awaited me. I could read, write, say my tables and do easy sums. I knew that God lived in the sky and could see my every action, which displeased me. Mummie would not let me see her in her bath; why then should God see me in mine? I knew it was naughty to lie and yet I lied. My imagination was vivid, my desire to present events as I would have them be, acute. So lies streamed out of my mouth and neither appeals to my better nature nor punishments stopped the stream, though presently I learned to lie with tact.

It was part of my creed that to be cruel to or neglectful of an animal was unthinkable, that everyone should be kind to the poor and not only kind but polite, and that to be rude to servants—though I sometimes was—was vulgar. It was wrong to be greedy—and how greedy I could be—and wrong not to eat what was put before me. Pease pudding, a loathsome yellow mess. Now, be a good girl. . . . Dot, do as you are told or . . . consternation . . . disgust. . . . But in me satisfaction that in the end I had punished them for their obstinate disregard of my wishes. I had also learned that one must not buy what one cannot pay for and that one must be modest. There was no mixed bathing in our nursery. If one is to believe that "virtue" is a virtue, then perhaps Puritans and the Fathers of the Holy Catholic Church are right in their insistence on the necessity for the teaching of modesty as we understood it. Nowadays some think that nakedness and modesty are not akin. Are they right? Thank heaven one cannot know everything or even be expected to pretend that one does, and so I ask the question but leave it to be answered by someone else.

Further I had observed that when people were busy or

irritable it was unwise to pester them with questions, and that in any case it was difficult to obtain an answer which one could accept as true. Although it was wrong to lie, it seemed to me that I was by no means the only person who did it.

On the whole I concluded that I would be good, provided that to be so was neither too dull nor too difficult.

CHAPTER III

We arrive at Clifton—The navvy who drank soup—She had murdered her baby—The new house—The first bathroom I had ever
seen—We go to school—Clean, tidy, ladylike and very plain
—Education in the 'seventies—The school concert—Life in a
mid-Victorian vicarage—Half a crown a week to give up witchcraft—The village poor.

A TRAIN journey interspersed with picnic meals was
an excitement. The arrival at lamp-lit Clifton was an
excitement. Next day we found ourselves in a
house with quantities of stairs and in front of it a
stone terrace, Royal York Terrace. At the foot of the
Terrace was a road and, in the wall supporting the houses,
doors and barred windows. What lived inside those doors?
Bears? I wondered at myself that I could still be so childish. Of course there were no bears . . . yet. . . . In casual
tones I asked my big sister what they kept under terraces.
"Sculleries and coal holes and places where they brush
boots."

Royal York Terrace was "apartments" and our dinner
table was adorned by a huge "cruet," an article new to me
which made a great impression on my mind. 6d. a week
was charged for "cruet."

In a fortnight's time we moved into our new house in
Cornwallis Crescent, which also had quantities of stairs and
a terrace. It was, I think, a Georgian house; it had a beautiful view away down to Bristol and a picturesque sloping
garden, common to all tenants. The dining-room opened on
to the terrace, the drawing-room looked over it, and from the

27

attic windows the view was vast and the sense of height almost alarming.

One of my memories of the time during which we lived in this house is of running a soup kitchen. I can see as plainly now as I saw him then, a tall, painfully thin navvy with a strained, enduring look, sitting in the hall drinking hot broth and eating slices of bread. That was during a hard winter when there was much unemployment and consequent want. My father and mother, ill off as they were, said that no one who asked for food should be turned away. I think there was some arrangement with the Charity Organisation to provide further assistance, but, at any rate, to save the servants we children were proud to act as servers.

Our staff then consisted of a tall, stout, cheerful Devonshire woman; a thin, sad, elderly house-parlourmaid, a nurse, and a boot boy—the cook called him a "limb." The parlourmaid, Hannah, I learned later, after giving birth to a child in secret, crazed with pain and misery, had killed her baby. She was a kind friend to us and looked with a lenient eye upon the "rampagins" of a house full of children.

The cook, Mrs. Snow, was a dear soul too and made Cornish pasties and Saffron buns and would have made clotted cream had we been able to afford it. "Keeping down the house books" was one of the bugaboos of Mummie's life. Every week did she produce them for my father's inspection, a procedure trying to both.

Our food was plain, our house simply furnished, and I recollect that Mummie declared that never did she have some homely dish such as liver and bacon but my father brought someone home to lunch. That was some half century before the introduction of the liver treatment for pernicious anæmia and the insulin treatment for diabetes, treatments which have sent the price of liver and sweetbreads soaring. It was in the very early days of imported meat and great was the fuss when my father suggested its use. Butchers with polite scorn said they did not keep it and there appeared in *Punch* a picture of a lady, who, having bought imported meat elsewhere, apologises to her butcher for the smallness of her meat bill owing to presents of game. "Yes, M', it's plentiful in July" returns Mr. Butcher.

I recall my brothers perched on bicycles with huge front and minute back wheels. The boys went to Clifton College and hated being day boys because they missed so much fun by having to come home to meals. Carli drew at the Bristol Art School and studied with my father; I also did lessons with him. He taught efficiently but, nevertheless, I hated my lessons because he laughed at my mistakes and sometimes repeated them in public. One day I translated "Richelieu était porté dans une litière" as "Richelieu was carried in a milk jug." I did not hear the last of that for some time. This teasing I could not take good-humouredly; it was the beginning of such tiresomeness on my part as eventually caused me to be sent to a day school.

While we were at Cornwallis Crescent, the death of two girl friends made a mark on my mind. They were away at the seaside and after a storm went to a lonely part of the sands to watch the unusually high waves. They stood at what they no doubt considered a safe distance from the sea. Suddenly a huge wave rushed upon them. . . . Night after night I woke drowning in that cruel wave. For years I could not bear to approach near to the sea.

My last memory of Cornwallis Crescent is a dream memory. Enemies were pursuing me. I rushed up what seemed to be never ending stairs, my heart almost tore my breast open with its beating and then I reached the attic. The window was open, I climbed upon the sill, looked out

29

over the Bristol docks to the country beyond. My enemies were clutching at me. Then suddenly a feeling of serene power flooded into me. I lifted my arms and floated away. Always after that in times of stress I have struggled for control, knowing that eventually power would be mine. But sometimes, alas, not before too much has been said, too much has been done.

Why we left Cornwallis Crescent I do not know; perhaps the new house was more convenient, certainly it was nearer the College. It had a small dull garden back and front, a semi-basement, three sitting-rooms on the ground floor, two bedroom floors, and a bathroom, the first bathroom I had ever seen. There were gas brackets, in the dining-room and in the drawing-room hideous gasoliers with white opaque glass globes. Our house was extremely ugly, a duckety-mud coloured sort of a house. My mother could, and if she thought it right to do so would, go without, but to make "an appearance" on nothing was beyond her. Besides, she did not like making an appearance. She liked things to be and to look what they were. She could have no more done wonders with a few tacks and a pot of paint than she could have murdered Margaret's pet rabbit, which lived in the back garden and wriggled his nose just as dear James had wriggled his. Our house was a clean, tidy house and no more. Margaret and I were now sent as day boarders to a school kept by a handsome elderly lady with two handsome daughters. Mummie, who had the same kind of taste in dress as in houses, dressed us in hideous clothes and plaited our hair in tight pigtails which were tied together with brown ribbon, looped back and again tied at the nape of the neck, just as Carli's had been when she was confirmed. We looked clean, tidy, ladylike and very plain.

We liked being at school, though being children with

30

hearty appetites we disliked the midday dinner at which we were invited to partake of a second helping but never did. Public opinion was against second helpings; only girls who were on particularly intimate terms with one another would admit that they could be so gross as ever to desire a second helping.

At this school I, now aged twelve, was put into a class of girls from fifteen to sixteen, who thought it impertinent of me to be there. However, I soon forgot most of what I had known, so that put matters right.

Why we were not sent to the High School, where the education was admirable, I do not know. Possibly my parents shared an idea which then was prevalent that at High Schools girls learned to be rough. It may too have been more expensive than the private school to which Margaret and I were sent.

At that time the famous Miss Dorothea Beale was Principal of the near-by High School at Cheltenham, and the pioneers who desired better education for women were working industriously to achieve their ends, so it is probable had I gone to the High School I might have become a well-educated girl.

When I was a schoolgirl in the 'seventies it was generally thought that girls were less capable of being educated than boys, and that any but a smattering of accomplishments made them less likely to be good wives and mothers. Indeed, the faintest tinge of "Blueness" was considered to make them so unattractive that it might prevent them from receiving any invitations to become wives and mothers. It was considered quite funny for a girl to wish to go to College[1]. Why should she, unless the poor devil had to

[1] The building of Girton was begun in 1870, Newnham in 1874. See *The Cause* by Ray Strachey and *Girton College* by Emily Davies.

earn her living as a governess? Even then, surely she could learn enough to teach girls without going to College like a young man. Only Heaven knew what would happen if women went to College—or rather probably more would be known about the matter in Hell.

I recollect nothing about my lessons except that two afternoons a week we "did drawing" in the dining-room after dinner had been cleared away, on a table covered with American cloth. We drew with crayons from copies. My copy depicted a Swiss Chalet, cows, a hay cart and some hens. The Principal, one of whose subjects was drawing, would come and sit beside me on the form (which I, anxiously, felt might collapse beneath her, for she was a woman with a presence who wore black merino, a lace collar and a cap shaped like a helmet), and "do" a little bit.

It is supposed that at girls' schools the conversation is not always such as was then known as "quite nice." At this school I never heard a word which would have brought a blush to the cheek of the purest female.

My scholastic career was brought to an end at the age of fourteen because I was ill. I had asthma and sat up night after night in an arm-chair before the fire. My eyes were in a bad state, a fact which, had it been realised earlier, would have saved me torment at the red puffy hands of a large, fierce widow woman, trimmed with jet, who reviled me because I played so many wrong notes. "Can you not *see* that that is an F?" she would cry, rapping my knuckles with her pencil, and then, as I leaned forward in my efforts to see the score, "Now don't poke like that. Do sit *up*, child," all in a crescendo of fierceness. Under her tuition I learned to play "The Turkish Patrol," "The Last Rose of Summer," and a duet called "Bluebells," which I performed at the school concert in the company of a fat girl singularly like an amiable pig in a maroon velveteen frock, who thumped solidly in the bass while I, clad in a starched white muslin inherited from Carli and still tightly pig-tailed, ambled uneasily about in the treble. Any guest who had a sense of humour and no ear for music must have enjoyed that concert.

When recovered of my asthma, as I was still obliged to rest my eyes, I went to stay with various relations.

Paito's father and mother were still living in their pleasant vicarage at Albury in Hertfordshire. Although but thirty miles from London, it might have been three hundred. Only one working man in the village had been to London. The nearest station was perhaps five miles away, the train service so bad that another station still further off was generally used. Unless an antiquated fly with straw on the floor was hired, the guests were fetched in the phaeton, a heavily-built, four-wheeled carriage with a front seat for two fitted with a hood which could be put up or down, and an unprotected seat behind. Any luggage too large to be put into this vehicle was fetched by the carrier.

Grandpapa was tall and as heavily built as his phaeton, with a red face and beautiful curly white hair, whiskers, chin beard and a shaved upper lip. He wore a top hat and white tie; only young clergymen wore clerical collars then. He had inherited a comfortable little income and, just as he went up to Oxford someone had left him a couple of thousand pounds. So he had lived richly and horsily, winning a bet that he would drive a four-in-hand keeping the wheels of one side of the coach on a track of half-pennies. By the time that he took Orders the loose thousands had been pleasantly squandered. He further impoverished himself by building a vicarage which cost far more than he had expected it to cost and consistently living beyond his means. The Vicarage was situated on a slope with park-like fields before and behind, garden, shrubbery, stables and outhouses, and contained a hall, parish room, drawing-room, dining-room and study, three best bedrooms, a nursery and servants' wing, and commodious back premises. Its architecture was vicarage-y. The wall papers were vicarage-y too. That in the drawing-room was buff-coloured with a pattern of gilt fleur de lys. There was an upright piano with a front of faded red fluted silk and a stool which twirled up and down. Once I twirled it with such a will that the top twirled off. I had killed the piano stool. What would they do to me? A green sensation took pos-session of the pit of my stomach. That rat-in-the-trap feeling of being helpless in the hands of grown-up people who can do just as they please is a horrible one. Aunt Mary, who was always kind though generally uninterested, screwed the top on again. The feeling of relief made me feel faint and limp and always after that if I "touched"— "No, don't touch that, Dot"—I touched with care.

The carpet was of a faded red with a vicarage-y design in fawn colour and a hole hidden by a small Berlin wool rug. There was a handsome mahogany bookcase, a sofa, my aunt's harp, a gentleman's chair for grandpapa, a lady's chair for grandmamma, "occasional" chairs for other people, a davenport, a gilt mirror over the mantelpiece, and a work-table with a faded red silk bag beneath. Grand-mamma, whom I acutely disliked, was attenuated and had a long, thin, pointed nose. She wore full skirts, paramatta boots with patent leather toe-caps, a cap with lappets and a lace chemisette and undersleeves. She painted in water colours, played the piano, composed music, and wrote poetry, and I often wished her dead, though other people, I am told, adored her.

My aunt, no longer young, was plump and indolent, had a beautiful singing voice, did all the things her mother did and was what is called "temperamental." She should have been an opera singer but, being born into such a family at such a time, was firmly clamped into a vicarage. We rather liked our aunt Mary, though later, as she became more and more temperamental and unreasonable about money, we found her a trifle trying.

At the Vicarage, life revolved round the Church, the school, and the village. Everyone "visited," everyone "took" something. Grandmamma took a Mothers' Meeting. Aunt, wearing a pork-pie hat, and the Curate, who drank glasses of hot milk with roast pork, took evening school for boys, Grandpapa took the services clad in a short stiffly-starched surplice from which his black trousers protruded with an effect almost of indecency. Grandmamma took the Savings Club; Aunt took the choir and played the harmonium. Sometimes all of them went to parties or friends came to tea. One could read *The Times* (but not young girls like me) and *The Guardian* and books that were recommended as being "sound." The food was good and plain, served on a polished mahogany table from which, at the 7 o'clock dinner, the cloth was removed before dessert, which consisted of biscuits, home-grown fruit or oranges and now and then figs, almonds and raisins or home-made damson cheese.

Grandpapa drank port and dined once a week with old Squire Parry who gave men's dinners at 6 o'clock and in whose stables Tom Firr, the celebrated huntsman, was trained. Now and then there were dinner parties to which the ladies also went, stately balls at Panshanger and at Hatfield and lesser jollifications at lesser houses. There was no tennis court at the Vicarage, but I remember that at one house to which I was allowed to go, Mr. Archer Houblon, a local magnate, played tennis in a top hat.

At Easter, if we children were on a visit, Grandmamma asked other children to tea; but not on Sunday, for there was no Sunday party-giving in such circles in those days. We hunted for Easter Eggs which the hens laid, the cook boiled, and Grandmamma painted red, green or blue and decorated with little landscapes, bunches of flowers, or animals. Having found the eggs we ate them for our tea.

I remember that at one of these parties Margaret and I wore dresses which aunt Charlotte had bought for us at Jolly's. They were very grand, made of white Bolton sheeting, the underskirts box pleated, the overskirts turned up fish-wife fashion and much bunched at the back. The edge of the fish-wife draping was faced with red, and the dresses had red belts, red buttons, and red collars inside which was some scratchy goffered lisse frilling. "Tuckers" were worn inside the high collars of all our frocks. These noticeable toilettes were completed by Tuscan straw hats turned up at the back with bows and streamers of red ribbon, white gloves and black silk stockings and laced-up boots. I was fat and Margaret was thin and, with our hair tightly drawn back and pigtailed, we must have looked a striking pair.

The cook who boiled the party eggs presided over a large stone-floored kitchen in which was a large coal range. Before it lay a black and red rag carpet, and red Turkey twill curtains gave a cosy effect. The bread was homemade and on baking days a widowed ex-cook came to help with the baking and the housework. She was a brisk woman with sparkling dark eyes, who never took off her black bonnet, merely untying the strings, and she wore pattens on which she click-clacked from kitchen to washhouse, where was the brick wood-heated oven. On baking days I was allowed to visit the kitchen and make plaits of dough, which were baked and served for nursery tea.

Although the house was a fair size, lighted by paraffin lamps, and everyone had a daily hot bath carried to their room, there were but two servants, aided twice a week and on special occasions by the widowed Emma, and in the daily task of boot and knife cleaning, water pumping and coal carrying by the man of all work. Neither Grandmamma nor aunt ever did any domestic work, but everything seemed to get done satisfactorily. Jawker, the man of all work, was our enemy. The sow having died leaving nine little piglets, Carli and I moved them to a home in a cucumber frame in the wash-house and brought them up by hand, carefully hardening them off, and when they could feed heartily, we proposed that they should return to the sty, which was to be cleaned, aired, and furnished with plenty of clean dry straw. Jawker, the old devil, dumped our pig babies into the damp, dirty sty, and although next day we brought them back to the cucumber frame all but one died of pneumonia. That one followed us about like a dog and learned to do all the usual doggish tricks. Alas, we could not take him back to Clifton. I sadly fear he ended as all pigs do end—and should no longer be permitted to end now that the humane killer has been invented.

Dick, the little brute, once went to see a pig killed. Boys are like that.

Grandpapa was a muscular Christian and had a way with him, and if on a Saturday night the hullabaloo at the "Labour in Vain" grew too violent he would be asked to look round, and thought little of taking two young men by their scruffs and putting them into the ditch conveniently placed on the other side of the road. He had put an end to that sordid Saturnalia, Patmore Fair, simply by saying that it should not take place again, and had commanded old Betty, the village witch, to bring forth her witching books and burn them on the stone-paved path of her front garden— a sad loss to some museum, for they had been handed down from generation to generation. Betty could not read her books, but nevertheless, deprived of them, declared herself unable to compass any more witchcraft, and demanded and received 2/6 a week to make up for her lost income.

In the little church, in those days, the men sat on one side, the women on the other, the children on benches under the belfry in charge of two of the Sunday School teachers. The old men wore smocks and spotted neckerchiefs and a few of them rough beaver hats; the younger men and lads wore clumsily-made dark suits or corduroys, which when new stank horribly. The old women were dressed in cottage bonnets and shawls and full-skirted gowns of black or grey stuff buttoned down the front, and they carried a Prayer Book or Bible wrapped in a clean handkerchief and a flower posy or spray of scented herb. Young women and girls were a trifle more fashionable in their attire than their elders.

At haytime the women worked with the men, at harvest time they gleaned. Until the church bell rang the gleaners were not allowed to enter the fields.

There was a good deal of drunkenness and a good deal of suffering.

A Parish Nurse was then unknown and neighbours helped each other in times of sickness. Hall, Vicarage and the larger farmers distributed gifts to the respectable poor, and the unrespectable and the Dissenters went without. In winter there were Penny Readings now and then, and in summer the boys, aided by the Curate who was probably quite the worst player in England, played a game resembling cricket.

CHAPTER IV

The books of my youth—Storing the mind with beauty—Studying
" Art "—Admirers—That humiliating ball—My conduct had
been "marked"—" It was God's will "—Religion as it was
taught to me—We did not powder our noses then—Bustles—
On being a nice girl—It was anxious work being " nice " in
the days of my youth.

DURING the next few years life had its moments,
but for the most part it was flat. I was delicate,
listless, at times morose, and at that difficult age
when one is neither child nor woman. Again I studied
with my father. I did not wish to learn, and naturally
he disliked a reluctant pupil. It is regrettable that I had
not the sense to avail myself of his thoughtful and culti-
vated mind. But one thing he did, for which I have
thanked him ever since, he taught me to make friends of
books. My indolent mind recoiled from what I called
"hard books" but he always insisted that if I read fiction
it should be good fiction and by the time I was twelve the
works of Scott, Dickens, Thackeray, George Eliot, Trollope,
Kingsley, Marryat, Hans Andersen, Harriet Martineau,
and Jane Austen were familiar to me.

Why, when I was allowed to read "The Mill on the
Floss" and "Adam Bede," Mrs. Gaskell's "Wives and
Daughters" was withheld from me until a later date I do
not know.

My Peel aunts were shocked at the extent of my reading
(they thought I did not realise this, but I did) and gave me
"The Heir of Redcliffe" and "The Daisy Chain" which

I perused for lack of anything better and despised. Re-reading them many years later, I realised their excellence, but at that time I appreciated but one of Miss Yonge's works, "Countess Kate."

The first book which I remember was that hateful Sunday book with the sacrificial picture, the next "Struwel-peter." In my memory clearly "there he stands, with his horrid hair and hands." Thackeray's "Rose and the Ring" and that lavish breakfast table brimming over with boiled eggs and muffins, and Lear's "Book of Nonsense" come next. As long as I remember anything I shall remember the "young lady of Smyrna, whose grandmother threatened to burn her." That she should have seized on the cat and said "Granny, burn that" shocked me to the core.

I also read "Sandford and Merton" and two primly pleasant pious works entitled "Leila on the Island" and "Leila at Home." A little later there was Mrs. Orr Ewing's "Jackanapes" and "The Story of a Short Life," over both of which I sniffed and sobbed.

Now I regret that I did not learn poetry by heart. It is a solace during long nights of pain or mere wakefulness to repeat to oneself beautiful words. But for some reason the only lines which are firmly set in my mind are those relating to the little girl who had a little curl right in the middle of her forehead, who when she was good was very, very good, and when she was bad, she was horrid, and a verse which has for subject a respectable family taking a walk.

F for a family taking a walk,
In Arcadia Terrace no doubt.
The parents indulge in intelligent talk,
And the children they gambol about.

At a quarter past six they return to their tea,
Of a kind which would not be attractive to me,
Though my appetite passes belief;

There was cold leg of mutton and warm lemonade
And a large pigeon pie most skilfully made
To consist almost wholly of beef.

A respectable family taking a walk
Is a subject on which I could dwell;
It contains all the morals that ever there were
And sets an example as well.

So much of life is pigeon pie which consists almost wholly of beef, is it not?

This gem, however, belongs to a later period of my life.

Now, had I to deal with the education of the young I would teach them beautiful verses from the Bible and other sources, the repetition of which brings peace.

"For I am persuaded that neither death, nor life, nor angels, nor principalities, nor powers, nor things present, nor things to come, nor height, nor depth, nor any other creature, shall be able to separate us from the love of God, which is in Christ Jesus our Lord"—Romans viii 38, 39.

At the time of which I write, that is when I was about fourteen, other literature interested me. I discovered in the bookcase in my mother's room—forbidden ground— two enthralling volumes, Dr. Chavasse's "Advice to a Wife" and Dr. Chavasse's "Advice to a Mother." They puzzled me; they puzzled me very much indeed. When I knew my mother was out I would stand by the bookcase, poised for flight in case I heard the hall door open, devouring avidly the worthy gentleman's words.

Soon after that my father ceased to "give me lessons" and a clever old lady who held a class for nice young ladies took me in hand. At first, being still delicate and easily tired, I cried miserably over my home tasks, every one of which had to be learned in French. From the time the pupils entered Mdlle. Hyman's doors, they became French girls. That little woman was a born teacher, and soon I began to enjoy working under her direction and in the companionship of other girls. I also went with Carli to the Bristol School of Art, where I drew in charcoal from casts. My future artistic efforts never got beyond painting Christmas cards—I was quite clever with robins—milkmaid's stools, tambourines, drain pipes and palm leaf fans, all objects which one might think no sane person would wish to paint, but which were fashionable at that time. Carli scorned my efforts—she intended to be a real artist and already drew from the respectably-draped model.

Some music lessons now came my way—a course of twelve, I think—and I was also taken to orchestral concerts in Bristol, where the audience talked so vigorously that one evening the conductor suddenly stopped his orchestra. A penetrating voice informed us "We always fry *ours* in oil."

As a little girl I had often fallen in love. Now, being fifteen and looking older, I found that "males," as our housemaid called them, fell in love with me. I felt deliriously pleased about this because, having been richly teased by my brothers, I felt doubtful of my charms, and, being of my time, I knew I must try to get married. Not to be married was to announce oneself a failure. Even my father, a nice-minded man who respected women, referred to unmarried girls as "young ladies on their promotion." I knew also that one must not appear to wish to be married though really one was secretly longing to be so. My brothers, of whom I was fond and who were fond of me, used to tell me that I was fat, that I danced like a coal heaver hopping in a public house, and that when I sang I had a voice like a cheese mite. Naturally I felt anxious and was relieved when other people seemed to think otherwise.

A dreary elderly Colonel paid me dreary attentions, a spotty youth, son of an old friend of my mother's and then at a tutor's, succumbed to my immature charms. A rather horrid young man, then home on leave from his regiment and acting in some theatricals, to which I was allowed to go because Paito and Carli were performing, brought me sandwiches and lemonade at the party which took place in the green room, and on meeting me again at the tennis club asked me to go for a walk with him on the Downs. Palpitating with excitement, feeling steeped in vice, I went. He tried to kiss me. Deeply offended I walked home alone. Yet I admit that I longed to meet him again. . . . However, my morals were strict and I took no further notice of him.

I did not like any of my admirers, but I did like having admirers. It was comforting, it made me feel that should my brothers again call me suet pudding I could bear the insult calmly. I do not know if my parents observed what was going on for certainly I did my best to conduct my affairs with caution, but just then Aunts Charlotte and Marianne desired Carli and myself to visit them and go to a Ball. Just think of that, to a Ball!

Carli was now a grown-up young lady, and balls were nothing new to her, but to me the doors of Heaven seemed to be opening. I was allowed to go to the ball because the two young girls of the house, aged fifteen and sixteen, were to be present. Probably it never occurred to the aunts that strange girls were unlikely to find many partners, that local girls would know all the local young men, and that others would come with parties and dance with the girls of their parties.

Off we set in the brougham, Carli in a blue, I in a white frock made of grenadine, modestly scooped out at the neck, my hair, for once loosed from its plaits, tied with a blue ribbon.

Two young men, one a mere boy, were introduced to my

43

sister, and she, kind girl, introduced them to me. The elder of the two regretted that he had no dances left, the younger, at the age when he would rather have danced with his grandmother than with a schoolgirl, viewed me with dislike but sulkily went through with it and later, because he knew hardly anyone else, still more sulkily asked me for another dance.

The aunts, who were popular, chatted with their friends and introduced their young nieces. A kind stout papa asked me to dance, a kind thin papa with a beard, whom no one could ever have mistaken for a real partner, asked me to dance. Someone's schoolboy brother said he couldn't dance but there were some jolly good meringues, so we ate several, and returned to the place where the aunts should have been. Thinking that I was disposed of, they had gone to supper. Alone I sat feeling larger and larger and as if everyone in that accursed ball-room was staring at me. Then appeared a stout lady in black satin and jet and a formidable cap. "Let me introduce Mr. Smith," said she, and did. Mr. Smith was like an ape, his collar was wilted and his gloves split. He did something with his feet but dance he did not. I said I was tired, he said he was tired too and should we sit out. We did. I loathed him with a furious loathing and he fell in love with me. Poor man, I suppose he had to fall in love with someone. I sat out four dances with Mr. Smith and then, thank God, we went home; and as if I had not suffered enough Aunt Marianne said that my conduct had been marked. I longed to shriek "Fool," and to burst into tears. But being a well brought up young girl I merely replied, "I am sorry, Aunt Marianne," and dear Aunt Charlotte patted my hand and said "Well, never mind, my dear, you looked very nice and ladylike."

When, while tears ran down my face, I was unlacing my

sister I asked her what she had done during those awful
hours and she said that she had danced fairly often, looked at
the pictures in the gallery with a curate who liked art, eaten
almost as many meringues as I had and had a nice little nap
in the cloak room. Only the knowledge that I had three
admirers at home saved me from utter despair that night.

. . . . . .

Three days later Mr. Smith came to call. Three days
later he came to call again. Then my aunts thought our
visit had better end.

. . . . . .

I had for some time been allowed to walk alone in the
morning in "quiet places," so one day my mother, who had
collected a little group of poor people, asked me to take some
jelly to a sick man. "There is no need for you to go in.
Ask how he is and say that I hope to come and see him
to-morrow." But his wife who opened the door would
not let me go. In I must come. I sat in a stuffy little room,
listening to someone coughing, coughing, coughing. "'E
coughs, and 'e coughs till 'e coughs 'is liver up in pieces,
'e does, poor fellow."

Night after night I woke hearing that cough. When I
learned that he was dead I was thankful. My mother let
me send a wreath. The widow wrote to Dear Missie on
black letter paper with a little white square in the middle,
signing herself, "your ever obliged Mrs. Jenkins."

I asked Mummie why some people should suffer so.
She did not know. It was God's will. I thought a good
deal about this. During the long services in the church to
which we went—my father was one of the Churchwardens—
I shut my ears and thought. I had been confirmed a year
earlier, had tried to feel what the clergyman who instructed
me had told me that I ought to feel. Honestly I had tried

and failed, and now I no longer believed what I understood to be the Christian Faith. I told no one that I had done this dreadful thing. I continued to go to church, but take the Sacrament I would not.

I have wondered since what religion represented to my parents. Did they believe that the flood enveloped the whole of the world and drowned every human being and animal save those in the Ark? Did they believe that Eve was tempted by a subtle reptile to eat an apple? Did they believe that at the Day of Judgment all peoples would rise from the dead like those in a picture by Doré exhibited in Bond Street, admission 1/-, and that the wicked would be condemned to everlasting torment and the good to wear wings and play harps? I cannot think that they did; and yet that was what they taught me. When I became engaged I asked my betrothed what he believed. He, being a parson's son, had received religious teaching of a like order, but in greater quantity. He said he had never believed nor disbelieved; he had never thought about it. As life unfolded we were forced to think, to learn that man cannot live by bread alone.

.   .   .   .   .   .

By this time I had developed an intense interest in my appearance. In the secrecy of my bedroom I did my hair this way and that, put cold cream on my face, dabbed powder on my nose, and tried the effect of improving my eyebrows with the aid of a hairpin blackened in a candle flame. In those days nice young girls did not powder their noses. If they shone, they shone. I made some underclothes and wanted to trim them with machine-made lace. Mummie looked severe. "Certainly not." She hoped that I would wear the underclothes of a lady. Real lace possibly, otherwise tucks or a neat Swiss edging. I tried to smarten up my few frocks and tied the strings of my bustle so tightly that it stuck out aggressively and waggled when I walked. It was the sort of bustle which was made of steels run into some kind of stout material, and sometimes the steels wore through and poked out. The cushion bustles came in later.

We wore high-boned collars which rubbed raw places on our necks, and stiff stays, and we skewered our hats through our hair with long bonnet pins, our gloves were tight and our boots buttoned. For tennis we wore long skirts with bustles, washing shirts with stiff white linen collars, ties and mannish straw sailor hats. The meeting place of skirt and shirt was hidden by a petersham belt, and as skirt bands would sag at the back they were kept in place by an ornamented safety pin stuck through the belt.

Our hair was brushed smoothly back behind the ears, and on the top of our heads we wore a tightly-curled Princess of Wales fringe. This was like the fringe a sheep wore and still does wear. The back hair was arranged on the top of the head behind the fringe.

In the evening our stays were pulled still tighter, and heavily boned satin bodices were laced over them. The decolletage was, in the case of young girls, decorously cut and a great to-do was made about fitting the short sleeves decently under the arm. We were closely chaperoned and warned to beware of the wiles of men who encouraged girls to be fast and then despised them if they became so.

One was not supposed to dance more than three dances with the same partner. It was very difficult to be a nice young girl, and yet not too nice. To be too nice led to dullness and young men, though in theory they approved of dull girls, in practice left them to be wallflowers. Indeed, unless you were a beauty or an heiress, it was very anxious work being a young girl in the days of my youth.

CHAPTER V

Young girls in the 'eighties—Pinning up improper pages—Tennis parties—Temperance Meetings—The murderous footman—A Sunday school class—My ancestry—Brave Jane Lane—Anne Hyde, Duchess of York—A striking likeness—I visit London— A brave and good woman—We did not walk alone—Out of the brougham stepped a stout, dignified gentleman, The Prince of Wales—The murder in the shocking street—We leave Clifton —A summing up.

MY eyes were still delicate. I had no desire to learn and no one wished to pay school bills for a girl who did not benefit by such expenditure. Also with one sister grown up and busy drawing and going to balls and parties, and the other sister now away at school, it was inconvenient to have me at home so I continued to pay visits to kind relations amongst whom was another sister of my mother's, Mrs. Hart Dyke, wife of the Revd. Percival Hart Dyke, afterwards Canon Hart Dyke, who was very kind to me. I was much attached to her and to my pretty cousins, one of whom was already out, the other on the brink of being so, while I, so far as going to garden and tennis parties was concerned, was conveniently out or in as the occasion demanded.

I still looked forward to coming out at a ball in all the glory of a tight white satin bodice, and tulle waterfall skirt. Mabel, who had come out at a Hunt Ball, had enjoyed herself. I think that, owing to the delicate health of her mother, she had been chaperoned by a cousin, Lady Glyn of Gaunts, but at all events someone had written to her mother to say that Mabel had behaved so nicely and quietly and looked

48

so lady-like. "What did they expect?" queried the scornful, irritated Mabel, "Did they think I should gallop about like a cart colt and look like a barmaid?"

Although Maud was not yet quite out the governess had departed and the schoolroom had become a sitting-room with the piano turned with its back away from the wall and veiled with a curtain of crazy patchwork. A *portière* of patchwork hung over the door. The mirror over the mantelpiece was painted with bulrushes and kingfishers and use had been found on other articles for several tins of Aspinall's enamel. On one end of the mantelpiece, which was clothed with art serge edged with ball fringe, was arranged a flock of plush monkeys for which there was then a vogue.

In this chamber of horrors which we greatly admired we played the piano, sewed, and now and then read novels. The newspapers were still forbidden and the novels were tried out by Aunt Markey, and if in one, otherwise innocuous, she found something not fitting for our budding minds, she clipped the pages together and bade us not undo them. Did we obey her? We did not. This habit was not confined to dear Aunt Markey, for when I was seventeen and had an admirer who was interested in mesmerism and lent me a book on the subject, he, proper youth, went to the trouble of sewing up certain pages. Naturally, I neatly unpicked them and returned the book re-sewn, being careful to use the original needle holes. The information contained in these censored pages was to the effect that mesmerism if practised on the expectant mother might possibly affect the unborn child. In those days, nice girls did not recognise babies until they were born. That troublesome process over, it was quite proper to gush over them. If the expected infant was being hatched by a sister or very great friend, one might knit woolly boots for it and possibly obtain some interesting information regarding its pre-natal career but, generally speaking, to be unborn was indelicate.

I cannot remember that my cousins did any parish work, but here perhaps memory misleads me. I do recollect that Maud, sighing, once declared that the life of a clergyman's wife was a moiling, toiling business and that she would never marry into the church and shortly after did so.

I always hoped that I might marry a Duke but, naturally, I never did. There are so few Dukes and so many girls who want to marry them.

In their girlhood days the cousins gardened and did the flowers and engaged in the occupations which I have already described and spent hours over their clothes, choosing designs for a clever local dressmaker to copy, re-trimming hats, and writing to London for ribbon, buttons, feathers, stuffs.

In the afternoon we generally mounted into a wagonette drawn by a pair of smart cobs and went to garden parties which seemed to occur every day, or friends came to play tennis with us.

Occasionally there were Temperance Meetings, for my uncle was an earnest preacher of this necessary virtue. That was the time of the Blue Ribbon movement, and we all wore tiny pieces of blue ribbon and sang temperance hymns, prayed and were addressed and provided with tracts.

Aunt Markey, although probably not more than forty-three, already wore a little shawl and a cap. She had very beautiful eyes and could show spirit now and then. I like to think of her when as a young married woman expecting her first child she was confronted by her striped waist-coated, plated-and-crested-buttoned footman who had gone mad for love of a haughty housemaid and now appeared in the drawing-room with a carving knife to inform his mistress

BRAVE JANE LANE, AFTERWARDS LADY FISHER, WHO HELPED KING
CHARLES II TO ESCAPE AFTER THE BATTLE OF WORCESTER
from Sir Peter Lely's portrait in the National Portrait Gallery

Jane Lane's riding whip was shown at the Charles II Exhibition in 1932 and now belongs
to Mrs. Peyto Shrubb. The bowl and papers referred to on the opposite page are the
property of Hugh Peel Lane Bayliff, my elder brother

that he should first cut her throat and then his own. "John," said Aunt Markey, her eyes flashing as she reared herself from the sofa, "You will do nothing of the kind. Put down that knife at once. I feel very ill and shall require you to fetch the Doctor." And John put down the knife and fetched the Doctor. But what befell him after that, alas! I do not know. None of the Misses Peel was of a temper to be bullied by footmen, mad or sane. It is pleasant to look back upon that summer when day after day the sun shone and one was young and shielded from care and sadness.

That same year there was a last visit to Albury. A tall, lusty, noisy curate had taken the place of the little milk-drinking man with the straggling walrus moustache. Aunt, in a small round hat and rather old-fashioned clothes, bridled a little when she talked and walked with this fine large male, but Grandmamma, I know not why, administered to him many acid snubs. Otherwise everything was just as it always had been. At nine forty-five the parlourmaid brought in a huge Bible on a salver, placed it on a table by Grandpapa's side and said loudly, "Prayers are on the table, Sir." Grandpapa who had been asleep and snoring woke up with a startled snort and stiffly lowered himself on to his knees. We followed his example, omitting the snort. The servants knelt facing the wall close to the door. Grandmamma knelt close to Grandpapa because sometimes now he fell asleep as he prayed and then she tweaked his sleeve until, waking with another snort, he would continue to pray at the gallop. The village was also just as before, and now I took a class in the Sunday school. I took the big boys, shy, shambling louts with greased hair brushed into a crest, and because some of them had forgotten their "larnin," as they described it, which meant that they could not read, I told them Bible stories and illustrated them with

E

scrawls done in coloured chalks on large sheets of paper. So tall was Goliath that he had to have a second piece of paper tacked on for his legs. These works of art were the prize of him who had best "larned his piece"—a few verses from the Bible. Still, in the mid-'eighties, this Hertfordshire village might have been three hundred miles rather than thirty from London, and the date in the seventeen hundreds rather than 1885.

It was during this visit that, having talked a good deal about our Peel relations, my aunt, Mary Lane Bayliff, suggested that she also had some interesting connections. It seemed that the Lanes were descendants of Jane Lane who had helped King Charles II to escape after the battle of Worcester. Grandpapa had inherited the riding-whip of that brave young woman and other family treasures including the pearls and the lace of a certain Dorothy Lane whose portrait—it was said to be by Gainsborough, but I doubt that—hung in the Parish Room over a lovely old harpsichord. Dorothy Lane was an ugly old lady, so ugly that my father and his brothers shot at her with their bows and arrows, but, being bad marksmen, hit her only once before this sport was brought to an end. Grandpapa, being then a bachelor, allowed his only sister Aubrey to set forth into Holy Matrimony accompanied by the pearls, the lace, and Jane's riding-whip. Some treasures remained, how-ever, notably a silver bowl of Charles I's reign—so soft that one could bend it—and some Commissions signed by the Duke of York (afterwards James II) for a couple of young Hydes.

Aunt claimed James II's first wife, Anne Hyde, daughter of the Earl of Clarendon, as an ancestress.

A century or more later it is supposed—though aunt did not tell me this—there was a family scandal of whom one of the Georgian Dukes was the hero but as it was a Royal scandal no one minded. So marked was the resemblance of a descendant of this temporary union that when he went into the Navy he was frequently mistaken for a certain Royal sailor and mobbed by those tiresome people who never know when to show respect for Royalty and when to be content with feeling it. I do not vouch for the truth of this family tradition but I do vouch for the resemblance.

Grandmamma's folk were rich bankers and lived near Manchester and had much to do with the musical life of that city. One of her uncles was a great admirer of Mozart. He travelled extensively in Germany, and, so it is said, had brought a hitherto unknown work of the Master to this country.

One of Grandmamma's sisters married Sir John Lubbock who obtained Bank Holidays for hard-working people. My Aunt Mary, when staying with the Lubbocks, used to drive up to the Bank with her uncle in a carriage with four horses, as was Sir John's custom.

"So," said aunt, "you have relations of whom you may be proud on both sides of your family."

I doubt if I thought much about my forbears then, but now I am glad to claim kinship with so brave a woman as Jane Lane, and with a man who did so well for his country as Sir Robert Peel the second.

From Albury I went to London in the company of Grandpapa, who deposited me at the house of Aunt Susanna Peel in Victoria Square. This aunt was an invalid, stout, brunette, with luxuriant hair then going grey. She was waited upon by a hideous, yellow-faced, frizzy-haired French maid called Auralie, who often offered her a green glass smelling-bottle with a large silver top and tucked a gregory powder-coloured shawl round her knees.

Susanna was a brave and good woman. Her history, as I heard it years after, was this. She had loved a handsome young cavalryman cousin and he had loved her. Her father, with some excuse, did not approve the suitor. She waited faithfully for her lover but he was not faithful to her and spoiled both his life and hers. His wife was obliged to be put under restraint, and he, left alone with his baby girl, did his best for her, but of necessity it was a poor best. Then Susanna, now her own mistress, intervened. Against the advice of her friends she adopted the child Emmie, and every day William visited them. He suffered from angina and one evening after leaving her house nearly died on a doorstep in Eaton Square. Again Susanna came to the rescue, "You will live here," said she, and nothing that anyone said changed her decision. So handsome, blue-eyed, and now grey-haired Captain William Peel took up his abode in a room built out at the back of the dining-room in Victoria Square.

Everyone said, "Susanna, you cannot do it," but because it had clearly been so right that she should do it, having said their say, her world accepted the arrangement and honoured her courage.

A week after William's death his wife also died.

Except for a stay of two days with two old ladies, the Misses de Lauzun, friends of my Bayliff grandparents, this was my first visit to London. Emmie and I did lessons in the morning with a governess who also took us out for a walk. In the afternoon Auralie exercised us or the cook, a respectable stout widow, looking very like Susanna in a bonnet and mantle formerly belonging to her employer, would turn chaperon and escort us to Madam Tussaud's or Westminster Abbey. A cousin took us to the Zoo; Aunt Susanna hired a carriage and we all drove in the Park and Uncle William, eyeglass in eye, his hat rakishly tilted, pointed out to us the celebrities. We waited with excited impatience for the Princess of Wales to drive past.

Once we were allowed to go out alone, through the Square, across Buckingham Palace Road, and into Gorringes to buy a pair of gloves. We felt that anything might have happened to us . . . the excitement was delicious.

We went to a theatre in London. I had once been to a pantomime at Bristol, but this was a play, a real, grown-up play, called "David Garrick." We also went to see a girl in tights shot from a cannon at the Westminster Aquarium and some performing fleas. We lunched one day at the Army and Navy Stores, then but lately opened. London was full of excitements, and not the least of them was to stand at the open drawing-room window, veiled by the lace curtains, and watch for a large shining horse which drew a little shining carriage, out of which, while a tall footman stood hat in hand, stepped a stout dignified gentleman, the Prince of Wales, who had come to visit one of his friends, and the lady who, after running away with him, had lately become his wife. And then there was the day when these intriguing neighbours, he wearing a deep black band on his hat and she closely veiled and holding a handkerchief to her eyes, entered a carriage taking with them a tiny blue plush-covered coffin with silver nails. . . .

In London, too, there were murders. Our murder happened one night in a little street at the back of the house—as close as that it happened. "Ah, la, la, it ees a shocking street," Auralie had often told us. There were brawling men, screaming women, crying children. But that night one of the women screamed for the last time, and the man who had murdered her when drunk went to the gallows sober, and that must be a gruesome thing to do.

I never stayed at Albury again, for first Grandmamma and then Grandpapa died. I never stayed in Victoria Square again, for Uncle William died, and Aunt Susanna and my lovely little cousin went to live at Folkestone; and I never stayed in Herefordshire again, for dear, dear Aunt Charlotte died and Marianne went to live at Torquay.

My mother hurried to her beloved sister's bedside to watch Charlotte die as she had lived, loving, spirited, and to the last enjoying a joke.

It was after all this dying that we left Clifton. Why we left I do not know. I was not quite seventeen, and was at that tiresome stage which most girls go through. I used to give the impression that I thought I knew better than anyone else about everything, and yet in the secret recesses of my mind I knew only too well that I did not and went hot and cold with shy self-conscious misery.

As a matter of fact, I was, compared with the girl of to-day, preposterously ignorant, and innocent too, which is a very different matter. Innocence is a spiritual attribute which one may keep all one's life, no matter through what dark ways life may lead one. But in what way does ignorance help? Sometimes intuition and imagination may serve as well or better than knowledge, but for the most part knowledge brings power, the power to use oneself rightly. But here was I, a tall pink-and-white-faced girl, ignorant, innocent, tiresome, gauche, happy, unhappy, and always hungry for new experiences.

I wish I had known how to be kinder to my father and my mother then. . . .

CHAPTER VI

I come out—What we wore and how we behaved—"God knows I never wish that time back again," said the Queen—Visiting the rich and great—At Twickenham—How odd to earn money— I become engaged—*The Queen* Newspaper—*Hearth and Home* and *Woman*—"Why do you not learn to write?" asked Arnold Bennett—Women would not trouble to learn their job, said he —Three-quarters of an author's business could be learned— Twelve miles from a s-s-shop—Writers of renown—When George Moore's books were terribly shocking—Lady Duff Gordon and Mrs. Elinor Glyn—A wedding outfit—Mothers-in-law and marriage.

WHEN we left Clifton the boys had gone out into the world—Hugh, because he had no liking for life lived in towns and without a horse, to British Columbia; Dick to a crammer's at Heidelberg. Carli, I think, was in Italy with a friend, and Margaret was at school. We went to Folkestone to be near Aunt Susanna, staying in apartments in Castle Hill Avenue. My mother, always direct of speech, called them lodgings, which distressed our genteel landlady.

I came out at a Military Ball at Shorncliffe Camp. This time it was all a ball should be, more indeed than I had dared to hope a ball could be. Emmie, who had just been presented, wore her Court dress of white tulle with a white satin bodice and trails of white Gelder roses, and I, because we were feeling very poor just then, wore an almost new ball dress of my sister's which she had not needed to take abroad. It was a pretty dress of filmy lace flounces with the regulation boned bodice. An admirer sent me a "spray" of gardenias wired and with their stalks wrapped in silver paper. We went to the ball in a fly. All Folkestone went to balls in flies, which generally smelt of straw. We each danced every dance but never more than three dances with the same partner.

There were other balls that winter, and at these our conduct degenerated; we danced many more than three dances with some partners.

Such an excitement, such a fuss did balls cause. It took so long to do one's hair and sometimes it would not go right and had to be done all over again. We curled our fringes with curling tongs and sometimes straight little bits stuck out and once or twice we frizzled pieces off. Occasionally an inexperienced helper would lace one up wrongly, missing a hole and have to unlace and begin anew, or a button of our long white kid gloves would come off at the last moment.

As far as memory serves me, we lived what sensible people call an aimless life. It did not seem aimless to us. Our aim was to enjoy ourselves morning, noon, and night. But I did not always manage to do so. I fell in love with a young man who loved another, and only the young men I did not like fell in love with me.

Is early girlhood a happy time? It is an exciting time but also an anxious time. One feels unsure. I personally would never wish to be a young girl again. I feel as Queen Victoria felt about her girlhood, "God knows I never wish that time back again." Then, just in the middle of a specially gay winter, I fell ill with measles; retarded measles the doctor called them. They made me feel very ill, caused my auburn-brown hair to turn dark, and my heart to go too fast or too slow and sometimes to turn somersaults.

Soon after that my family went to London but I stayed on at Folkestone with my aunt and cousin. Susanna now lived withdrawn into herself. If she had ever possessed worldly wisdom, she had little of it left. She cared nothing about people but adored little dogs. Trundling up and down the Leas in her bath-chair or drawn up by the railings while the chairman rested, she studied with interest all the little dogs that passed. A lady in an adjoining bath-chair had a Skye terrier which won Susanna's heart. An acquaintance began and ripened. We were invited to tea in a house on the Leas. The lady, a pleasant person, was, so our aunt discovered later, not quite an acquaintance with whom two young girls should have been seen.

We were allowed to run very wild at Folkestone and oh! how innocent our wildest runnings were.

There were fast girls then. We were not of them, but it was difficult not to be considered fast in that gay, gossiping little seaside town where life was lived so much in public.

Soon Emmie married and Aunt Susanna went to live near some cousins in Hampshire.

For a few more months this life of visiting, of party going, of freshening up my few party dresses continued. How difficult it was to be sufficiently well dressed, to afford railway fares and tips, to live amongst people all of whom were richer than oneself.

Carli and I were, I imagine, amusing girls; we could sing, act, paint, tell fortunes and make ourselves pleasant to elderly people, for unlike many girls we honestly enjoyed the society of our elders; so we did not suffer from lack of invitations.

My first experience of Society with a large S was at a great house on the borders of Shropshire and Wales, Brynkinalt. It was all very grand; a huge hall and gallery, wide stairs, gold plate, a groom of the chambers. All the ladies but ourselves had maids, the men valets. One by one my small stock of boots and shoes went away to be cleaned and never returned. I rang. Probably the bell rang in the ladies' maids quarters. I was keeping my hostess waiting. Oh! the anguish. A frantic dash down the back stairs, an obliging footman, and at last my boots and shoes. What agitation lest the housemaid should not appear in time to do me up and I should be late for the stately dinner, served on those silver gilt plates which never were hot and on which knives and forks squeaked shrilly.

I recall a dinner party of twenty, a tablecloth of exquisite damask, and all down the centre a mat made of the decapitated heads of miserable begonias bordered by maidenhair fern, and in the centre trophies of silver gilt. Table centres were fashionable then. They were made of satin or tulle or velvet or live mangled flowers. When the visit ended, how dreadful it was to have to tip that most superior housemaid.

Before I left, kind, grand, severe Lady Trevor, who was my hostess tipped me Five Pounds—riches. I did not know if I ought to accept such a magnificent present; then suddenly her severity melted, she became just a friendly soul, kissed me, told me that I was a dear child, that my red sailor hat was rather flighty looking, that young girls could not be too careful, and that when she was a young girl with a small allowance her godmother had always tipped her. That was an amusing visit. I must own, however, that in some of the mansions of the rich in which I was a guest the conversation was not gay. The respectable rich are apt to be dull, and often the richer people are, the more do they love economy. On one occasion my sister and I dined with some important folk in company with two other ladies—a squire's wife and a parson's wife—with their menfolk. How we small fry would have loved to hear of the doings of the great world, to know what that terrible Mr. Gladstone said to the

Queen, and if Mrs. Langtry really was as lovely as people said. But instead the after-dinner interval before the arrival of the men was spent in a dreary description of our hostess's efforts to discover the cheapest shop at which to buy little boys' sailor suits.

Imagine, too, my disappointment when I was invited to spend the day with old friends of my father's who, as the phrase goes, rolled in money. They took me to the Academy. Then, although it was raining and my best frock and hat were becoming more and more speckled, they waited for an omnibus and in it we returned to eat mutton in a vast, drear house in Grosvenor Place. They asked me, who of necessity seldom travelled in any other vehicle, if it was not quite amusing to go in an omnibus, which people of their kind seldom did. They also said that they did not go to the theatre often because it was so expensive.

By this time my family had settled themselves at Twickenham, which was a different Twickenham from that of to-day, a more countrified Twickenham with large houses set down in large gardens and quite a rural little patch between it and Richmond.

There are many things in life one never knows. I do not know why we went to Twickenham. Possibly because Carli found it an easy place not to be in, for she had a season ticket and spent pleasant days drawing in Mr. Furze's studio at Vauxhall.

By this time I was beginning to realise how tiresome it was to be badly off. Poor we were not, but in comparison with other people of our world, badly off we were. Yet no one seemed to think that anything could be done about it. If you were a girl, as you were so you remained unless you made a good marriage.

Then suddenly one of our numerous cousins, Mrs. Talbot

Coke, took to writing on House Decoration in *The Queen* Newspaper, and suggested that Carli should illustrate her articles, which the clever girl did. If one person could write why not another? I had a liking for my pen. As a small girl at Wyesham I had written in printed characters in a copybook a novel called "Three Figures of Mourning," a fine title, but before its time, for the vogue of Russian dreariness had not then set in. At the age of sixteen I had written a sickeningly sentimental novel called "Poor Teddy," which was a falling off in the way of titles.

Now, on the way to stay with friends, I had bought at a railway bookstall a clever little paper called *Woman*, which later on was edited by Mr. Arnold Bennett. A prize was offered for a Dress Article. I opened my travelling-bag, found pen, ink, and paper (there were no fountain pens then), wrote an article, and won the prize. A week or so later I received a letter asking if I would care to call on the Editor with a view to writing further articles. From that time, except that I still lived at home and was boarded and lodged, I became financially independent. My parents were surprised, and so was I. It seemed that they had two clever daughters instead of one.

Naturally it was strange to think of their daughters earning money, but undoubtedly the money was very useful and even nice girls were now beginning to go about by themselves and to be independent. We were independent by the help of the train, for, except for a few abandoned females in bloomers, ladies did not yet ride bicycles, and omnibuses did not rush about the roads of Twickenham and its surrounding suburbs.

During this time my father was in failing health; he became weaker and weaker. There were not many people he cared to see except old friends of his soldiering days,

Sir Sanford and Lady Freeling, who often came from London to visit him. The Freeling children were our friends, their children and our children are friends, their grandchildren and our grandchildren are well on the way to a fourth generation of friendship. A near neighbour, whose visits gave great pleasure to my father, was Sir Mountstuart Grant Duff, who lived with his wife and family at York House. Tiny Grant Duff, now Mrs. Huth Jackson, and I became friends, and we are friends still. It was at a party there that I first saw the Duchess of Teck and a shy Princess May, now Her Majesty Queen Mary. Other old family friends were Mr. and Mrs. Woodroffe, who then had a house on Kingston Hill. Beautiful Mrs. Woodroffe's parents and our grandparents had been friends, her daughter, Mrs. Barrington Crake, is one of my best and kindest friends, and her daughters Lady Montagu of Beaulieu and Mrs. Cyril Cubitt are carrying on the tradition.

And then my father died. It was the first time I had seen death. There was nothing terrible about it. He looked beautiful and peaceful.

After his death life for me went on as before, though to Carli the shock of his death brought a nervous illness, and she travelled with Lady Freeling. Margaret came home from school and occupied herself with music.

I was now engaged to my second cousin Charles—generally known amongst his friends as John Peel. All the relations disapproved. It was a most foolish engagement, they said, as indeed from a worldly point of view it was. But in spite of the wise advice we received we went on being engaged. It was true we had no money, but we both intended to earn some.

I now wrote for *The Queen*, which was then edited by dear old Miss Lowe who wore a mushroom hat tied under her chin and looked like Queen Victoria. *The Queen* had a great prestige. Advertisers humbly asked for space in the paper. Once I, going to a certain shop to write a notice of its wares, was kept waiting and not too politely received. I told Miss Lowe what had happened. She struck the bell on her desk. "Ask Mr. Dash (the Advertising Manager) if he will be good enough to speak to me." "Will you kindly tell Messrs. So and So that we are unable to accept their advertisement. I require that representatives of *The Queen* shall be treated with consideration."

Now Mrs. Talbot Coke had a newspaper of her own—in fact she had three papers, *Hearth and Home*, *Woman*, and *Myra's Journal*. Her articles were read all over the world. Wherever English women were, there were decorative schemes chosen for them by Mrs. Talbot Coke. I wrote for both *Hearth and Home* and *Woman*, which now was edited by Mr. Arnold Bennett, though I think he was still Mr. E. A. Bennett then. He was a plain young man, a raw young man and afflicted by a violent stammer, but one who already knew what he meant to do. Under his direction *Woman* was a brilliant little paper.

I entered his room one day with an article. He took it, read a few sentences; then looked up at me. He leant back in his chair and his limbs stiffened, as happened when his stammer overcame him. "W . . . w . . . w . . . why do you not l . . . l . . . l . . . learn to write?" he enquired. Probably by then I was earning considerably more than Mr. Bennett, but I had the sense to know that I could not write, and that he could. I replied humbly that I would gladly learn. How did he think that I should begin? "I will teach you," said he. Kind man, he little knew what a task he had set himself. Presently, "Did you not learn grammar?" "I think I know the difference between a verb, an adjective and an adverb." He sighed . . . no, it was a hiss rather than a sigh. He hissed with exasperation. "You must learn and I certainly shall not try to teach you. I know a Miss So and So who might be able to give you lessons." Miss So and So did give me lessons. She taught grammar to Board School children, but she never taught me. I seemed to be incapable of learning grammar. A combination of words sounded right or sounded wrong, and, thanks to my father's refusal to let me read trash, my ear was accustomed to the sound of words well used.

Arnold made me write articles; he made me strike out superfluous words; he made me put away what I had written, produce it again and then decide if I had written what I meant to write or if I had merely imagined that I had written what I meant to write. He asked me why I wrote "can" when I should have written "may." I did not know. I am not sure that I know now. He spoke of the balance of sentences, the weakness caused by over emphasis. He read the articles which I brought to him, recast sentences, cut out a word here, a word there, substituted the right word for the wrong, until from muddles of words they became ordered presentments of fact or opinion. He suggested to me that words did not mean what one thought that they sounded as if they might mean, they meant just what they meant; that, and nothing more. He said that women were idle and would not take the trouble to learn their jobs, that authorship was a trade as well as an art, and that authors who wrote what no one wanted to read and muddled contracts and excused their foolishness on the plea of artistic temperament deserved to go hungry and generally did.

(I believe, however, that in spite of his fierce words he was a generous helper of those who needed help.)

He said that three-quarters of an author's business could be learned, the other fourth must be born in him. He instanced a woman who wrote begging him to help her to become a journalist. "But what can I write about here,"she asked, "buried in the country, twelves miles from a shop?" "The fool," said he, "what better subject could she want than Twelve Miles from a S...s...s...Shop?"

The work of many writers who were to become successful appeared in *Hearth and Home*. Mr. Robert Hichens, whom I had known as a boy at Clifton and whose "Green Carnation" and "Garden of Allah" brought him renown, and, if my memory is correct, Mr. Eden Phillpotts were amongst them.

The late Mrs. Aria then edited the Dress pages of *Hearth and Home* and also wrote a clever weekly article in *Black and White*, an excellent paper long since defunct. I devilled for her, and an admirable teacher she was. Through her I met various members of her clever Jewish circle—her sister, the late Mrs. Julia Frankau, novelist and authority on colour prints, and mother of Mr. Gilbert Frankau, now well known as a novelist, then a boy at Eton who had, I think, pluckily rescued someone from drowning in the Thames, and one of her brothers, Mr. Jimmy Davis, author of several well-known musical comedies.

I also met the late Mr. George Moore, a thin, reddish-headed man with a vague-looking moustache, whose books were considered terribly shocking. Now earnest church workers read them unmoved. Miss Hope Temple, writer of songs which had a great vogue was another friend of Mrs. Aria's, as were Mr. Le Gallienne the poet, and beautiful Mrs. Roy Devereux, who wrote "The Wares of Autolicus" in the *Westminster Gazette*. I did a little devilling for her, and through her introduction worked for Mr. Harry Furniss, the artist, who was then editing a paper, but what its name was I have forgotten.

I made what was for a young woman journalist in those days a comfortable little income, and as my young man had now become an electrical engineer we thought that four years was long enough to have been engaged and announced our intention of marrying.

I began to buy a trousseau. Crêpe de chine had not yet "come in." Diaphanous garments were, I think, introduced to Society by Madame Lucile, then Mrs. Wallace, afterwards Lady Duff Gordon, who also introduced a new make of stay which kept the figure flat in front and emphasised its size below the waist at the back. That was how we described it then. To-day we should say what we mean plainly. We should say we went in in front and stuck out behind. I had met Mrs. Wallace a year or so earlier when we had organised a week's programme of amateur operetta at the Richmond Theatre in the cause of local charities. She was our star dancer, a pretty, graceful little woman with a talent for designing dresses and making them. With her she brought her sister Mrs. Elinor Glyn, who a year or two later wrote "The Visits of Elizabeth." It appeared in *The World*, and in book form was refused by one publisher and accepted by another who made a considerable sum of money out of his venture. Mrs. Elinor Glyn, red-haired and extraordinarily striking, became a celebrity, but never again did she write anything to compare with those delicious "Visits of Elizabeth."

A posse of Mrs. Wallace's admirers came to see her dance and one night gave a supper for her at a Richmond Hotel. She asked me to come and I was allowed to accept if suitably chaperoned. It was a party such as made me open my youthful country-bumpkin eyes.

I must admit, however, that in those days they opened easily.

When I bought my wedding outfit, the underclothes of girls such as I were made of white cambric, trimmed with lace and threaded with baby ribbon. We wore woven combinations, and flannel petticoats which were embroidered and scalloped with white filoselle silk, and stiffly-boned stays. Waists were small. Although I was all but 5 feet 8 inches in height my waist measured 22 inches. My going-away dress was made of a brown material called Zibeline, my hat of brown felt was trimmed with sable tails and gardenias.

We put a vast amount of trimming on our hats then, and they were perched on the top of our heads. I had a sealskin jacket and a sumptuous sable tie sent to me from British Columbia by my brother Hugh. Although I was disgusted by cruelty, I do not think it ever occurred to me to wonder how those poor little sables had been caught. To-day I would not wear the fur of a trapped animal even were it given to me.

My wedding dress was of white satin, the skirt bell-shaped with a stiff frill, tacked on the inner side of the hem to make it set properly. The Court train was of brocade. I wore orange blossoms and my mother's Brussels lace veil. Our relations continued to disapprove of our approaching marriage but they did it so nicely. My mother was devoted to Charles, his father and mother were kindness itself to me. So many young women seem to find it necessary to quarrel with their mothers-in-law. I loved mine and she was always the dearest friend to me. She was a woman who had seen a good deal of the world in her youth. As a baby she went with her parents to Constantinople, where she was christened. Her father, then Captain Wake Walker, R.N., had been lent to the Turkish Government to reorganise the Turkish Navy. Whilst there she was painted by Sir David Wilkie, R.A., and carried through the streets to his studio in a basket by an eunuch. At the age of seven she returned to England when her father, then Vice-Admiral Sir Baldwin Wake Walker, Bart., R.N., was appointed Surveyor of the Navy and afterwards Controller and lived in London for the twelve years during which he held these posts.

One of her sisters having married Mr. Bacon Frank, of Campsall Hall, Doncaster and Earlham near Norwich, she came to stay at Campsall, met the Rev. Francis William Peel, Rector of Burghwallis nearby, then a widower with eight children, married him and lived happily ever after, adding four more children to the already large family. My soon-to-be-husband, having finished the task of electrifying the town of Antwerp, was now at Dewsbury. He applied for leave, which was granted. The wedding day was fixed. An old friend of Clifton days, Mrs. Bengough, lent us her house in Wilton Place and we arranged to be married at St. Paul's, Knightsbridge.

Then I fell ill. I had influenza very badly. The wedding must be put off. It should not be put off. I rose from my Twickenham bed and with my family came to London. Our friend and doctor, the late Dr. Leeson, arrived the next day and by means of a strong pick-me-up administered while my veil and wreath were being arranged enabled me to walk up the aisle and down again.

I am told I was married by several clergymen at St. Paul's Knightsbridge. I may have been, but all I remember is that I came out of a mist to find brother Dick, who gave me away, knocking an elbow into my ribs, and whispering, "Stick it out, old girl, stick it out," and then went back into the mist again.

We went away in the wrong carriage, the coachman making no protest, and that evening my small bridesmaid succumbed to an attack of measles.

Waking about four o'clock next morning and feeling desperately influenza-ish, I was fed by my devoted bridegroom, lovely in pink and white striped pyjamas, upon Brand's jelly. My careful mother had included the jelly in my outfit, but had forgotten to add a spoon. Being a resourceful lad, Charles was not deterred by that, but used my shoe-horn instead.

CHAPTER VII

At Dewsbury—Pigs begin to scream—Three widely different worlds
—The artistic London world, the manufacturing town world,
the country house world—Jacob and John Bright—Down a
coal mine—Country Squiredom—The parties of that day—
Country houses—The host ate some more rice pudding—Mrs.
Town Councillor gave a high-tea party—" You do see life in a
bar "—" Love don't last, comfort does," said the pretty horse-
breaker.

WE spent four happy days together, and then one of
my newly-acquired husband's engines at Dewsbury did something which it should not have done.
Being a man and therefore a slave to machinery and obedient
to its whim, though he said evil words about it, he left
hurriedly. I returned home, caught a chill and was more ill
than before. Recovered, I set out for Dewsbury. Whereas
furnished rooms were "apartments" at Folkestone, in
Dewsbury they were "rooms," and very scarce; that is to
say the kind of rooms we should have liked. Our rooms
were on the outskirts of what seemed to my eyes a squalid
town enclosed in a grey mist. Over the greasy cobbled
streets horses slipped and strained, hauling drays loaded
with rolls of cloth and bales of shoddy, and four times a day
the operatives, the women with shawls over their heads,
flocked noisily in and out of the mills. Their life was lived
in obedience to the hooter. Wizened children played in the
streets and in a dreary place called a park, to return to the
care of some old woman while their mothers were at the mill.

Our new home was neat and clean, with stiff Nottingham

lace curtains tied back with blue ribbon, an aspidistra on a tottery bamboo table in the window and a chiffonier.

But oh! the cold of that little house. The water pipes froze and burst, the water in the jug in my bedroom froze, I froze. I arrived on Tuesday and on Thursday pigs began to scream. Poor things, of course they screamed; they did not want to die, and to die so cruelly. With the unseeing eyes which men have, my Charles had not noticed that opposite our lodgings was a pork butcher's shop. He was out all day, he did not hear those agonies. I flung on my outdoor clothes and walked the streets, to return, to listen . . . and when all was still to go home again.

Aunt Charlotte had always gone out for the day when a pig was killed. Now I had to do the same; and at Dewsbury there was nowhere to go but the streets.

Once, driven forth by pig squeals and by the necessity for buying some mutton for Charles's dinner, I visited the butcher, a stout, suety-looking, blue-aproned man. Accustomed to London ways, I thought that I should order mutton which would be brought to my door by a small replica of Mr. Butcher. But no. My small joint was loosely wrapped in a piece of blood-smeared newspaper and chucked at me. Carrying this unsightly parcel, I wandered on. A few yards away I found a small and dirty girl sitting upon a three-legged stool in front of a baker's shop window. I felt that I might come to do likewise if the pork season lasted much longer. Alas! it had only lately begun.

I bought some buns and gave them to the child. She took the bag, stared up at me with blue, questioning eyes, then slowly her lips curved into a brief, sweet smile. Picking up her stool she trotted away.

That evening I talked to Charles about pigs. He said pigs had to be killed like that, but I knew that they had not.

Not because I had studied the gory subject, but because women, being intuitive beings, sometimes do know what they have no reason to know. And now I know that I was right; but still, in spite of humane killers, some people will go on murdering pigs brutally.

As I was still a journalist, I had plenty to do and found it necessary to go up to London for one night each week; and generally we went away to stay with friends and relations of my husband's—whose home was near Doncaster—from Saturday until Monday morning, and for the Christmas holiday, to which he was able to add his deferred leave.

I now lived in three widely different worlds—the artistic London world, the manufacturing town world, and the country house world. In London books and plays, pictures and music mattered; in Dewsbury trade mattered; in country houses hunting and shooting and Tory politics mattered. I do not remember that we ever stayed in a Liberal house. I thought of Mr. Gladstone as an enemy of his country, or, more truly, I accepted that opinion of him and never thought about him at all. I was not interested in politics because I did not know what politics were. Just as History in my school days meant Kings and Queens, wars and long lists of dates, politics meant matters over which elderly gentlemen became excited, exclaiming that the country was going to the dogs. I was not even sufficiently interested to ask, Whose dogs? What dogs?

But when I come to think of it, it is untrue to say that I never stayed in a Liberal household. When I was fifteen or sixteen, Carli and I stayed with Miss Jessie Fothergill, niece of John and Jacob Bright. She had taken us to see the Bright Mills, where plush was being made, and afterwards to lunch with her Uncle Jacob, whose food was such as a greedy young person accustomed to the plainest fare would appreciate. No roast mutton and bread and butter pudding here, but chicken done in some delightful way and ice in the shape of peaches. I regret now that I remember the splendours of the meal, but little about Mr. Jacob Bright.

On that occasion I had the honour of shaking hands with the great John, who looked in to see his brother.

Ignorant wretch that I was, I knew nothing about him. Now, when studying Victorian History I read such words as these: "I am not afraid of the future. We have not, as the chosen people of old had, the pillar of fire by night to lead us through the wilderness of human passion and human error, but He who vouchsafed to us the cloud and the fire has not left us forsaken. We have a guide not less sure, a light not less clear; we have before us the great principles of justice and mercy which Christianity has taught us, and the advantages of philosophy and experience have alike been sanctioned. Let us trust these principles. Let us believe that they exist for ever unchangeably in the Providence of God, and, if we build our national policy upon them, we may rest assured that we shall do all that lies in our power to promote that which is good, and which the patriotic amongst Englishmen have in all ages prayed for—the lasting happiness and prosperity of this great nation—" I regret that if did not use my opportunity to better advantage and fix upon my mind a picture of a great man.

Until I married I had thought little about anything but clothes, amusements, young men, and religion; and about that I had as yet come to no conclusion other than that one must try to do the best one could.

Now on the long weekly journey to and from London which my work necessitated, and in the lonely hours during which I walked about Dewsbury while my husband was working, I had time for thought. I began to read not only

novels, but memoirs and history, and, because I now saw
something of factory life, the history of the Industrial
Revolution.

Twice when staying in the vicinity of Yorkshire villages
I went down a pit. Down, down, down in the cage, then
to walk through black tunnels, sometimes so low that we
walked bent almost double, now and again crouching
flattened against the wall while a tub, pony drawn or pushed
by a boy, went by.

The coal was hoisted to the pit head in tubs two at a
time or, in the bigger pits, four at a time; not as in some
modern pits in two-deck cages, each deck carrying nearly
three tons. Earlier, when the pits were shallow, women
carried the coal in baskets up rough spiral staircases, and
women naked but for trousers were harnessed to the tubs.

I saw men lying in cramped attitudes, hewing as best
they might. The overseer who showed us over one pit told
of an accident when twenty-three men had been killed. . . .
"I found m'brother here . . . m'son, he was lying there . . ."

When the shift was over, blackened men carrying their
dinner cans went lurching stiffly home to little back-to-back
cottages. Later one might have seen their women bathing
them out in the yard. There were no gardens to make for
the eye a resting place. Gardening is not a mining tradition;
but even in this place the doorsteps were whitened, the
windows shining and draped with clean lace curtains.

The children were shy and savage, the women stared,
dogs nosing about snarled as they slunk by.

It became difficult sometimes to adjust myself to such
different worlds.

The artistic highbrows despised (though they envied)
the aristocracy and the squirearchy and spoke of village folk
as Chawbacons and Yokels. Nine times out of ten they

knew nothing of country life, of the men so skilled in the ancient and difficult craft of husbandry, the women so able, so patient, so well loved by their girls, who seldom failed when out in service to send home something to mother, and by their loutish lads. Under friendly curtsying and hat-touching was the self-respect which allowed them to show respect for others with no loss of dignity.

The squirearchy in its turn was as a rule ignorant of the writer, the artist. To many of these healthy, hearty men with behind them the tradition of family, public school, university or a few years' soldiering, an artist was a strange being, one who took a paint brush and painted a picture or took a pen and wrote a book. Of the passionate desire to express, of the exhaustion of the brain and body caused by mental creation, they realised nothing. Because a man wore his hair long or an odd hat, anything else he might do, or at all events anything else he might do until fame won him the right to be peculiar, counted for nothing. He was one of "those artist chaps," one of "those writer chaps." As for trade, it had to be, but thank God, factories, offices, and shops were none of their business.

These men were, for the most part, honourable, kindly, respectful of the rights of the people who worked for them, but often, because of their limited knowledge of life, harsh in their judgment, and then, as now, able to sort cruelty to animals into two sections, cruelty and cruelty necessitated by sport, which is not only allowable but even praiseworthy.

Although I, too, had been brought up in this tradition, I was beginning to dislike it. I felt that the killing and, worse, the maiming of animals and the trapping of all the little beasts known as vermin should not be regarded as sport, that is amusement. When it is necessary to kill, then kill quickly, but not for fun. Charles did not share these ideas. He was a good shot and spent the great part of his holiday shooting. I like better to think of other aspects of country life. The first time we went to stay, after our marriage, at a big country house for a ball, I wore my tiara, three small diamond stars surmounting a diamond bandeau. That tiara was the pride of my life. We young folk went to the ball in the omnibus and took hours getting there and back, for the roads were covered with snow which balled in the horses' hoofs. The two chief ladies drove in the brougham.

Except that we drove to them in horse-drawn vehicles, Hunt Balls then were much what Hunt Balls are now, but dinner parties were different. They began earlier—at seven-thirty or a quarter to eight; everyone was paired off strictly according to rank, and walked in procession. The menus were longer. There might be two soups, two fishes and two entrées, though this two and two business was beginning to be old-fashioned. Then came the joint, game, two or even four sweets, and a savoury and, in some old-fashioned houses, cheese and celery and old ale as well.

Modish folk dined a little later and were content with one soup and one fish, but at large parties generally provided two entrées. Bridge as an after-dinner amusement came in a little later, but it took a considerable time to penetrate into squiredom. In the houses of the rich and gay, Baccarat might be played. In such houses one met with elaborate and luxurious bathrooms, lace-trimmed sheets and pillow cases— fashions looked upon with aversion by folk such as our relations.

Then one might find one bathroom in a country house, and sometimes electric light, but for the most part candles and paraffin lamps, baths in the bedrooms and great crackling fires, which, in the houses where comfort was studied, were lit at 7 o'clock in the morning and kept up until bed-time, and in houses where comfort was not studied were just beginning to burn when one came upstairs to dress for dinner. What with making up fires and carrying cans of hot water before breakfast, luncheon, tea, dinner, and bed-time, housemaids worked hard for their living. I remember well a dinner party at an old-fashioned house. We drove to it one night when the swans had elected to leave their lake and stand on the bridge and hiss and flap their wings at the horses, who shied and all but overturned the carriage. Recovered from this alarm we joined an assembly of sixteen squires and their ladies, clergy and their ladies, nice girls and sons home on leave. The host, a grotesque, jolly old man with long grizzled whiskers, had a large rice pudding in front of him. Now and then an awkward footman in white cotton gloves brought him another clean hot plate and he ate some more pudding. The incompetent butler fussed about; the footmen who had come with the guests seized upon the dishes and served their own people. The man on my right never achieved any fish; and he only secured some pudding because I whispered to Charles' Uncle Fred's George as he was handing it to me that he was to find a plate and hand the pudding to my hungry neighbour.

I like to recall too, walking home in the late afternoon by roads where the wheel ruts were frozen stiff, the rough grass by the roadside white with frost, the sun setting redly in a greenish sky, the leafless trees dark against it, the russet of bracken, the tang of burning weeds, the smell of turnips freshly chopped for cattle, a shepherd trudging home with his dog.

Half an hour later there would be tea in the great hall, the women in tea gowns, the men still in their tweeds . . . .

Then back again to Dewsbury, where we knew no one

until one of the Town Councillors with whom my husband had dealings bade his wife call upon me. Finding me in a modest lodging she was condescendingly kind. When in answer to her question I told her that I hoped eventually to live in London she was sorry for me. Why live in London when one might live in Dewsbury, or, better still, in Leeds? This lady asked us to partake of high tea in a house on the other side of the town which, it appeared, was the fashionable quarter. I was ushered into a richly-furnished bedroom to take off my hat. On the mirror of the dressing-table hung a "tidy" made of perforated cardboard embroidered in cross stitch and tied with crimson ribbon. There was an array of white crochet mats.

The drawing-room was crowded with mahogany furniture. On the sofa which was covered with tapestry in shades of vieux rose and green, were muslin cushions threaded with pink ribbon. There were aspidistras, a palm, some artificial carnations, and some shiny oil paintings of blue-sashed little girls with kittens and of lovers saying good-bye. And why not? My godmother, who was a fashionable ladyship, lived in Grosvenor Place, where fashionable people did live then—it had yet to become a favourite situation for engineers' offices and clubs, and she had a drawing-room full of fine furniture cheek by jowl with trashy little tables crowded with small silver articles, palms in blue china pots, and a piano covered with a piece of brocade which was a resting place for quantities of photographs, mostly in silver frames. A painted drainpipe full of bulrushes was placed in the angle of a beautiful French screen and on the mantelpiece was a "slip" of plush and on the slip a colony of monkeys made of crimson chenille, together with some remarkably fine bronze and gilt candelabra.

Mrs. Town Councillor gave us a magnificent feast—cutlets, crumpets, raspberry jam, a silver basket full of cakes, tea, claret and, so Charles said, some admirable liqueur brandy. There was a plush table-centre and on it a peculiarly florid épergne with more artificial carnations in it.

Mrs. Town Councillor was so pleased with Charles that she asked us to come again, and next time it was a real party, and after our high tea we played a race game or listened to music. As the piano was crowded with photographs and palms and the kind of little silver vases which scarcely hold any water so that the flowers in them soon die, it was rather twangly jangly music, which was regrettable, for the girl who played was a fine musician.

Our host called his wife Mrs. P. and spoke of her as "my old lady." With men he was Rabelaisian, with women his conversation was decent and, because decency cramped his style, dull.

One of the guests with whom I made friends was a delightful woman. She came from the Brontë country and knew all there was to know about the Brontës and their books.

After I had endured the pig-screaming for a few months, one of our new friends persuaded a lady in reduced circumstances to let part of her house to us, and there we lived in comfort and gentility.

On the occasion of one of my visits to London, I arranged to stay with my mother for a day or two, but was recalled by a telegram. My husband had influenza. It was too late to leave that night; so next day, Sunday, I started and found the train was almost given up to a couple of touring companies. Finally I discovered a carriage in which there was but one occupant, a lady in a rich fur coat with rugs and bags and newspapers in profusion. When the time came to eat my modest sandwich and piece of cake, she opened a handsomely fitted basket and produced chicken and ham, fruit, cake, wine and a box of chocolates tied up with pink ribbon, and begged me to share this feast.

It was Arthur Roberts, a famous musical comedy star of that day and for long after, who divided women into three classes, the blue-eyed, the black-eyed, and the perox-ide beauties. My new acquaintance was one of the last. Her conversation was genteel, she crooked her little finger as she helped herself to fruit or chocolates. Presently she ceased to be genteel and became confidential and racy. Her husband had a large horse-jobbing business and riding school in London and livery stables at Market Drayton. She showed off horses both in London and in Leicestershire. Horses she loved and spoke of with understanding. She found a horse lover in me, for ever since the days of Phyllis and Marianne's wild Welsh pony I had ridden anything on four legs which I could get hold of.

As the fair unknown continued to drink sherry, she confided to me that she had been a barmaid, first in a bar near Tattersalls, then in a street off Piccadilly. "You see life in a bar," she assured me. "Not that a lady can't always be a lady," she added, "still, I must say you do see life in a bar. There's chances too. If a girl's careful and knows when to give 'em their heads and when to ride 'em on the curb, there's chances. And I took mine. A bit of trouble with 'im now and again, but nothing to speak of. Live and let live's my motto. Now you, my dear, you're just the girl for the bar—style and all that. You'd soon get your chance."

"But I am married already."

"Oh, well, are you, my dear? Hubby nicely off?"

"No, we're quite poor."

She looked pityingly at me, "Well, love in a cottage's all very well, but give me comfort. . . . Love don't last, comfort does. You can pop a diamond ring if it comes to it, but where's all the lovies and dovies of last year when he's off with the other girl? And it mostly comes to that. Sooner or later, men being what they are, that's what it comes to, and that's where a bit of solid comfort comes in. Well if it ever should happen that you ever want a change, you can think of me." She handed me her card, "I'm not one to forget a girl if I take a fancy to her."

I think many people thought me rather an odd young woman in those days. I was often gauche and spoke when I should have been wiser to be silent, and was silent when I should have been wiser to smile and prattle. They would have thought me odder still had they seen me hobnobbing with this pretty horse-breaker.

CHAPTER VIII

Life in Notting Dale—A horrid story—The memory of a brave and kind woman—Happy go lucky and sane—We take a flat—Ellen goes mad—Albert Charles Alexander, what chance in life had he —Alice, a girl like a Persian kitten—We go to Teneriffe—The Dragon tree—Oh! that enchanted time—A Gaiety girl—The Poulet Marengo was cooking.

IN the early summer of that year both Carli and Margaret went abroad: Carli to stay with Hugh and his wife on their ranch in British Columbia, Margaret to travel in Eastern Europe with Lady Freeling. Our sister-in-law was a wonderful woman. Never having experienced anything but comfortable town life, she had married a rancher who lived 150 miles from anywhere, cooked, cleaned, washed, sewed, kept her house in exquisite order and became a remarkably fine horsewoman. She was then expecting her first child, and Carli, disliking the idea of finding herself in a situation with which she felt unable to deal—for it takes some time for a doctor to travel 150 miles, and babies are not the most punctual of beings—apprenticed herself to a midwife in Notting Dale.

My horse-breaking friend thought a bar a place from which to see life, but what she saw there was nothing to what my sister saw in Notting Dale. Poverty, drunkenness, vice, squalor, humour, and loving-kindness were what she saw.

Sent in advance of the midwife to a woman already in the pains of labour, she found her in some sort of a dirty nest— for bed it was not—a ragged umbrella by her side. Earlier

83   G

her drunken husband had beaten her because his supper was not ready. Now she was armed to resist further assault. A frightened, sullen little girl of nine was doing her best to keep five other children quiet. Later all were bundled out on to the icy cold stairs. A neighbour took the two youngest into her own crowded den. The husband returned still drunk and banged the children about. My sister, a tall upstanding girl, dealt with him. By the power of her eye and of her tongue and the authority of her starched cap and apron, she dealt with him.

When all was over, the midwife gone, and Carli left to tidy up, she brought the children in; they fell asleep like dogs on the floor. My sister asked the little nine-year-old drudge, "Would you like to see the baby?" The child burst into hysterical sobs, "I 'ates 'em, I 'ates 'em. It's babies, babies, babies, and it's me that 'as to mind the bloody little bastards."

In another such den a nurse called to a premature case found four children asleep and three adults drunk in the one room. She turned them out and went begging for newspapers and old rag. Except for a cup or two and a cracked plate, a frying-pan and a kettle, the only other utensil was what you might expect it to be, a splendid, rose-patterned relic of some luxurious toilet set, its handle broken, its edge chipped. It served many purposes beyond its own. Nurse, asking for it two days later, found a pudding baking in it. A horrid story? Yes, but there are such homes as that to-day; though maternity nurses, who know—none better—the life of the poor, assure me that only where there is drunkenness and gambling is such squalor unavoidable.

After the departure of Carli and Margaret, my mother, who had been going to turn her little housemaid into a maid and spend the summer visiting, became ill. I hurried to her.

Oh! the uncomplaining courage of that woman; her thought for others; her anxiety that I should not leave my husband too much in order to be with her. But he loved my mother, and encouraged me to stay with her, and came to us whenever he was able to do so.

My sisters came home, and soon we had only the memory of a brave and kind woman. But why do I say that? I do not think that one loses those one loves by death. But when we were both earning good salaries I did regret that my mother could not have lived to share our prosperity and to take pleasure in her grandchildren. In many ways she had led an uncongenial life, and we should have loved to give her happiness.

After my mother's death, we went away to the seaside for a few days but were recalled to the deathbed of my father-in-law. It is pleasant to think of all the good and kind deeds done by Francis William Peel and his wife Emily. One of his daughters has written a description of their life at Burghwallis Rectory. Some day the student of social history will give thanks for it. For one reason and another, our financial affairs suffered by Mr. Peel's death. The allowance which he had made us ceased, and there was practically nothing to take its place. Things improved a little some years later, but for the time being, except for my small share of my mother's income, we had to depend upon our own energies to produce a living.

In those days there was work for those who would do it and, as we found, little difficulty in earning sufficient for our needs. Nevertheless, the sudden cessation of what we had regarded as our safety income was, naturally, a shock—but one which taught us some understanding of the anxiety suffered by those for whom the dividing line between enough and nothing is a month's or a week's notice.

When those who enjoy sufficient and certain means bemoan the happy-go-lucky ways of the small wage-earner, they talk of that about which they know nothing. When the wage is both small and uncertain, the happy-go-lucky spirit is the only one with which to face life if one would remain sane.

When the time came to leave Dewsbury, we said good-bye with regret to some of our new friends, and returned to London, where we took a flat in Greycoat Gardens, Westminster. We paid £80 a year for a first-floor flat with two sitting-rooms, two bedrooms, a bath-dressing room, and a good kitchen, and there was electric light. I was as proud as a dog with two tails of my new home. My bedroom was quite in the mode, with pink striped paper powdered with talc so that one strip was plain and one shiny, curtains of ivory holland and under-curtains of ivory-spotted net, ivory-enamelled furniture with Carton Pierre enrichments, and a pink carpet. The drawing-room—which overlooked a pleasant old garden—had a paper with a design of fritil-laries in two shades of the palest green as recommended by cousin Charlotte Talbot Coke.

By 1925 flats had become quite a commonplace, though ten years earlier, like all else that is new, they were not considered too respectable. Their chief drawback was that in most of them the back rooms were as dark as dungeons.

I engaged a general servant who asked £22 per annum. Ellen said that she could cook, and that was true; but unfortunately, from our point of view, she did not say she was expecting a baby by a young man who refused to marry her. In the hope that he would change his mind, she entertained him in our absence. He left richer than he came by a pair of race glasses, a set of dessert knives and forks, a silver flask, an overcoat and some sleeve links.

86

When we discovered this, our poor little Abigail rushed out of the flat saying that she would drown herself. I fled to the Police. A stout Inspector seemed to think it unlikely that she would drown herself. At 11 o'clock that night she returned, dry in front but soaking wet from head to heel at the back. It looked as if she had tried to commit suicide in a puddle.

Next morning she remained locked in her bedroom and refused to respond to any of our enquiries. Again we called on the Police, who recommended us to send her to a home where girls in such circumstances were received.

We returned to find Ellen mad; a sly, smiling kind of madness. She had made a pie with a lovely crust and still smiling carried it into the dining-room. Its inside consisted of hay. Even though the cook is mad, one eats, but that pie we could not consume.

The drawing-room looked odd. Ellen had placed small pats of butter at regular intervals on the walls and strewn the floor with bread and cheese. She was removed that afternoon—still slyly smiling. Later she brought a deplorable rat-like boy baby to see me. He wore a rakish cap like a cake tin with rosettes of baby ribbon over his ears and a crazy ostrich tip nodding over his left eye. I tickled him under his poor little chin, and he smiled the gaping, appreciative smile which babies do smile. His name was Albert Charles Alexander. What chance in life had he? Yet miracles happen, and perhaps one happened for Albert Charles Alexander.

Then came to us Alice; an eighteen-year-old girl like a Persian kitten. We loved Alice and Alice loved us. She knew everything, more indeed than it was possible that she could know, and she made a delicious *Poulet Marengo* with a suspicion of garlic in it. This child became a family friend. When, after marrying a railway guard who retired and kept an inn, and bringing up a family, she died, we mourned our loss.

In the days of our comparative riches, Mrs. Alice came to stay with us. She told me that our household was terribly extravagant; that were she housekeeper it would be very different. And it would have been, for she was one of those talented persons who can make lovely soup out of a cabbage leaf and an eggshell.

But our household was not extravagantly managed as servant-keeping households go. It then consisted of a nurse, a man-servant, housemaid, and cook, ourselves and a child of five. We spent 12/- a week per head on food and cleaning materials, and lived well.

Shortly after the coming of Alice, my husband was required by his firm to go to Teneriffe, to put electric light into a villa then being built by one of our numerous cousins, Colonel Owen Wethered. Carli, who was now settled in a flat in Chelsea, took Alice to live with her, and we set sail for Teneriffe, cousin Alice Wethered having kindly invited us both to stay at the Villa Miramar, where they were in residence, while Charles dealt with the electric light at the new villa.

The sea is no friend to me. Whenever I take ship, tempests rage. This time we had to start four days earlier than we had expected in order to pick up the mails, and what passengers there was room for, from a boat which had come to grief and put into Vigo.

To increase our speed, extra coal was required and was piled in bags upon the deck. Off we set in a small ship which smelt of bacon and cabbage, varnish and hot oil, and was so designed that the passengers had to walk through the saloon to reach the bathrooms. Nowadays, luxurious boats are at the service of visitors to the enchanted island of Teneriffe. In the Bay the weather became violent; the coal broke loose, smashed in the skylight and filled the passage outside our cabin. When the door was eventually opened coal poured in to mingle with our possessions, most of which now lay on the floor. The only peaceful hours of that voyage were those spent in Vigo Bay. It was a warm star-light night when we arrived. There were spicy smells, and the sound of a guitar and of a tenor voice singing a passionate love song floated out to us. How heartening it was to feel that a stationary world still existed, and that some day one might again set foot upon it.

About midnight we continued our voyage, to meet, between Madeira and Teneriffe, such a tempest as made me wish that I were dead. But we had something to be thankful for. The waves moderated sufficiently for us to be slung into a lighter and landed. Had they not done so, we should have been obliged to continue our journey as far as the Cape.

At Santa Cruz a carriage with three little horses harnessed abreast, the harness tied together with string, and a driver dressed in black broadcloth, wearing a black sombrero and heavy gold earrings, awaited us. We stopped for lunch at Laguna and arrived some hours later at Orotava.

Hedges of scented geranium, of heliotrope, old Spanish villas with paved courts and pergolas of Datura trees from which hung long wax-white flowers. Here a splash of scarlet cactus, there the blue flowers of the Agapanthus. Golden days and silver nights, the croaking of frogs. . . . .

When my husband had finished his work, we decided to resume our interrupted honeymoon. There was, we were told, a picturesque and comfortable inn at Ecod, a village farther along the coast. To Ecod then we would go.

The scuttling trot of the three ponies which drew our

ramshackle vehicle ate up the sunlit miles; occasionally the driver lifted up his voice and sang, often he cracked his whip. Away to the right was the sea, to the left the high ground, and towering above, the snow-whitened Peak. Now and then we heard the ripple of water, and from the face of a rock, a waterfall fell, or through some miniature valley, thick-grown with maidenhair fern and heavy-scented narcissi, a stream trickled. Once we caught sight of a great clump of arum lilies. Just then the ponies shied, the driver cursed and cracked his whip, and round the rocky bend of the road came padding a melancholy, supercilious camel, loaded with great white wooden crates.

It was midday, and the sun had baked the dusty cushions of the carriage until they felt hot to the touch, when we drew up with a flourish at the door of the inn at Ecod. The green shutters of the low, pink-washed house were shut, and the place looked sleepy, almost deserted save for some chickens squatting in the dust at the side of the road. The driver cracked his whip again and again, and presently a smiling, dark-eyed girl, a red and yellow handkerchief round her head, a large check apron enveloping her figure, came to the door. The señor and señora were welcome, most welcome. The midday meal was about to be served. That was the salon; upstairs the chamber of the señora. Would it please the señora to descend when she was ready?

The salon, with its boarded floor, its three or four little tables with their blue and white tablecloths, smelt of the sun, of coffee, and of garlic. The green jalousies were closed, but through their wooden slats the sun shone, making bars of yellow light upon the floor.

On our table there were pink oleanders in a glass vase, and the pink of the flowers was repeated in the fluted silk panel of a little old upright piano in the corner of the room.

After we had eaten we sat in the garden at the back of the inn, where scarlet cannas bloomed. The wall was covered with Banksia roses and amidst the dark shining leaves of the orange trees hung golden fruit.

Later we strolled down the road past the ramshackle barracks from the balconies of which women looked down. At the doors children played, and a soldier was singing in a rich southern voice, a tune with odd twists and catches in it. On the little hill by the Church an enormous Dragon tree grew, its fleshy grey-green leaves thrusting themselves heavenwards. It looked like a bewitched tree in a fairy story, and its sap was red, like blood.

On the last evening of this enchanted time we sat upon an upturned boat in the little bay. The sun sank in a riot of rose and purple, and just before the quick-coming dusk fell, the sea shone out in streaks of brilliant metallic green. Some swarthy-faced fishermen in striped jerseys, red caps, and dangling ear-rings, had lit a fire; and as the daylight faded the flames flashed and flickered, and from an insignificant detail became the salient point of the picture. The men laughed and talked in their harsh Spanish tongue, and then began to sing the same tune with the catches and twirls that the soldier had sung.

The next day our baggage was replaced in the shaky, rattling carriage, and again the ponies broke into their shambling trot.

.   .   .   .   .   .

When we arrived at Santa Cruz we learned that the boat would be at least two days late, so we took up our quarters at the Hotel, to find three other English people, two remarkably good-looking women and a youth. We dined at the same table with them, the other tables being filled by Spaniards, business people of the little town.

The elder of the two women was Miss Alma Stanley, a celebrated Gaiety showgirl.

The next morning we met again at *déjeuner* and found her an entertaining companion. Leaving the *salle-à-manger* we went into the hall to drink coffee and, hearing excited voices, looked out. A small crowd had collected and in true Spanish fashion were shrieking and gesticulating. Suddenly a knife flashed and a man fell dead.

That evening the police appeared. Men were posted at the front and back doors and their officer retired into the little office with the manager. At first we thought this visit had something to do with the murder. Then Miss Stanley appealed to us to help her. She had played a practical joke on the young man of her party, who thinking that one of the hotel servants had committed a theft had called in the police. Charles was able to settle the matter with both police and hotel proprietor and so saved Miss Stanley from what might have been a tiresome situation.

As we waited not only two, but three days for our boat we saw a good deal of Miss Stanley, who told us her history. She declared that at the age of sixteen she had been sold to an elderly lover. "After that I had no mercy on any man," she said, but I doubt if that was true, for she was a woman with a kind heart.

She made us promise that we would visit her in her dressing-room at the Gaiety. The poor soul was already suffering from phthisis but a few weeks later we saw her name on the Gaiety posters and went to pay our promised visit. She looked desperately ill and we were not surprised to hear a few weeks later that she was dead.

. . . . . .

Arrived in London again there was a fog. Then it began to drizzle. The roadway was like ice. Our horse fell. Charles and a policeman and the driver put it on its legs again and we proceeded at a walking pace. Every few yards an omnibus horse was down. How I hated to see the struggles of the poor brutes.

At the flat Alice waited, beaming with joy; fires were burning, lights lit, spring flowers blooming. It was evident that the *Poulet Marengo* was cooking.

CHAPTER IX

London in the 'nineties—Dress—Society—Habits and customs—
The early days of the motor—Bloomers and bicycles—At
Hurlingham and Ranelagh—They ran pell-mell to see an aero-
plane—The Season—Mrs. Grundy—Bridge—" You are requested
not to star-re at the King "—We were more ignorant then—The
Oscar Wilde case—The Beardsley Period—An illogical standard
of morality—Drawing-rooms and Courts—Her Majesty Queen
Victoria—Her Majesty Queen Alexandra—Her Majesty Queen
Mary.

IN London again, with Alice to direct our domestic
affairs, we settled down to work. My husband was now
at Crompton's London Office, and I took the place of
Mrs. Aria as Editor of the Dress pages of *Hearth and Home.*
In addition to this work, I continued to write domestic
articles and to do some free-lancing, writing a few short
stories and articles, and now and again book reviews and
theatrical criticisms—or rather, I should say, notes about
books and plays, for to criticise I was insufficiently informed.
My notes, however, pleased the publishers and managers.
London in the mid-'nineties was a London so different from
that of to-day that under normal conditions it might have
needed two hundred rather than thirty-eight years to effect
such changes as have taken place. The well-to-do then
were more smartly dressed than they are to-day. Fashionable men wore frock coats and striped trousers, a pearl pin
in their cravats, shining top hats and patent leather boots.
There was no lounging about Piccadilly or Bond Street or
St. James's Street in tweeds, and no one would have thought
of going to a restaurant or the stalls of a theatre in day

clothes or even dinner jackets. Smart young men had private hansoms or hired a hansom by the day with a Jehu in a buff-coloured box-cloth coat with large pearl buttons, a button-hole, and a very curly, very shiny top hat.

Young ladies in Society seldom walked alone except in retired situations, and never in Bond Street, Piccadilly or St. James's Street. For a girl to drive alone in a hansom was still rather fast, and never did a lady travel on the top of an omnibus. It was not until garden seats and roomy staircases took the place of the ladder and knife-board back-to-back seats, and skirts became more manageable, that women ventured to the top of the omnibus; and even after omnibuses were improved, it was some time before women of good class travelled outside. Grand ladies did not travel in omnibuses at all. They had broughams, victorias or barouches, and the Park in the late afternoon was a parade of beautifully dressed women, fine horses and perfectly appointed carriages.

Few people protested against the tight bearing reins which tormented the horses, because they made these unfortunate animals look so "smart." To be smart and to look smart was then and for many years after the ambition of all those with social aspirations. In the season it was fashionable to gather in the Row before luncheon and watch the riders, and such ladies as might be driving themselves, and again in the afternoon—but now north of the Achilles Statue—to see the Princess of Wales drive through.

A vast amount of entertaining took place, Sunday being the favourite day for the less formal parties. Sunday luncheons were attended by men in frock coats and by small-waisted women wearing bell-shaped skirts which touched the ground, sleeves tight fitting until they burst into fulness which was gathered on the shoulders, high, boned collar bands, and a hat or toque perched on the top of hair arranged in a curled fringe and a cluster of sausage-like curls rolled over the fingers and pinned rather high at the back. Young men paid their duty calls at Sunday teas and sowed the seed of further invitations. After tea everyone sat in the Park between the Achilles Statue and Stanhope Gate. Dinner-giving at restaurants had not become generally fashionable, though there was the Amphytrion, a dining club patronised by the Prince of Wales, and the Orleans, where the food was admirable.

Invited to dine at the Orleans one night, I felt very "smart"; but for the most part people dined in their homes, and the lesser folk had Sunday supper as now.

The week-end habit had not become general, though at certain houses conveniently near London large parties assembled. The platform at Taplow, near which was Cliveden, would be blocked with guests, their servants and numbers of huge dress baskets which were necessary when dresses were frequently changed and of a kind to take up much space.

The difficulties of transport in wartime and the intro-duction of the knee-length chemise dress, and now the fact that everyone goes everywhere by car or motor omnibus, and that fewer people employ men-servants, have reduced the week-end luggage of the ordinary woman to a suit case and a light-weight hat box.

In our early married days to go out in a motor car was an excitement. We women wore motoring caps or bonnets, and wrapped our heads in gauze veils, took our knitting or a book, some biscuits and chocolate, knowing that we might sit for hours by the roadside while our men-folk tinkered with the insides of these wilful machines. We returned covered with dust, for roads had not then a tarred surface.

The clouds of dust caused in dry weather by a flock of sheep, a wagon, or even a carriage, is a sight which we seldom see now. Then, if driving in open carriages, ladies wore dust cloaks generally made of biscuit-coloured tussore.

Our motor expeditions were further diversified by the rearings, prancings and boltings of such horses as we met. These conservative animals were terrified of horseless carriages. A modern-minded squire who bought one of the first motor cars and appeared at a meet in it caused a veritable stampede and was almost cut by the County. Gentlemen of static minds refused to allow cars to be brought to their front doors; the motoring visitor must leave his disgusting vehicle in the road. Earlier, horses had been terrified by the bicycle, which in my early girlhood was ridden by men only. I recollect when I was a young girl two women in bloomers came bicycling through Albury village and stopped to inspect the church. A crowd collected and several boys threw stones at them, encouraged by their mothers who thought it a right and proper way to treat such shameless hussies.

This mode of progression began to be popular about 1896 when smart women mounted the new safety bicycle, and in specially cut skirts with deep inverted pleat at the back, a shirt, high collar, and sailor hat would convey their bicycles to Battersea Park and there mount them. Later every young woman had a bicycle; and so began the downfall of the chaperon, completed by the motor car and the War.

In the 'nineties golf was not generally played and people did not rush out of London to get exercise and "keep fit." Country clubs did not exist, unless Hurlingham and Rane-lagh could be considered such. Every Saturday afternoon in the streets leading to these resorts there would be a pro-cession of barouches and victorias, the enticements other

than those of a lovely garden and tea being polo, and at Hurlingham—until the Princess of Wales, by refusing her
patronage, caused it to be stopped—the shooting of trapped
pigeons.

Only on special occasions were other entertainments
offered. When one of the new aeroplanes flew over the polo
ground at Ranelagh the spectators in all their finery ran
madly to the appointed place of its descent. There were no
stands from which to watch the polo at Hurlingham, rows
of chairs being sufficient for the lesser number of people who
then availed themselves of these clubs.

All through the season the windows of fashionable
London houses were adorned with flower boxes and striped
sun blinds, and at night door awnings and red carpets were
set out.

From four o'clock, before which hour cards and notes
had been left (for this was a card-leaving period and the
telephone was a novelty), until six-thirty women drove
from house to house to find each crowded with women and
elderly men who drank tea, iced coffee, or cup, or ate sandwiches, cakes, strawberries and cream, and ices, listened to
professional musicians, and gossiped.

Tea-visiting over, the lady of fashion would perhaps
take a turn in the Park and a short rest before dressing for
dinner in a gown cut well off the shoulders and, although
short sleeved, never actually sleeveless.

It happened that I was in Switzerland in 1910 when a
party of *chic* French women appeared in sleeveless dresses
cut low under the arm. They caused a sensation, a shocked
sensation. Now a bodice which has no back and hardly any
sides excites no comment.

The vagaries of fashion cause one to ask, is there such
a thing as decency in dress, or only custom? In my youth

had a woman worn the kind of evening dress or bathing dress which she wears to-day she would have created a riot. We bathed in a loose trousered garment with a tunic reaching nearly to the knees, and even when so clothed hurried into the sea and, our bathe finished, hurried out again and into a dank smelling, sandy floored bathing machine. Some women could look indecent clad in black paramatta, elastic-sided boots, a shawl and a poke bonnet, others could never look indecent, though they might look unusual: which may in reality be a synonymous term for indecency in the eyes of that Victorian female deity, Mrs. Grundy.

Surely Mrs. Grundy must have regarded the Victorian bathing dress as her *chef d'œuvre*. Apropos of that, the history of Grundyism is interesting. The good lady was not truly a Victorian for she was created by Thomas Morton, a play writer who died a year after Queen Victoria came to the throne. She was a character in "Speed the Plough," one of the most famous of the twenty-five plays written by him. Perhaps no woman had for over a century a greater influence than Mrs. Grundy, who was born at a time when people were becoming weary of loose living and ready to welcome the Victorian virtue of respectability, which at its best was something fine, and at its worst a loathly hypocrisy.

Dinner parties during the season were large and formal, but the two-and-two procession of dishes was now *démodé*; soup, fish, two entrées (one white, one brown), joint, asparagus or a mousse of foie gras, a sweet, a savoury and dessert, at which ices were served, sherry, hock, champagne, port, and liqueurs with the ice were now considered sufficient.

After dinner the men stayed downstairs for a considerable time while the ladies chatted; and when the men re-appeared, chatted a little more or played Bridge, which was then becoming popular. Evening receptions or private concerts followed, or balls where tiara'd chaperons lined the walls. Mothers did not then look but a year or two older than their grown-up daughters. The mode of dress was more ageing, and slimming cures, other than a yearly visit to Homburg or Marienbad or some less fashionable spa, were not part of a woman's routine.

Homburg was the favourite resort of the Duke of Cambridge—the uncle of Princess May, who later was to marry Prince George, Duke of York—and of the Prince of Wales, and therefore, of course, of numbers of other people.

It was after the Prince of Wales became King Edward VII that he abandoned Homburg and adopted Marienbad, then a small picturesque place where His Majesty could obtain rest and freedom from the attentions of the mob. Care was taken to protect the King from too near approach on the part of those drinking the waters, for the King, generally attended by Sir Stanley Clarke and the Hon. Sidney Greville, would drink and take his promenade along with the rest of the world.

On one occasion I was doing a cure at Marienbad with Miss Alys Hay, who at that time was almost blind. The King approached and stopped to speak to a friend. I, naturally turned away, but Alys, who had no idea that His Majesty was anywhere in the vicinity, did not. Before I could attract her attention, a fierce little man in a Homburg hat hissed in her ear, "You are requested not to star-r-r-re at the King." "I have never even *seen* the King", protested Alys, continuing to stare directly at him, an incident which evidently much amused His Majesty.

But although slimming treatments were not then in fashion, there were middle-aged women who went on looking young and lovely; but these were the exception rather than the rule.

Social duties—who talks about social duties now?—were taken very seriously. Hostesses kept books in which they noted the menus provided at their parties and the names of the guests. One did not give two cutlets in return for one.

Mothers manœuvred so that their girls were seen at the right places and not at the wrong, that the right people were seen at their own parties. The gulf which yawned between the right and the wrong was deep. Society is in essentials much as it has always been, but because life was more stable and because taxation was so much lower, spending incomes larger, and the telephone, the car, and the aeroplane had not practically anihilated distance, it was more formal, more dignified then than now, and the conduct of the young girls was more staid and controlled. "Unpleasantness"—a favourite word—of any kind was ignored. People might do and often did do those things which they should not have done, but they must sin tactfully; open scandal there must not be. If they made scandals they were, unless very important folk, cold-shouldered or cut. Appearances were vastly important.

Divorce was not approved by Queen Victoria and divorced women could not appear at Court; but now Lord Salisbury had suggested to Her Majesty that Royal recognition should be denied to the man guilty of matrimonial misconduct.

As a rule, however, it was agreed that "men were men", and the less said about it the better.

Respectable women of all social grades might ignore the existence of the underworld, and young girls need not know anything about it, and often actually did not.

Unless a young married woman lived in a fast set, she might remain ignorant of much that "decent" men thought it advisable she should not know. Not until I had been married for some years did I know that venereal disease and sexual perversion existed. No respectable newspaper mentioned them, and although plays and musical performances might be vulgar, even gross, no reference to these subjects was permitted. The music halls were content with mothers-in-law, twins, drunkenness, and the "gay" life as subjects for joke. We waited for the Rev. Dick Sheppard to preach his sermon on "The horrible things at which people laugh"—and still do laugh. Many years later I saw a play, "White Cargo". A brilliantly clever doctor is drinking himself to death in West Africa. His drunkenness has cut him off from his world, has sent him into exile. The mail comes in. Even yet he hopes that someone will remember him. The other men have their letters, but there is no letter for him. He turns to the whisky bottle. The audience laughed.

By 1895 it would have been difficult to escape knowledge of the unsavoury subject of sexual perversion, for the Oscar Wilde trial became the *cause célèbre* of the day. I had never met Oscar Wilde, though I had seen him on several occasions and enjoyed his plays. His looks were not prepossessing, but people said that the charm of his conversation and of his smile was so great as to wipe out from the consciousness of his listener any feeling of repulsion which his appearance might excite. The trial, the subsequent life and death of this highly-gifted victim of mental processes which are still obscure were tragic indeed.

Those interested in the subject should read the brilliant description of the trial given by Mr. Marjoribanks in his "Life of Lord Carson" published a year or so ago. They might also read some of Wilde's works, not forgetting "De Profundis," which was written while the unhappy man was in prison. Let us pray to whatever gods there be that we may be pitiful of all distress.

Mr. Edward Carson, now Lord Carson, who appeared against Wilde, had known him in his early Dublin days. The first time that he saw him in London, Wilde was driving. Both he and his coachman wore white flowers in their buttonholes. He nearly drove over Carson, stopped and spoke to him. Some years afterwards Carson was walking in Paris. To avoid a wildly driven fiacre, he stepped back quickly on to the pavement and knocked heavily against someone. Turning to apologise, he saw a man lying in the gutter and recognised the painted haggard features of Wilde,[1] then living in Paris, and, as witty to the last he described it, "dying beyond his means."

It was by an extraordinary chance that Wilde's downfall was brought about. The police for some reasons unconnected with him were watching a certain shop. A girl employed there who was, as Victorians used to say, "no better than she should be," was asked by one of the detectives if she was doing well in her profession. She said "No," explaining that members of her trade were now in competition with certain other persons. She gave an address, and from that moment Wilde's fate was decided.

At the conclusion of the trial there were disgraceful scenes outside the Old Bailey, where women of the unfortunate class danced and sang.

History does indeed repeat itself. Much the same scenes occurred on the occasion of a trial of the same order in the late seventeen-hundreds.

[1] Lord Alfred Douglas has written to the papers denying this story.

103

Years after and shortly before the publication of his life of that great criminal lawyer, Sir Edward Marshall Hall, I met Mr. Marjoribanks at the house of Sir Malcolm and Lady Hogg, and regretted, as all who had met him and knew his books must have done, his untimely death at his own hand, which occurred during an acute attack of nervous depression brought about by overwork.

The 'nineties became known as the naughty 'nineties. Possibly people were no naughtier than they had been at any other time. The title was chosen, no doubt, because it made a good alliterative headline, and possibly because of the Oscar Wilde scandal and the drawings of Aubrey Beardsley. The 'seventies and 'eighties had produced the Romanticist period; the 'nineties was the Beardsley and Yellow Book period. While Romanticism had been a revolt against the ugly materialism of the Manchester School of Thought, to which nothing mattered but wealth, the Beardsley period was a revolt against a manufactured Romanticism.

The principal figures of the group whose work appeared in that famous magazine were Aubrey Beardsley, a consumptive lad, formerly a clerk, who died at the age of 26, by which time his exquisite black and white work had become world famous, Arthur Symons the critic, a little circle of poets which included Lionel Johnson, Ernest Dowson, and Richard Le Gallienne, the famous caricaturist Max Beerbohm, and John Davidson, whose "Ballad of a Nun" was read by everyone.

The only members of the group whom I met were Mr. Beerbohm and Mr. Le Gallienne; Mr. Beerbohm at a dinner of literary celebrities, including Mr. Somerset Maugham and Mr. Pett Ridge, the only woman star amongst them being Miss Ella Hepworth Dixon. This party was gathered

THE EYES OF HEROD
One of Aubrey Beardsley's illustrations to Oscar Wilde's 'Salome'

together by Mrs. George Warrington Steevens, whose husband, the famous War Correspondent of the *Daily Mail*, died during the siege of Ladysmith. Mrs. Steevens doubtless had invited my husband and myself to listen to the celebrities, but the party failed because the celebrities were too many and the audience too few. After the trial of Oscar Wilde, although he had never written for it, the publication of the Yellow Book was discontinued. Mr. Osbert Burdett in his brilliant work, "The Beardsley Period," is of the opinion that the Victorian convention came to mask a corruption which it was a return to sanity to reveal. "This is the revelation of the early Beardsley drawings, which became an extraordinary illustration of Gautier's text, that *la correction de la forme est la vertu.* That is the final virtue of Beardsley's famous line, which was employed to re-capture the Vision of Evil for a century which, in losing it, had lost also the vision of good."

"The theory of the man and the moment is justified of Beardsley too in this; his genius appeared at the moment when the line-block also was perfected."

But if the 'nineties were made remarkable by the Yellow Book group they were also, as Mr. Burdett points out, made remarkable by other writers: Mr. Wells and Mr. Kipling, Mr. Shaw and Mr. Arnold Bennett, Mr. Meredith and Mr. Thomas Hardy.

Looking back on London as it was then, vice certainly was paraded in a manner which is not now permitted. Certain streets, and those not of the secluded kind, but the great thoroughfares, such as Piccadilly, Regent Street, Leicester Square, and the Strand, were a display ground for unfortunate women. At this time I worked at the office of *Hearth and Home* in Fetter Lane, Fleet Street. Although I was quietly dressed, and I hope looked what I was, a respectable young woman, there was scarcely a day when I, while waiting for an omnibus, was not accosted. I perfected myself in the art of staring blankly through the ill-mannered persons who offered their undesired attentions. Only once, and then because I was annoyed that some manuscript which should have gone to press that day had been lost, I spoke my mind. "Will you come out to tea with me?" asked one of these pavement pests. "Why should I come out to tea with you?" I replied. "You are a vulgar, impertinent person. If you speak to me again, I shall give you in charge."

I am not sure how the law stood in those days. Certainly women could be taken into custody for accosting men on the evidence of the Police alone and without any complaint from the man who had been accosted. This kind of thing, as we all know, continues, but not in the blatant fashion then permitted. The general point of view regarding sex morality was utterly illogical. Beautiful Josephine Butler had done much to educate the public with regard to morality and to better the position of women, but yet it was generally conceded that men could not be moral. Indeed, many people held that celibacy was impossible to a man without injury to health. It did not sound right for Christian people to say this openly, so the matter was put lightly—"Boys will be boys," and "Young men must sow their wild oats." Provided they ceased to be boys and to sow wild oats after they married, what more could anyone ask of them? The fact that men who were not moral necessitated the existence of women who were not moral was put aside. It was one of those unpleasant subjects which the Victorians were so clever in avoiding.

Yet there was a large class of despised women known by several opprobrious names, a danger not only to the men with whom they consorted but to their wives and off-spring, despised not only by respectable women but by the men for whose convenience they existed. These unfortunates, for that was the name which truly described them, were hardly dealt with by the law and were practically in the power of the Police.

. . . . . .

It was in the May or June of the year after my marriage that I was presented. Drawing-Rooms then took place in the afternoon and refreshments were not provided. The business of dressing began quite early in the morning. There were not then the number of hair-dressers' shops that there are now. Very great ladies might have their own hair-dressers whom they took with them when visiting their friends, but generally speaking the lady's maid did her lady's hair. If a lady did not keep a maid, she did it herself, employing a hair-dresser only on special occasions. On Drawing-Room days fashionable hair-dressers might begin their rounds as early as eight o'clock in the morning.

We wore full evening dress made strictly according to regulations, Court trains, and feathers, and carried the large shower bouquets which had lately become fashionable. The Court train was long, lined, padded, and trimmed, and therefore more sumptuous looking than the shorter trains which are worn to-day.

The attendance at Courts since the War has grown so numerous that it has become necessary to shorten the trains in order to facilitate the quicker passing of those who wished to pay their respects to Their Majesties.

We started for the Palace long before the luncheon hour, and our carriage took up its place in the Mall. Members of the great families still used their State carriages, driven by a white-wigged coachman who sat alone on the hammer cloth, while a couple of footmen in State liveries, their hair powdered, stood at the back. Persons of lesser degree also prided themselves on the smartness of their horses and carriages and the liveries of their coachmen and footmen, who wore posies of flowers in honour of the occasion.

Such a fine show attracted crowds of sightseers, whose comments were occasionally difficult to bear with equanimity.

Arrived at the Palace, those who knew the ropes generally left their wraps in the carriage to avoid the delay caused by reclaiming them from the cloakroom. At the foot of the Grand Staircase we met a friend and her mother. Sally was one of those girls to whom things always happen at the wrong moment; when half-way up the staircase her flannel petticoat fell off. It was a modish garment, gored into a shaped band and embroidered. Without a moment's hesitation she stepped free of it, gathered it into a bundle, and threw it at one of the Beefeaters who lined the staircase on either side. Never shall I forget the face of that man, as, mouth open, eyes staring with horrified astonishment, he clasped that petticoat to his breast.

If I remember rightly seats were not provided, and as everyone was anxious to reach the Throne Room before the departure of Queen Victoria, who when tired would leave the Princess of Wales to represent her, there were some unseemly scrambles.

At the entrance to the Throne Room each lady handed her card to the Gentleman appointed to receive it, while two other Gentlemen took her train from her arm, upon which it had been folded, and arranged it. Our names were announced and we entered the Throne Room.

I am glad I was not too nervous to take in the scene; the half circle of Royalties and their ladies and gentlemen brilliantly dressed, brilliantly jewelled, and in the centre a little red-faced sad-looking old lady in a widow's cap, and old lady-like, black evening dress, high in the neck and with sleeves reaching below the elbow, across her breast the Garter ribbon.

Her Majesty was not a beautiful old lady. She had a rudder-like nose and her blue eyes protruded. Yet such is the power of personality, a personality formed by the living of an upright life, that I doubt if anyone who ever saw her could forget Queen Victoria. After passing the Queen, upon whom one must not turn one's back, one progressed in a sideways fashion, pausing at intervals to make the required number of curtsies. After that there was nothing to do but to go home again.

The next event on the programme on a Drawing-Room day was the Drawing-Room Tea at which relations and friends gathered to admire us in our finery.

After the accession of King Edward, Drawing-Rooms became Courts, and took place in the evening. A luxurious buffet-supper, accompanied by particularly good champagne, was served from tables set out with the Royal gold plate.

I attended a Court after the accession of King Edward, wearing a home-made train of white brocade lined with pale pink satin and garlanded with La France roses which I bought at Stagg and Mantle's in Leicester Square where artificial flowers were both good and cheap.

I attended yet another Court after the accession of King George V. After the War for a time Garden Parties took the place of Courts. My elder daughter was presented at the first Garden Party after the War. It was a marvellous gathering, not only of English people, including representatives of the Women's War Associations, but of notabilities of the Allied countries. The guests numbered several thousands, and refreshments consisting of tea and coffee, ices, sandwiches, cakes and fruit, were served from a series of buffets placed in tents. Messrs. Lyons were the caterers, and the good things provided were dispensed by neat waitresses in black dresses, white aprons and caps—those same girls who now are afflicted with the title of "Nippy's."

When I presented my younger daughter, now Denise Welman, Courts were again held in the evening. We watched the Royal procession leave the Throne Room. That night Her Majesty Queen Mary wore a gown and train of cloth of gold, the train of enormous length, a tall crown of pearls and diamonds, a high collar of diamonds, and ropes of pearls, the only touch of vivid colour in her dress being the blue Garter ribbon.

After the dreariness of the War and early post-War years, the ceremonial of a Court, even though shorn of some of its former splendour, because the trains were shorter and there were few bouquets, was like a scene out of a fairy tale.

CHAPTER X

We move to Chelsea—A nurse who was too kind—" 10/- a head for
House Books "—Edwardian extravagance—The cost of living
—" My husband is a disagreeable, greedy man "—In Paris—
Clothes, food and night life—The Empire Promenade—Monte
Carlo in the 'nineties—" Can't we meet again ? " he asked—
£1,000 in his boots—It was a good day, that.

THAT winter we left Greycoat Gardens and moved to
a house in Chelsea where our first child was born.
I was seriously ill, partly owing to unavoidable
causes and partly, though I did not then realise it, to bad
nursing.

The nurse who took charge of me was a pretty,
charming, inefficient woman, unsparing of her trouble, and
devoted to the baby. She did not stop short at being
charming to me but, as he told me years after, extended her
attentions to my husband. The fact that he could not see
his way to accept her advances seemed to have caused no ill
feeling, and we all parted the best of friends. Her ignorance
of her duties did, however, cost me dear in the matter of
health for some considerable time.

Our beloved Alice, who had refused to listen to the
blandishments of her railway guard until after the birth of
"our" baby, as she always referred to it, now left us to be
married. It was not easy to replace her satisfactorily, and
I soon discovered how easily money may be wasted by bad
kitchen management. I began to study the question closely,
making experiments which rather tormented the cook, and
wrote for *Hearth and Home* a series of articles entitled " 10/-

a head for House Books." These articles excited considerable interest. The authors of some of the letters I received were angry with me because they could not keep their expenditure within 10/- a head per week and declared that my figures were incorrect; others who kept within that limit were vastly pleased both with themselves and with me because they did so.

Amongst my correspondents was one who accused me of being a mischief-maker in households, and likely to encourage divorce, while another complained that the nonsense I wrote had made her husband more tiresome than ever about the bills.

I assembled these articles into a book and sold it to Messrs. Constable. Arnold Bennett, who had the true journalistic mind which can concern itself with all subjects of the kind that news editors describe as of "human interest," recast the preface for me and said the title was odd but the book good. It sold all over the English-speaking world, and only went out of print when war prices upset my calculations.

At that date, and indeed, until 1912 or 13, when prices began to rise slightly, it was possible for a competent housewife, even in a servant-keeping house, if the cook was willing to do her part, to provide an early cup of tea, a breakfast dish and the usual toast, butter and marmalade, an 11 o'clock refresher for the maids, a substantial luncheon which was also the nursery and servants' dinner, a simple tea, and a three-course dinner for eight people, two of whom dined late, for 10/- per head per week; the 10/- to include the cost of food and cleaning materials only. To keep within this limit it was necessary to buy all provisions to advantage and to use them to advantage.

In a two- to four-servant middle-class household (including a nurse) the standard of living expected by the maids was not as high as it is now.

During the War the cost of food rose by 129 per cent. above 1914 prices, and in 1920, the year of the highest prices, to 191 per cent. above 1914 prices. At the time that I write these words—March, 1933—it is again possible—given clever management—to provide plain food of the kind to which middle-class people are now accustomed at the 10/- rate.

During the course of our married life, because I have controlled the domestic departments of *Hearth and Home* and *The Queen*, and now control that of *The Lady*, have organised the *Daily Mail* post-War Food Bureau and been Director of Women's Service in the Ministry of Food, I have had unique opportunities of learning how the people of this country live.

In the rich years of the late Victorian and Edwardian periods, the extravagance in many large houses was appalling. The owners of these establishments had neither the time nor the desire to look into the details of their household expenditure. Other people were employed to attend to that, and it was not surprising that those to whom even small sums of money mattered very much should use their opportunities to provide for their later years. The perquisite system was carried to great lengths; indeed in numerous cases the term perquisite was a polite synonym for what was neither more nor less than theft.

In allowing such a state of affairs the careless rich created social plague spots. Every boy and girl who took service in their houses was contaminated by the atmosphere, and it was not only the servants whose standard of moral values was harmed, but the inhabitants of the neighbouring villages.

When Mr. Lloyd George's policy began to impoverish the great land-owners they were forced to enquire into the upkeep costs of their households. Then and after the War, when War Taxation completed the work which Mr. Lloyd George had begun, I received numbers of letters asking for advice from writers who stated that unless their expenditure could be lessened they must shut up their houses. In many cases, to shut up the house at all events temporarily was the only thing to do, for the staff trained to extravagance could not adjust itself to new ideas. The letters I received through my newspapers were confidential and destroyed after being answered, but I remember the contents of several to which reference may be made without abusing the trust of the writers whose names, indeed, I have forgotten.

In one case, it was found that in a household numbering thirty persons, not including guests and their servants or the cost of parties, the expenditure for food and cleaning materials worked out at £4 per head per week, and this although mutton, game, rabbits, garden produce, milk, cream, butter and eggs were obtained free from the estate. At prices such as ruled during the first ten years of the twentieth century it was impossible that any person could eat even £4 worth of food each week and remain long alive. In this case effort was made to put matters on a different footing, but in the end, though greatly against the desire of the owners of the property who were distressed at the amount of unemployment which would be the result of such a step, this house was shut up.

I think it is Frances, Countess of Warwick who, in one of her books, refers to the extravagance of a ducal establishment, where for a week-end party three turtles costing £20 each would be sent down from London and perhaps only partly used. The rotting corpse of one of these reptiles was commented upon by a disapproving farmer who re-marked that "it did cost as much as a cow."

In another case where economies had to be made dis-section of the house accounts showed that the number of eggs used was unreasonable. The *chef* never troubled to teach his underlings to examine each egg as it was broken. For a dish for which perhaps thirty or forty eggs might be needed, one after another they were broken into a large bowl. If one tainted egg went in, then the whole bowlful would be thrown away.

Commission on all goods ordered was regarded as the perquisite of the upper servant who gave the order. It was putting too much faith in human nature to suppose that the average person would refuse to avail himself of the opportunity of making easy money, though in justice to the servant one must bear in mind that he saw nothing wrong in the perquisite system, but many did draw the line at deliberately ordering goods to be given to their friends or thrown away.

Generally speaking, even when luxurious living was required in the dining-room, which meant it was also enjoyed by the upper servants, an average sum of £2 per head per week throughout the household throughout the year should have been sufficient to buy every article of food required. In lesser houses where the management was good, 25/- a head for the dining-room, £1 for the nurseries, school-room, and housekeeper's room, and 15/- a head for the servants' hall, allowed for as good living as most people require. The same estimate is applicable to-day.

If I include letters received by the *Daily Mail* Food Bureau as well as those which came to *Hearth and Home* and *The Queen*, and still do come to me at the offices of *The Lady*, I must have replied to many thousands of letters.

I enjoyed answering that correspondence. Housekeeping is the world's basic profession, and the better we keep house the better people we shall be. Yet no one showers O.B.E.'s on worthy women who stay at home and bring up families, or upon those equally worthy women who go into service and give not only the work of their hands but often the love of their hearts to those for whom they toil.

It always has amused me to note the naïve way in which my correspondents take it for granted that I have magic knowledge of their affairs. They write asking me to budget for them, but forget to mention if they live in the town or the country, the amount paid in Income Tax, or indeed any such details as might make it possible to supply them with a helpful answer. On the other hand others confide in me the innermost secrets of their lives. "My husband is a disagreeable, greedy man," wrote one poor soul, "but naturally I never tell him so," a restraint which I fear would not have been practised by me had I suffered in like manner.

During the five years we lived in Chelsea, life was full of incident. I had plenty of newspaper work and made the most of every opportunity which came my way to gain experience, preferring such as kept me at home rather than that which took me away. Our baby was a great delight to us, and although she had an excellent and devoted nurse, I disliked leaving her.

While yet an infant, she also had an interesting experience. We had chartered an omnibus and had made up a party to drive about and see the Jubilee illuminations of 1897, and then come home to a late supper. As we did not like to think that the servants should not also see all that was to be seen, the supper was put ready, the house locked up, and off we started. Our precious child slept placidly throughout the entire proceedings, which was more than she did on occasions when Nannie went out, for little Miss Peel early learnt to take advantage of her absence and the weakness of her doting parents.

In this same year, 1897, I paid my first visit to Paris. A young, rich and beautiful cousin and her husband had taken a sumptuous flat in the Avenue d'Iéna. The staff consisted of a very old lady whose head was generally tied up in a duster and who wore a black stuff dress, a black apron, and list slippers; her still more ancient husband, who also wore list slippers and a bibbed apron; a smart young footman; and my cousin's maid. The old lady was the cook, and an admirable cook she was; the remainder of the work fell to the lot of the two men, and everything was as well done as it would have been in an English house where double the number of servants were employed.

How I did enjoy myself in Paris! My cousin, who dressed remarkably well, took me with her to the great dress houses where she bought her clothes.

To see well-dressed French and American women was a valuable education to me. Indeed, it was because my news-paper would profit by it that my editor granted me leave of absence. French women, then as now, dressed quietly for the street. Their neatness was exquisite and every detail of the toilette was carefully thought out; English women on the other hand were apt to overdress and to be untidy. They did not think out the ensemble and often spoilt the effect of a good dress and hat by an ill-chosen handbag or the wrong stockings and gloves.

While in Paris we dined at the fashionable places, amongst them the Café de Paris, where there was a wonderful Tzigane band, the leader of which afterwards eloped with a well-known Princess. The Princess could not have had very good taste, for the way in which this theatrical-looking

person ogled the women in his audience was revolting.
Had she eloped with the entire orchestra I could have
understood it, for they played entrancingly.

I learned a great deal about food as well as about
clothes on the occasion of that visit, and learned, too, something of the night life of Paris. If one is to live life to its
full—and that I was determined to do—one must have
some experience of all sections of society. The entertainments which we witnessed were certainly not of the lowest
order, but sufficiently disgusting to make me feel saddened
that large numbers of people should make a living by
prostituting their intelligence and that a still larger number
of people should enjoy such entertainment. Yet if one must
"see life," I prefer to see it in Paris rather than in Berlin
or London. I remember long afterwards that the late
Luigi Naintre, that perfect *maître d'hôtel*, so well known in
the West End of London, told me that the post-War night
life of Berlin was more terrible than anything he had seen
elsewhere.

In my young days public fancy dress balls were held at
Covent Garden. I wished to go to one; so we gathered a
party together and went. Towards the end of the evening
people lay in the passages drunk, and altogether it was rather
a sordid affair. I also desired to see the promenade at the
Empire Music Hall. Young girls did not go to music halls;
but married women might go to a box or to the stalls of
certain houses. I was allowed to hurry through the Empire
promenade, my tall husband on one side and a tall cousin
on the other. This place was nothing more or less than a
a meeting place for women of the town and men who wished
to enjoy their society; but for some extraordinary reason the
Empire had become a National Institution, and when Mrs.
Ormiston Chant made her famous protest against it, she

excited much opposition for daring to interfere with what some of the newspapers referred to as the Club of the Empire. Truly a respectable club, to paraphrase the words of Queen Victoria who when her newly-married daughter departed to Germany with an eighteen-year-old lady-in-waiting, remarked "Truly a respectable Court. The bride seventeen, the lady-in-waiting eighteen."

A year or so later than the Paris visit, I paid my first visit to the Riviera. This book seems to be a record of kind cousins. On this occasion I stayed with cousins who had taken the late Lord Salisbury's villa, La Bastide, on the hill above Beaulieu. Never shall I forget the after-dinner drives to Monte Carlo, a fairy-tale town of domes and jewel-like lights, with at its foot a moonlit sea. Never shall I forget, too, expeditions along the upper Corniche Road into the snow-covered hills. Often the sun was so hot that when we picnicked by the roadside we were glad to shelter beneath our green-lined umbrellas.

One day there came riding past a regiment of Chasseurs Alpins. My cousin was a strikingly beautiful woman and at the sight of her the sun-burned faces of the blue-clad men of Southern France lit up with delight and their white teeth flashed in appreciative smiles. The Colonel set his horse cavorting and kissed his hand gallantly to the ladies.

Monte Carlo then was very different from Monte Carlo to-day. The Sporting Club did not exist, nor, as far as I remember, did the Cercle Privé in the famous Casino. The company in the rooms was not quite of the same order as throngs them now, though even then the German tourist was in evidence—the women in stuff dresses, their long skirts held up by means of a clip attached to a cord girdle, boots of a sternly *pratique* order, and small sailor hats. At night guests were desired to wear evening dress, but who is to say that a check stuff dress turned in at the neck and garnished with a lace collar is not an evening toilette?

I remember lunches at Ciro's, dinners at the Hotel de Paris, evenings spent in the Rooms where celebrated women of the half-world such as Lianne de Pougy and Cleo de Mérode flaunted their beauty, their exquisite dresses and jewels. Of the three most beautiful women I have ever seen, I saw two at Monte Carlo. One was a tall girl of perhaps two-and-twenty, with brown hair and limpid blue eyes, and the complexion of a child, untouched by paint or powder. She should have been picking roses in an English garden. Then she was the mistress of an Indian Prince. We were lunching one day with a party of friends of whom Sir Squire Bancroft was one. This girl passed; there was a little babble of laughing gossip about her. "Poor girl, poor girl," was all that Sir Squire said. I liked him for that.

The second beauty was an Indian woman, unusually tall. As she came swinging up the rooms the crowd drew aside and stood staring. Her exquisite brown shoulders and arms were revealed by the bodice of a low-cut 1830 crinoline dress of dead white satin, she wore heel-less sandals, long diamond ear-rings, and a rivière of diamonds round the pillar-like brown throat which supported her haughty little head.

The third beauty I saw in my childhood at Clifton. She was the nurse of some children who played in the Zoological Gardens. I used to stand and stare at her, and sometimes she would smile at me. Emma Hamilton was once a nursemaid. Later when I first saw a portrait of Emma as the spinning girl, I found my little Clifton girl again.

Monte Carlo was a glamorous place where money lost its normal value; the tables were piled with gold and silver pieces which came and went at the caprice of a whirling ball or the colour of a card. The days were made lovely by the sun, the sea, the great baskets full of carnations, stocks and roses offered for sale by sunburnt, smiling women, and the perpetual smell of freshly-ground coffee which came from the service door of the Hôtel de Paris, where a man in a blue blouse sat roasting it and singing a gay song, added to the fascination.

Sooner or later all the world was to be seen in the Rooms, in the Square or on the Terrace; though there I never went because of the pigeon shooting. At Monte Carlo I saw for the first time Lady Randolph Churchill in the height of her dark, Southern beauty, lovely Miss Muriel Wilson, Mrs. Langtry, and a man whose face I have never forgotten. He was Mr. Carson, now Lord Carson. Often, as in the case of the Clifton nurse, I have seen faces and found them again in portraits of men or of women of a former age, but never in any picture gallery have I seen a replica of Lord Carson's strange and compelling countenance. I think he invented his own face. He would sit at the tables, a "cartwheel" in his hand—I never saw him play high—waiting and waiting, on his sad, kindly face a withdrawn expression. Then, almost reluctantly, he would stake.

One evening the Rooms were so crowded that I could not get near enough to play at my chosen table. A tall, fair, powerfully-built Englishman standing near me took advantage of someone moving from the table to make way for me to approach it. I played for some time and won; once or twice the unknown helped me to rake my winnings in. When I moved from the table I thanked him. To my surprise he followed me, "Be careful where you go with that amount of money on you," he advised. "Thanks, I am joining my cousins, I shall be all right," I replied a little stiffly. He looked at me for a moment. "Monte Carlo isn't London. One does things in Monte Carlo that one doesn't do elsewhere. Can't we meet again?" I wondered if we could. There was something very attractive about that Englishman. Of course he might be a crook but I did not think he was.

After I had agreed to that meeting I went to look for my host. He seemed pleased, but walked as though his boots were tight. They were. He had won £1,000, changed it all into notes, and packed them away in his boots. "Who is that tall fair man over there?" I asked. "So-and-So— quite a nice chap—why do you want to know? Does he love you?" "I think so," I laughed. "Bless you. It's good to be loved," said he.

We did meet again; we spent a day up in the hills, lunching at a little inn under a pergola of vines at a table spread with a blue and white check cloth, upon it a long *bâton* of bread, a basket full of oranges, set off with a spray of fresh orange blossom and toothpicks in a wine glass. As we sat there eating an omelette, followed by veal cutlets and drinking a pinkish fragrant wine made in the hills above Mentone, a bank of white cloud formed, blotting out the world beneath.

That was a good day. I enjoy the memory of that day. After I married there were no more love affairs for me, but I have watched the course of many. Ninety-nine times out of a hundred they create more trouble than they are worth. And yet . . .

CHAPTER XI

A wonderful " buy "—Brompton Square—Life in the early 'nineties—
Prices—When Income Tax was 1/- in the £—The Coronation
of King Edward—Unexpected guests—A Suffrage debate—
A trio of Women's papers—The Hat Shop—Odd customers—
" Dear me and why not ? " said the lady, blandly—Miss Ellen
Terry buys a hat—The Merry Widow Model—How the working
girl lived—They liked to make expensive hats—Hypnotised
by clothes—Writing novels—Fallen girls—But it is hard for
men too.

WE stayed five years in the Chelsea house, and then
thought that circumstances permitted us to better
ourselves, so we bought a house in Brompton
Square. Dear Aunt Susanna had died and left me a little
money which made this purchase possible. I hoped then,
and always have hoped, that wherever her spirit took refuge
she found there the spirit of that handsome, blue-eyed,
crinkly-haired soldier man she had loved so devotedly, and
that once again they were young but this time together and
untorn by the miseries which wrecked their happiness in
this world.

Older and wiser people thought us foolish to take a
more expensive house, but we were young and confident.
We had always found ourselves able to earn money, and I
for one never doubted that we should always be able to go on
earning money, and so far my faith has been rewarded.
How thankful I am for some of my so-called foolishnesses.
They make such joyful memories.

When we married the craze for picking up old furniture
and china had begun. We were bitten by it and had already

made one or two good "buys" at Dewsbury, and were now
looking out for "pieces" for our new home. Passing a
house a few doors from our own one day, I noticed that a
sale was in progress and went in. There were a good many
people there and most of them looked like small dealers.
I stood by the door and was surprised to see some fine
pieces of old brocade and velvet sold. Then a bundle of
what looked like worthless old curtains was brought in.
It was too dark to see them properly, but as they were
carried past me I stretched out my hand, and felt that one
bit at least was embroidery, and fine embroidery at that.
The bundle was thrown on to the table and by chance the
embroidery was hidden. No one took any interest in the
lot and very slowly the bidding went up to 20/-. Then I
had an intuition that amongst that rubbish was something
good. I bid 30/-, someone else said 35/-, I bid 40/-, and at
that price the lot was knocked down to me.

When Charles returned from his office that evening he
was not best pleased to find a bundle of old curtains for
which we had no use. He viewed my purchase in a
different light when we found stitched to two of them
panels of exquisite needlework. Attached to the back of one
panel was a label on which was written, "A pair of
needlework panels, from the Cavendish-Bentinck sale, 8 feet
by 2 feet. £30 the pair."

We subsequently made enquiries about the late owner
of the goods which had been sold and learnt that he had
been a dealer in old furniture and curios with a shop in
Sloane Street. When he retired from business he had taken
some of his stock to furnish his house in Elm Park Road.

In his will he had left his house and contents to two
nieces who lived in the country and they had instructed the
auctioneers to sell them, neither party realising that some of

A LUCKY "BUY"—PRICE 40/-

The photograph shows one needlework panel in its entirety and the central portion of the second

the pieces should have been sent to Christie's and not sold as ordinary "household effects."

I had my panels cleaned and mounted. They hung in the Brompton Square drawing-room and now ornament our drawing-room in Montpelier Place. Not long ago we were offered—but no, I will not say what we were offered for them.

When we went to Brompton Square it had not so long before been a favourite haunt, together with St. Michael's Grove, now Egerton Terrace, of ladies of the half-world. Earlier still its reputation had been exceedingly black, rumour suggesting that many a man had been lured to what was then a rural neighbourhood, robbed and murdered.

I think my husband's uncle, Sir Baldwin Wake Walker, was one of the first respectable persons to install his family in a house in this Square. His example was soon followed, until in the early nineteen-hundreds it was considered quite a good situation.

Our home was one of the two last lodging houses. We proceeded to modernise it, adding a kitchen, larder, boxroom and storeroom, a large drawing-room, small sitting-room and bathroom, a service lift, electric light and a telephone, not as usual a piece of domestic equipment as it now is.

Neither architect nor builder suggested central heating, a second bathroom, or indeed any labour-saving arrangements.

The architect was uninterested in such details, and only by chance did we discover while yet there was time to defeat his plans that he proposed to carry all the hot water pipes through the larder and to make the service lift of such a size that not even a leg of mutton could have been put in it. It took the world war and economic upheaval to make architects realise that houses must be lived in and not only looked at.

This house when rebuilt contained a large basement, three sitting-rooms, what house agents now call a lounge-hall, and seven bedrooms. All the rooms were warmed by coal fires. There were nursery meals to be carried up and down, hot water to be taken to the bedrooms, and we entertained a good deal in a small way. Yet we found little difficulty in running the house with a staff consisting of a Norland nurse, a parlourmaid, a housemaid, and a cook. Later we kept a manservant who had been head footman of three, and asked £70 a year. The cook, and a very fair cook too, earned £28. If my memory serves me rightly, the Norland nurse's salary was £40. Norland nurses, who were women of the educated classes trained at the Norland Institute, wore a special uniform and were a novelty. Later, while our second child was in the nursery meal stage, we had a between maid.

Old account books show that we spent about 12/- a head each week on food and cleaning materials, and this sum included the cost of come-and-go guests, but not of parties. We bought coal at 15/- a ton taking six tons at a time, laundry charges were no more than half what they are now, and the cost of the upkeep of a house much less because labour was cheaper, and the rent and upkeep of shops and business premises very much less. There was penny postage, no insurance to pay for domestic servants, stamps on cheques cost 1d. each and, most important of all, Income Tax was but 1/- in the £. An income of £1,500 a year was, I think, equivalent to one of £2,500 to-day.

One of the first parties which we arranged to give after settling into our new home was on the occasion of King Edward's Coronation. We tucked in country friends wherever they could be tucked, and then the King fell ill and the Coronation was put off. When it did take place it all fell rather flat. We saw the procession from a stand on Constitution Hill, and the only person who made any great mark on my mind was the lovely Queen Marie of Roumania, to whom years after, when she was Queen Mother, I had the honour of being presented. Then she had lost the slimness of youth, but her beauty was magnificent and her personality overwhelming.

On the occasion of another party our tall, elegant butler Clements proved a friend in need. We were expecting friends to dine and were dressing when the maid informed me that Sir Somebody and Lady Something had arrived. This puzzled me for we knew no such people. Also it was now but twenty minutes to eight and our own party was timed for eight. We descended hastily to find an ancient lady in a cap and shawl and a still more ancient gentleman whose head drooped low on his breast as if from the weight of his flowing white beard. They said how d'you do and did not seem in the least surprised to see us. I began to wonder if I was mad. Did I know them? Had I asked them to dine? And what was going to happen now, for by no conjuring could our dining-table accommodate more than eight persons. It seemed terrible to say, "We don't know you and you must go away" to such a pair of pets. Then Clements appeared and bent over the old lady. "If you please m'lady, I think there has been a mistake. Mrs. ————from next door is expecting you to dinner at quarter-to-eight."

Just as obediently as they had accepted their unknown host and hostess did they allow themselves to be coated and shawled and delivered next door.

Next day Clements informed me that it had suddenly occurred to him that our extra pair of guests might belong to one of the "next doors." "So I popped over, Ma'am. I chose 47 because they keep more company than 49. The parlourmaid said they had lost a couple of theirs and I said we had got them."

Clements never walked, he "popped over," he "slipped out," he "just ran"

It was in the middle of the 'nineties that I decided to invite my friends to a Suffrage Debate and asked the Suffrage and the Anti-Suffrage Societies to provide two speakers. Having a liking for hearing both sides of any question, I looked forward to an interesting afternoon.

The Suffrage speaker made a brilliant speech, but the Anti-Suffrage representative crumpled. One of the few suggestions which she put forward in support of her cause was that as the Virgin Mary had not had a vote it was unnecessary for any other woman to have one.

It was daring of me to stage this debate, for Women's Suffrage was one of those subjects which excited passionate feeling. Many men, and women, too, thought that if women were enabled to use political power directly rather than indirectly by exploiting their sex or using the power of money or social position, the British Empire would crumble to ruin.

In my childhood it had been thought dangerous to allow women to go to College, to pass examinations and above all to trifle with mathematics, their brains being so constructed as to be unable to absorb such knowledge. It was a blow to this school of thought—or of prejudice—when in 1890 Miss Phillipa Fawcett, daughter of the blind Professor and Mrs. Henry Fawcett, later on President of the National Union of Women's Suffrage Societies, had been placed "above the Senior Wrangler." However, one could, if so minded, comfort oneself by hoping that Miss Fawcett was a freak.

Now we had ceased to be quite so excited about higher

education and were concentrating our attention on this question of votes for women.

Life was very pleasant during the first years of our stay in the Brompton Square house. We had almost enough money for our needs, interesting work, plenty of friends and acquaintances and occasional holidays.

In 1903 I became Editor and Managing Director of three women's papers, *Hearth and Home*, *Woman*, and *Myra's Journal*, which was an experience worth having. It lasted for three years, and then, owing to the death of General Talbot Coke, the chief proprietor, the papers were closed down, and I retired into private life until after the birth of our second child. A year-and-a-half later we had the sorrow of losing our third and last baby.

After regaining my health I decided that I would take a rest from newspaper work, but soon found that having been accustomed to regular occupation, time hung heavy on my hands. Too much amusement did not amuse me.

It happened just then that a friend, once Ethel Freeling, then Ethel Kentish, and now Ethel Hornsby, became a widow and was anxious to take up some occupation. We decided that we would start a hat shop. Both of us knew a good hat when we saw one, and there our knowledge ended. Undeterred by that, we took a shop and engaged a head milliner. She had been an assistant in one of the lesser Paris houses and was a sister of the maid of one of Ethel's friends. She was a very nice woman, and one who thoroughly knew her work, though, being temperamental, she needed careful handling.

We also engaged an accountant-stock-keeper, Miss Brown, who understood the routine of the business. Ethel and I learned much in that shop, not only about hats but about human nature and about friendship. She is to this day one of the best and kindest friends I have.

We discovered that company manners were often left on the doorstep of a shop (I fear I have left my own there at times) and that ladies of high degree did not hesitate to descend to trickery to obtain goods at other people's expense.

One of our funniest experiences was when a well-known social celebrity came into the showroom, chose one of our models, put it on, thrust a hatpin through it, and walked off. Our accountant had early warned us that we must always ask new customers for references. This lady's reputation was so well known that it was unnecessary to trouble to do that. The situation was explained to Miss Brown. She took up the hat which our undesired customer had left behind her. "Five good feathers," said she. "Cleaned and curled they'll be all right. Now, Madam, don't you let her have that hat back till she's paid for the new one. Not that she ever will. She used to play that trick with Madame G——. Still, you won't actually lose much on it. These feathers are worth nearly the cost price of our hat."

Lady ——— never did pay for her new hat. Nevertheless, on another occasion when she was going abroad, she appeared, quite unabashed, and gave a considerable order. We left Miss Brown to deal with her. Miss Brown told her politely that we were a ready-money firm, and that we should be obliged to ask for payment before the goods were delivered. "Dear me, and why not," said the lady, blandly.

Three times the goods were sent; three times the servant did his best to persuade our messenger to leave them. Then came a telephone message to say if the goods were delivered at 11 o'clock that morning they would be paid for and so they were.

On another occasion a beautiful and well-known young

woman ordered an expensive blouse which I had bought in Paris. Three days later it was returned rather crumpled. In the box was a note from our customer to a Mrs. So-and-So in Walham Green asking her to copy the blouse as quickly as possible and to return the model to us. Pinned to the lining of the blouse was a note addressed to us in which our client explained that she hoped we would not mind her returning it, but after trying it on she had found that it did not suit her.

Generally speaking, however, our clients were charming. Not the least charming was Miss Ellen Terry, who sat in the shop fascinating us while Mademoiselle altered a model until it conformed to Miss Terry's idea of what a hat should be.

It is the fashion nowadays to talk about good salesmanship, of which indeed there is none too much. I think we were good saleswomen. One day a beautiful woman appeared. She wanted hats to take to India. As it was then winter no suitable hats were forthcoming. "If you can allow me two days, Madam, I will send you six hats on approval. Please do not think you are under any obligation to take them if they do not suit you." That lady was Lady Hardinge the new Vicereine of India. We received the whole of her order for millinery, as well as one for a considerable number of blouses and oddments.

Another well-known woman, now Lady Susan Birch, who often came to us, was so popular that Mademoiselle herself would come down and wait on her; Miss Brown would come up from the office; even the trotter would peep round the door entranced.

A trotter was a little girl who went to the shops to match materials, and fetch odd reels of cotton or silk needed in a hurry, or small goods not worth ordering from the travellers of the wholesale houses who arrived in broughams or small omnibuses piled with boxes.

At first we bought all our models in Paris; but we soon found that, although English women demanded Paris models, what they really wanted, and what they generally got, if they had only known it, was a French model adapted to suit the English face and taste. Since the War, women of all European nations have come to look more like each other than they did, because they wear the same kind of clothes. When we kept a hat shop this was not so. French fashions were very much in advance of English, and women of the various nationalities were more individual.

In some of the well-known Paris model houses the small customer was treated with scant respect. In one of these my *vendeuse* told me airily that she would make me a couple of models as soon as she had time to attend to the order. I pointed out that I should like to see the models before I bought them, for although I knew that the reputation of her firm was such that the hats would be perfect examples of the milliner's art, they might not be saleable in London. The young woman was very hoity-toity. When I bade her a polite good-bye without giving an order she relented and ultimately provided me with two models which we copied over and over again in various colours and materials. The better model of the two was a hat with a very large flat brim, which Miss Lily Elsie popularised as the Merry Widow hat, and which I honestly think we were the first milliners to introduce to London.

The life of our work girls interested me. They began work at 8.30 and left off at 6 o'clock. In those days there was no fixed scale of wages. Head milliners in the great houses were well paid. We paid ours £4 a week, and our second hand 25/-. The rank and file earned from 8/-

to 16/- a week, and the little apprentices who made the head linings, picked up the special long pins which strew the floors of all millinery workrooms, and learned what they could, received half-a-crown a week. Some of our girls travelled to London by workmen's trains and sat in waiting-rooms, reading their novelettes until the workroom was open. It was not surprising that by 11 o'clock they needed food. In many workrooms no morning break was permitted and the girls would produce food from their pockets and try to eat it unobserved, with the result that material might be spoiled.

The girls were obliged to go out in the dinner hour in order that the rooms should be aired, in conformity with the orders of the Home Office. A printed list of Home Office Regulations hung in each room and women inspectors might demand entrance at any moment to see that they were not ignored.

Accordingly, girls who could not afford to go to a restaurant ate their meal where they could. We finally decided that an apprentice should make 11 o'clock tea and the girls should be allowed a ten minutes' break at 11 o'clock to go down to the kitchen and drink it. It took Miss Brown all her time to see that the break did not extend to fifteen or twenty minutes. We also arranged that our staff should have the use of a kitchen and a couple of gas rings, which enabled them to eat their midday meal in comfort.

Our workers were generally very gay; they would sing at their work, and chatter like a cage full of birds. The word of the head milliner was law, and any conversation not approved by her was brought to an abrupt end.

One might have thought that girls living under such conditions would have resented customers who bought hats costing as much as eight and ten guineas, for that was

not an unusual price when fashionable women wore afternoon hats on which there might be half-a-dozen feathers or
a lancer plume, that is, a feather as much, perhaps, as a
yard in length, on to each frond of which another frond was
knotted. On the contrary, the girls enjoyed making these
expensive hats and went short of food so that they might
copy for themselves these costly models.

I had not long been in the millinery business before I
began to realise how deteriorating to the moral sense is a
passion for costly clothes, both to the women who buy them,
to the girls who make them, and to the women who sell them.
Many a girl dreamed not of a husband who she would love
and who would love her, but of a rich husband who could
provide the garments for which she yearned. Then when
it became evident that a rich husband was unlikely to come
her way, perhaps a well-to-do lover might take his place.
Considering the small wage which they earned, the squalid
homes in which they lived, and the fact that the small wage
they earned left them dependent on their admirers for their
amusements, it was surprising that so many of these girls
did, as they expressed it, "keep on the straight."

As for our customers, many of them were absolutely
hypnotised by new clothes; have them they must. If a
husband could not pay, someone else would. If their moral
sense did not permit this, they would actually ask to hire
hats or promise that if we would lend them one for some
special occasion they would introduce a new client. The
vendeuses in their turn in order to sell their wares would
descend to all kinds of trickery and blandishment. I who
loved "good" clothes so well could understand all these
points of view and did not succeed in deciding how such a
state of affairs could be altered unless by passing a sumptuary
law and putting all women into uniform.

Eventually my partner fell ill and was obliged to have an operation and to retire from the business. Not long after, I too became ill, and that was the end of the hat shop. But no, not the end, for the experience gained in it was of lasting value. Also, when I recovered, it occurred to me to write a novel about it. This I did; it was well reviewed and later on published in a cheap edition.

As "The Hat Shop" had proved popular, my publisher demanded another book on the same lines. I called it "A Man and His Womenkind," which was the right title for it. I was persuaded to allow it to appear under the title of "Mrs. Barnett, Robes," a label which I disliked. It had its points but was a carelessly-written book and no credit to me; why the publisher's readers did not suggest that it needed revision, is one of the many things which I do not know.

My next novel was called "A Mrs. Jones," and it, too, pleased the critics. My fourth and last novel was accepted amiably by critics and public, though one woman wrote asking me to stop writing novels. "I like your cookery books, but I hate your novels," said she.

In order to obtain local colour for these books I procured an introduction to a lady who was employed by a certain Association to work amongst the unfortunate girls of the West End streets. We made friends and she told me much about her experiences and took me out with her once or twice. That woman was a saint if ever there was one; a hard-working, tolerant, humorous saint. She told me that it was not unusual for a man who had become interested in a girl to apply to Sister, as she was known, in the hope that the girl might be removed from the life of the streets. In few cases, however, could any kind of work which would appeal to them be offered to such girls. "The life gets its claws into them,"

Sister explained, "and after a time they are useless for regular work."

I pushed my investigations further, visiting Homes for what were called "fallen" girls. Almost all of these places were financed by religious bodies. There would be, perhaps, a Sister in charge of a receiving station, to which the police or any other interested person would send some stranded girl who had already got into trouble or was in danger of doing so. From this temporary shelter the girl would be passed on to a Home, in some of which a girl was taken before her baby was born, then sent to the Infirmary for her confinement, and received again with the baby afterwards.

In one Home which I visited, in a large bare room were rows of cots. Every baby appeared to be screaming as hard as it could scream. After a day's work the young mothers would return to put their babies to bed, and to wash their clothes. They had the charge of the infants at night, rose early to attend to them, and then went out to work again. Perhaps it was not wonderful that the life of the street, hard though it might be, appealed more to young girls than this fifteen-hour day of respectability. Yet what better could be done for them?

I visited too, an Infirmary in Soho, a similar Institution in South London, two others in West London. Dreary places all. In one was a lovely, fragile girl with twins, as beautiful children as you could wish to see. How could that delicate girl support herself and two children respectably? The man she had loved had disappeared. He was of higher social position than she, had lived with her for six months and left her penniless, knowing that she was bearing his child.

Well, life is as it is and we can but do the little we can do to make it more endurable for those on whom it bears too hardly. Sometimes it bears as hardly on men as upon women. Only to-day did I learn of a young man who had committed a burglary—the tool of a professional thief. This young man, of admirable character, had been out of work for many months. His wife, whom he loved passionately, nagged him—the poor soul was ill-fed and had to stint her two children of food, she had to see them shabby and to go shabby herself. At any time a trashy-minded girl, though with a certain vivid charm, she could not bear hardship grandly. Her husband met the thief in a public house. The thief got clear but his accomplice was caught.

The wife attended the Police Court dressed in the height of cheap fashion, silk stockings, fur-collared coat, pert hat and lipstick. Why should the man be driven to steal if his wife could dress like that? A kindly policeman explained, "Hired, M'm. They'll all go back to-night and no doubt she's borrowed to pay the hire. A little sense'd have showed her she'd better have come here looking quiet."

That night I was reading "Façade," a clever novel by Theodora Benson, and came across these words: "'Tis bad luck if you're found out just the one time you do something quite unlike the sort of chap you really are."

He was a courteous little burglar, that, for later he came to apologise to the lady he had burgled.

Fate was kind, and the matter ended happily, for a former employer for whom he had worked well made a job for him.

CHAPTER XII

Operations were different then—Sir William Watson Cheyne—
Sir Thomas Parkinson—The Lister technique—It was quiet and
comfortable being dead—"Come back, come back," he cried—
Wintering in Switzerland—The Children's Commonwealth—
They sent themselves to school—God knows what were the
memories of that child—The age of consent—Modern Babylon
—Oh, happy days—The tragedy of Miss Lucy.

THE illness which brought my shop-keeping to an
end became acute. No one knew what was the
matter. Someone suggested a treatment at Aix les
Bains, which was a cheery, cosy little place full of beautifully-
dressed French women and *chic* restaurants. There was a
good theatre, admirable music and gambling rooms, and
the surrounding country was exquisite. I went there, and,
in the intervals of having bad attacks of pain, enjoyed myself.

But the treatment did me harm rather than good.
When I arrived home again I was in severe pain. Dr.
Parkinson, now Sir Thomas Parkinson, was away, so his
assistant came to see me and declared that I was suffering
from gallstones. Dr. Parkinson on his return wished me to
see a specialist. An immediate operation was decided upon,
and I was ordered into a nursing home.

Dr. Parkinson had warned me that the operation was a
serious one. "You are not a foolish, hysterical woman,"
said he, "and I am sure you will wish to know how matters
stand so that you may make such arrangements as may be
necessary, though I hope and believe that all will be well."
Having made all my arrangements I entered a Home

which was extraordinarily unhomelike. Once inside I felt
that my responsibilities were ended; and that night, for the
first time for many weeks, I slept soundly, and naturally felt
extremely annoyed that I had to be awakened so early to be
prepared for the operation, which was to take place at nine
o'clock. A young nurse with pink cheeks and exquisite
black-lashed blue eyes appeared. Whilst she did what had
to be done she chatted amiably. "And are ye afraid of
dying?" she asked in her pretty Irish brogue. Had I been
the silly hysterical woman who dear Parky, as our children
called him, had told me that I was not, I think I might have
given that young woman some trouble.

Later in the morning the anæsthetist arrived, a tall
young man with a walrus moustache and a canary-yellow
woolwork waistcoat such as devoted young ladies then
worked for their beloveds. In order, as he said, to cheer me
he sat upon my bed and produced numbers of photographs
of starving Russian children. He had lately been in Russia,
where famine was raging. After some conversation with him
I was so thankful that I did not live in Russia that I could
feel resigned to being in London, even though I did have to
have an operation.

Then appeared Dr. Parkinson and his assistant, the
latter praying passionately that he who had been the first
to diagnose my complaint would be found to have diagnosed
it correctly.

Shortly afterwards the matron summoned my three
visitors elsewhere. Heavy footsteps now approached, the
sound of loud breathing was heard, and the star performer,
stout, elderly Sir William Watson Cheyne, made his
entrance. He said nothing, sat down by my bed, and seeing
a box of chocolates upon the table, opened it and helped
himself. There he sat munching and looking at me, and

there in my bed, my hair neatly plaited in two pigtails each tied with pink ribbon, lay I looking at him.

Sir William Watson Cheyne was one of the famous surgeons of the day. When Lister was introducing a new technique with regard to operations at King's College Hospital, Sir William, then young Mr. Watson Cheyne, was one of his assistants and enthusiastic admirers. In Lister's day an operation, even though it might be simple in itself, more often than not proved fatal owing to blood poisoning. The famous Professor Naussbaum, of Munich, then perhaps the greatest living surgeon, confessed that eighty per cent. of his operations proved fatal, but after adopting Lister's technique, his statistics of death from wound infection sank to zero.

Even after Lister came to King's, and St. Thomas's and Guy's welcomed him eagerly, the authorities of yet another large London hospital refused to accept his methods and many surgeons remained scornful of his new ideas. At King's a well-known surgeon while watching Lister perform a dangerous operation, rose and was on the point of touching the wound with an unsterilised finger when Lister pushed him back.

When Watson Cheyne was a young man and I a little child, surgeons performed operations in dirty old coats which they kept as being suitable for such occasions, merely turning back their sleeves so that they might work with greater freedom.[1] I wish that I had then known that my surgeon had been one of the pioneers of antiseptic surgery. I should have asked him to tell me of his experiences instead of chatting amicably about the weather, which was, when he had eaten his fill of chocolates, what we did.

Then Sir William disappeared, and soon the matron

[1] "Reminiscences of a Specialist" by Greville Macdonald, M.D.

140

came to say that the doctors were ready for me, and I, clad in a nightdress slit open up the back, a coquettish pink dressing-gown, "operation stockings" which were rather like fishermen's waders made of white flannel, and which I clutched, fearing every moment they would descend, made my *début* in the operating room. This at other times was a bedroom, for there were no operating theatres in nursing homes then. Without more ado I was assisted to climb on to the operating table. Everyone was very kind to me. Dr. Parky held one of my hands and the anæsthetist patted the other and then set to work. I talked and I laughed, becoming stupider and stupider, but still I could not stop talking. "I am very sorry," I explained, "but I *must* talk." "Talk as much as you like," replied Dr. Parky, "we shan't listen to anything you may say." And then the world faded. . . .

Later I thought I was dead. It was quiet and comfortable being dead. I had no regrets, indeed I had forgotten my earthly existence. Then I became aware that although I was dead, other people were still alive. I was far away, but I knew they were shaking my body and talking to it. After they had talked and shaken for a long time a few words penetrated my consciousness. "Husband," and again, "husband . . . so unhappy." It seemed a pity to have to come back, but when husbands are unhappy . . . A very great friend of mine once told me that she had died of double pneumonia in India. Her spirit had escaped from her body and was free. Somewhere from a great height it looked down upon earth and saw her body lying on the bed. Her husband was kneeling by it. "Come back, come back, come back," he cried in his misery. It gave her terrible pain to renounce her newly-won freedom, to return to that fever-wracked form.

It has been said that after the spirit leaves the body, for some short time it hovers near. Perhaps it is true. My convalescence was long, and before I had completely recovered I fell ill with pneumonia. Feeling the worse for wear, and with a pain in my back, I thought I would walk in the Park. About half way between Albert Gate and Hyde Park Corner I stopped to rest as the pain was acute. Once more the world faded. I recovered my senses to find that a crowd had collected. A kind woman took charge of me, asked a policeman to get a cab and took me home, or rather to the hotel in which we were staying as we had let our house and were about to take one in the country. I staggered to my bed. Fortunately, later a cousin came to see me, was told that I was ill, came up to my bedroom, and sent for a doctor and a nurse.

I wonder that my husband did not send for a packet of weed killer. Never was a man so kind as he to a wife who was for ever being expensively ill.

For four years after this escapade I spent a month or two of each winter in Switzerland taking the children and being joined by my husband for a fortnight at Christmas. What fun those winters were. A great friend, Winifred Herbert, came with me while our husbands hobnobbed together at home. How lovely it was to start out, she with her sketching, I with my writing things, our luncheon packets fastened on our luges, to sit and paint and write and eat in the brilliant sunshine amongst the fast-frozen snow on which the pine trees threw shadows of deepest blue, to pause on the way home and drink coffee and eat *croissants* and cherry jam at the village café. Even though he could only take so short a winter holiday, Charles enjoyed it to the full. He lost no time in learning to ski—indeed he put on skis and skied. Women skiers then wore skirts half-way between knee and ankle and knickerbockers beneath. The result when they took a toss was a trifle comic; undoubtedly the modern trousered outfit is more workmanlike. But it needed the War to accustom us to women in trousers.

Those Swiss winters mended my lung, and again I felt fit for whatever adventure life might provide.

Interested as I was in the Suffrage movement and as a professional woman coming in touch with other workers, I met many clever women, amongst them several whose lives were spent in helping to better conditions for underdogs. Owing to one of these contacts I paid a visit to the Children's Commonwealth in Dorsetshire, an experimental colony to which delinquent children were sent. Certain magistrates found difficulty in satisfactorily placing certain children both for their own sakes and for the sake of more normal children with whom they were unfitted to associate. The Commonwealth was started for their benefit. Life in this farm colony approximated as nearly as possible to life in an ordinary home, for children of different ages lived in cottages under the care of a house mother. To some extent they were allowed to manage their own affairs by means of a Parliament which discussed questions of general policy and discipline. The children were not forced to attend school. Other methods were employed. One summer afternoon I sat in the little garden of the guest house watching and listening to some young children who were making a garden. They were totally ignorant of gardening. One wished to grow a cauliflower. How did cauliflowers grow? After some discussion one of the children went to ask the Director of the Colony to advise him. Now, this little group of children had only lately arrived and had refused to attend school. They said they saw no object in going to school. The Director took his opportunity. He presented the would-be gardeners with a book, which none could read, and some labels on which they might write the names of the seeds which they had planted, well knowing that none of them could write. He regretted that other duties prevented him from helping them further, but explained that they would find all they needed to know in the book.

Those children decided to send themselves to school.

One of the gardening party, or rather a very young lady who had attached herself to the gardening party, was the Colony's pet, then aged two-and-a-half. She was the incestuous child of a little girl of thirteen, who after the baby's birth screamed so terribly at the mere sight of her that she had to be taken away. Another girl, pretty, fair, graceful, who was helping with the work of the guest house, had at the age of fourteen been purchased by four sailors. She seemed happy there, but was very silent. God alone knows what were the memories of that child.

Alas, this Colony came to an end. Although the reasons why it closed were tragic, much good work had been done in directing the attention of those in authority to reformatories and their betterment.

You may think that what I have just written should not be published in a book such as this. That is not so, for this is the life of a woman, not a pretty tale for schoolgirls. It is only by the knowledge of the existence of such horrors that they may be lessened.

I will remind you that when I was a baby girl playing in a lily garden, the age of consent was thirteen. If a child of that age entered a disorderly house of her own accord, even though it could be proved that she was innocent of any knowledge of such places, she had given legal proof that she had consented to her undoing. A Royal Commission sitting in 1871 had recommended a change in the law. Ten years later a Bill was drafted and formally introduced. It was opposed by Members who said that its supporters were visionaries who did not know the world. Five years later again, when I was a young girl, Mr. Stead, Editor of the *Pall Mall Gazette*, was begged by Josephine Butler and Mr. Benjamin Scott, the City Chamberlain, to save the Bill by publishing the facts of the situation. First he proved that they were as stated, then he published his experiences in his paper under the heading of "The Maiden Tribute of Modern Babylon." Fifteen years of patient protest had made little impression, but this publicity aroused such horror that in 1885 the age of consent was raised to sixteen.

In those fourteen years since the finding of the Royal Commission of 1871, when the police had given evidence of the magnitude of this traffic, how many children had been betrayed?

Do you women who now are citizens wonder that when I was young, we so passionately desired the vote?

Do you think that had there been women in Parliament then, it would have taken fourteen years to raise the age of consent from thirteen to sixteen?

. . . . . .

One year, after a bout of influenza, we went to Algiers, and being both in the nervous, irritable state which was a marked after-feature of that year's form of the disease, we disliked it and, to my subsequent regret, left without going on into the desert. Instead, we dismally waited for a still day, and then took ship for Marseilles, and very nearly did not get there, for half-an-hour after leaving Algiers, such a tempest suddenly arose as to cripple our boat. We chugged on with one engine and had to be towed the last few miles into port. The next Spring, on the same day, that same boat went to the bottom, and all those in her were drowned except one man, who went mad from shock.

Ill and jaded we arrived at Marseilles station, to be delayed from crossing the line to the opposite platform because the remains of a man who had been run over by a train were then being removed. Arrived at Monte Carlo, we went to an hotel perched high above the Bay of Monaco.

I write in London on a morning so dark that the electric light is burning, and make for myself pictures of days when the sun shone, and the oranges—those golden fruits of the Hesperides—hung amongst their shining green leaves, and the scent of stocks floated up from the garden beneath, and we sat oh! so happily together on our balcony drinking coffee and eating croissants and little curls of butter.

I think, too, of silver-spangled, sweet-scented nights. . . . Yet London has it compensations, and so has age.

I recall, too, lovely happy days in an English garden, the blue sky shaded by soft white cloud, the lilacs blooming, and under an apple-tree, pink and white with blossom, the luncheon table. It was our habit when in the country to live in Continental fashion, eating *déjeuner* at half-past twelve, and while we ate and talked over our meal, blackbirds and thrushes sang, and a lovely green-eyed cat with swishing tail crouched, then tired of useless endeavour, came purring to beg for just a tiny share of our feast.

Is there anything more beautiful than an English garden in spring, unless it be an English copse in autumn when the leaves are turning golden and russet, when the mist rises and the sun sets in a glory of red and gold, fading to a faint metallic green? How I have loved such beauty.

The mention of sunsets recalls to my mind a house from the stoep of which I have watched so many flush and fade, and memory also connects it with a tragic event which happened while we were living in Brompton Square, for it was on that stoep that I rested and recovered from the shock which I received.

I had been accustomed to employ a certain hair-dresser, and so had made the acquaintance of Miss Lucy, as she was called, who visited me at home for face massage and manicure. This young woman would describe her life in the shop, which she detested. Later she left it, hoping to make a living by working independently. One afternoon she came to me and I thought her looking ill and tired. Tea had been prepared for her, but she refused it, saying that she had indigestion. She began her work, standing behind me, when suddenly I heard the noise of a heavy fall. I thought for a moment that some object in the room below, possibly a picture, had fallen. I jumped from the bed and saw the poor woman lying on the floor. Fortunately at this moment my husband came in. Together we laid her upon my bed, and did what we could to revive her. As she showed no signs of returning consciousness, we rang up our doctor, but he was out. We tried several other doctors, and finally a very aged and apparently senile person arrived. After looking at the patient for some time, he said that he thought she probably had had an hysterical fit. "Keep her warm, let her lie quiet. She will soon recover," said he, and departed. At nine o'clock that night, feeling uneasy about her, I sent for a nurse. Leaving the still unconscious patient in her charge, I went to lie down. Two hours later nurse woke me. Lucy, still unconscious, was dying. We knew nothing more about her than her name and address. The woman at whose house she lodged knew no more than we knew. Then I remembered that she had told me she was a Catholic. We went to Brompton Oratory and found her Father Confessor there.

In time we learned something of her history. Her father, a ne'er-do-well, had deserted his wife and children. Lucy, the eldest daughter, had been adopted by a relation. She lived the life of a rich girl, chiefly in Nice and Cannes, occasionally in London. One day a letter came from her father. He was dying, he longed to see his daughter, whom after his fashion, he loved, and who loved him. The relation, who had suffered much at his hands, refused to let the girl go, said that if she disobeyed she should never return. The girl went and never did return.

Lucy died from long-drawn-out starvation, and at the last from congestion of the lungs and a broken blood-vessel in the brain. The landlady told us she had no friends and never went out except on business. Her one extravagance was the purchase of newspapers which offered money prizes for competitions, and the necessary stamps and envelopes. She told the woman that some day she knew she would win a prize—perhaps a thousand pounds. A thousand pounds! A penny for a paper, a penny for a stamp, twopence for a few envelopes . . . and that night to bed—hungry. But to-morrow, perhaps, a thousand pounds.

CHAPTER XIII

When Edward was King—His death and funeral—The Suffragettes
must "pester and be patient"—Lady Constance Lytton—When
the ladies appeared the gentlemen sang, shouted, jostled and
threw mud—Hence the sheep—In Holloway Prison—Girls'
Borstal—She was mad with jealousy and distress—Education
—Bridge and Bridge Clubs—The lucky day—A salary of £700
—Winning the Derby at 100 to 1—Intuitions—At Monte Carlo
and at Aix les Bains.

WHAT a rushing, glittering time it was, that of
King Edward's reign. The Court set an example
of splendour, and American, South African, and
Jewish magnates were made welcome. Social conventions
became less strict and, where rank, or position gained by
outstanding mental capacity backed by wealth had been
passports into exclusive society, now money, unbacked by
other qualifications, began to talk, though not invariably
to just those people to whom it desired to talk.

There was a vast amount of entertaining of a lavish order,
with red carpets and awnings, rows of men-servants and
champagne suppers. As the motor car came into more
general use, the week-end habit grew, and well-to-do folk
ceased to use the Park and went further afield for their
Saturday to Monday pleasuring. Even people of no account
like ourselves were affected. We went to quantities of all
kinds of parties and when we could get away took a holiday
abroad or rented a house in the country, sufficiently near
London for Charles to travel up and down to his office and
for me to keep in touch with my newspapers.

Then came the illness and death of King Edward.

149

Everyone, I think, felt sorry that he should have lived so short a time to enjoy the Kingship which for so long had been denied him, but his death did not mark the end of a period, as that of his Royal Mother had done, and neither was it mourned by members of the general public as a personal loss.

For some days before his death women had wondered what best to do about mourning; probably there would be a shortage of black clothes, and the price would then rise. Should they buy at once or should they wait until . . .? One friend told me that she should equip herself because never did she buy bright-coloured clothes but that she killed a relation. To buy black might save His Majesty's life. The only result of her loyal decision was that she had the pick of the market at a reasonable price.

King Edward's funeral was a red and gold and gorgeous pageant, but it did not touch the heart as that of the Queen had done. As the *cortége* passed I was struck by the way in which the visiting Royalties chatted with each other, and even laughed. His Majesty, ex-King Alfonso of Spain was the only one whose face bore any look of grief. The Coronation of King George and Queen Mary passed without special incident, and soon it seemed as if in Royal circles a steadier, more domestic atmosphere was being created. For the time, however, society in general went its way as before.

Throughout the twentieth century until the War the doings of the Suffragettes were one of the chief topics of conversation. Since 1906, when the Women's Social and Political Union, led by Mrs. Pankhurst, had made London its headquarters, the public had become more and more excited about votes for women. In that year Mr. Keir Hardy had secured a day for the introduction of a Women's Suffrage Resolution in the House of Commons, and the

Prime Minister, Sir Henry Campbell Bannerman, had been persuaded to receive a Deputation consisting of representatives of all the organisations supporting "The Cause," as it had come to be called. It was hoped that the resolution would be carried by a substantial majority, and that the Prime Minister would be so impressed that he would then make a favourable announcement to the deputation.

A Mr. Cremer opened the debate, taking the jocular tone which so infuriated women, referring to them as persons, the majority of whom were not bread winners, who had not to bear the burden and did not understand the responsibilities of life. . . . The women who were present began to fear that the resolution was to be talked out. "Divide, divide," they called from behind the grille, for then they were put inside a cage like animals at the Zoo, and "Votes for Women" banners were pushed through its bars.

There was a mild fracas and some of the women were ejected. It was regrettable that the militants, who up till then had done nothing more violent than interrupt meetings, did not realise that it was unwise to allow themselves to be irritated by a person whose purpose it was to irritate.

In spite of this fuss, the Prime Minister did receive the deputation, agreed that the women's case was conclusive and irrefutable, and proposed to do nothing about it. He advised them to go on pestering and to exercise the virtue of patience.

The deputation of "persons who had not to bear the burden and did not understand the responsibilities of life" numbered over 300, and represented all the organised women suffragists—a large number: 50,000 textile workers, 22,000 Co-operative women, 52,000 members of British Temperance Associations and 1,150 graduates—and was introduced by Sir Charles McLaren and led by Miss Emily

Davies, the originator of Girton College, who had been working for the better education and enfranchisement of women for fifty years.

That was the beginning of the real militant campaign. Although I did not approve of lawless deeds, I am convinced that in the end it was the spectacular propaganda of the militant suffragettes, under the leadership of Mrs. Pankhurst and her daughters, which did even more than the quieter efforts of Mrs. Fawcett's followers, or the War work of women to procure for us the status of citizens. The surest way of furthering a cause is to make martyrs of its advocates and the Government made martyrs of women who, after all, were only desirous of being put in a position to serve their country better than before.

One of the ugliest incidents of the campaign arose out of the case of Lady Constance Lytton. Enthusiastic though delicate, she was twice arrested and imprisoned, on one occasion in Holloway, and on another in Newcastle. She was not submitted to the ordinary prison discipline, and was on both occasions released before her sentence expired. But when she was arrested at Liverpool under a feigned name, no careful medical examination followed, and she was forcibly fed. Only when her identity became known was she released on medical grounds, to remain an invalid to the day of her death. That was a scandalous affair, and as far as the Government was concerned, a stupid affair, for it added many supporters to the cause.

I never had the pleasure of meeting any of the Pankhursts, though I did once or twice meet Mrs. Fawcett, afterwards Dame Milicent Fawcett, and felt that I should never be influenced by her leadership of any cause. She left me cold. That, however, was merely my reaction to her personality, for she was a very fine leader, far seeing, quick witted, calm and just. I also met Mrs. Despard and Mr. and Mrs. Pethick Lawrence.

Now that I profit by the brave, unselfish efforts of the suffragists, I feel ashamed that I did practically nothing to help them. The young women of to-day do not, perhaps, know enough of the women who worked so courageously for the benefit of their sex during the past century.

Talking the other day to a quick, clever girl who had been educated at good schools, I found that she had never heard of Mary Wollstonecraft, Caroline Norton or Josephine Butler, or of that group of educationists, Emily Davies, Lydia Becker, Miss Buss and Miss Beale, or of those others who made it possible that women should become doctors— Elizabeth Blackwell, Elizabeth Garrett (afterwards Mrs. Garrett Anderson), and Sophia Jex-Blake.

When I was a little girl of two—before I had seen the end of the world—the to-do about women doctors was at its height, and the famous riot of Surgeon's Hall, Edinburgh, took place. The men students wished to prevent the five women students from entering the building. When the ladies appeared, the gentlemen sang, shouted, jostled, threw mud and slammed the courtyard doors in their faces. The ladies remained calm; a janitor managed to open a little door and they entered and went to their classroom, which was in possession of more young gentlemen. The professor turned them out. A moment or two later a sheep was pushed into the room. "Let it stay," said the angry professor, "it has more sense than those who sent it here." The male students afterwards said they understood that inferior animals were not to be excluded from the classes— hence the ladies and the sheep.

I have always longed to know what the sheep thought of it all—that, alas! we never shall know. And why do we label animals, which never commit such vulgarities and sillinesses, as inferior? My young friend did not realise that in those days married women did not own their own money or furniture, and that if they earned money they did not own even that. They owned neither themselves nor their children—unless these were illegitimate.

She was amused by the story about the sheep and is now reading up the period, having begun with that admirable book "The Cause," by Ray Strachey, in which she finds food for mirth, for anger, and for thankfulness.

I think that now women are citizens they take a greater interest in the nation's affairs than they did when I was a girl and a young married woman. But now that they may become magistrates, and be called to sit on a jury, I should like to see them preparing for such duties by visiting prisons, reformatories, and the "homes" to which delinquent children are sent, and attending police courts, and possibly a murder trial.

To watch a murderer tried for his life out of a mere lust for sensation is a horrible act, but as part of the education of any person who may have the responsibility of sitting on a jury which is trying a murder case, it might be advisable to endure the experience.

It fell to my lot once to visit Holloway Prison, that dreary-looking building which has about it something of the appearance of a pantomime castle, and inside, because of its wire-netted staircase, something of the appearance of a parrot cage.

When I visited Holloway the suffragettes had called a truce and were helping to win the War, and Holloway contained only its ordinary population. It was clean, which it had not been when the suffragettes were imprisoned. A kind-faced matron took charge of me, and stalwart young women wearing caps and blue dresses, with keys chained to their waists, accompanied us on our round of the premises.

In each cell the bedding was rolled up, the few utensils arranged in meticulous order. Women were working in the laundry, in workrooms, and, the only cheerful place, the kitchen. They wore shapeless, depressing-looking clothes and ugly caps. We visited the infirmary. In a small, separate room was a woman with a few-months-old baby. She looked both evil and mad, and the baby's eyes followed her every movement. I think it was frightened of her, and I wished that the authorities had taken it away.

The prisoners I saw were for the most part petty thieves and prostitutes. I had been told elsewhere that girls who went to prison came out worse than they went in. I could well believe it for I could see little in that prison that should better them. Studying their faces, it seemed to me that the greater number were more or less mentally degenerate, but I say this tentatively, for it would be wrong to express any decided opinion without more knowledge than I possess to back it.

Another day I waited by the prison gates and watched the friends who came to meet those who had served their sentence and regained their liberty. The men for the most part were a revolting type, many being of the kind who live on the immoral earnings of women, and the degradation of their lives had put such a mark upon their faces as set them apart from other men.

In the years since I visited Holloway much has been done to improve the lot of the prisoner, and much remains to be done. I am interested in Prison Reform; but I am far more interested in such reforms as shall keep people out of prison.

A Borstal Institution is not called a prison, but if a

prison is a place where people are kept against their will, it is one.

When I visited the Girls' Borstal, at Aylesbury, Miss Lilian Barker was not yet in charge. Even then, however, there was a very different atmosphere from that of Holloway; but perhaps in some ways it was the sadder, because here the inhabitants were all young girls between sixteen and twenty-one, many of whom, as people say, "had never had a chance." Some of them, perhaps, had gone through such experiences as had those children in the Commonwealth in Dorsetshire. In their rooms photographs and other little treasures were set out, and there were no long hours of solitary confinement. The girls who would shortly be free were making their outfits, pretty clothes such as other girls wear; but in one room—they do not speak of cells at Aylesbury—was a girl with red-rimmed eyes, a face blue-white, clothes torn, her hair in crazy disorder. She was pacing up and down like an unhappy animal in a cage. She glared at us as we passed. That girl had lately been taken from her home. She was a thief, a liar, an immoral girl, but she loved her mother, and her mother had failed her. Not one letter had she written to the child. She had loved the boy with whom she was living, never once had he written to her. She was mad with jealousy of that boy, and with distress that her mother had thrown her off. Hysteria had overpowered her and she had attacked the officials, torn her hair, her clothes, and knocked her head against the wall.

Attached to the girls' Borstal was a little prison for women undergoing what is called a life sentence. In it was a murderess, who under terrible provocation had killed the man who had misused her. When she was permitted to walk by herself in the prison grounds she was so

156

frightened that, like a long-caged bird, she fled back to her cell.

.   .   .   .   .   .

In 1913 both our children were at school. I had found it difficult to discover the kind of schools I wanted; in fact I never did discover them. I then thought, and I have since seen no reason to change my mind, that children should be taught through their hands as well as their heads, and helped to realise why they learn what they do learn. I did discover two schools where the teaching was of this order, but alas! when I came to enquire into such details as baths and the care of the person the answers did not satisfy me, and I confess that the appearance of some of the pupils and their parents, who were visiting at one of the schools that afternoon, prejudiced me. This school was in the country—I may add that it no longer exists—and the children of suitable age cooked and did the house-keepi g and some of the housework, gardened, worked in the dairy, and in the carpenter's shop; they also ordered all necessary materials, kept the accounts, and were expected to make their departments pay. Thus history, geography, geometry, and citizenship were attached to the things of everyday life, and the meaning of and the necessity for education became clear.

Now that my little grand-daughter is at school, I find that she enjoys far more intelligent teaching than I was able to procure for my children. Her school is in London; she cannot, therefore, revel in the care of animals or help to run a dairy; but in every way possible she does learn that she is not merely at school, but is living an important part of her life which, if lived rightly, will help her to live its further stages for her own happiness and that of others. History and geography are not kept in separate compartments; they are taught as depending on each other, and history becomes a study of what we were and why we were so, what we are and why we are so, and how we may use it to mould the future. History to me was kings and queens, wars and dates. Our daughters were well taught at their baby schools, and after that taught in such a stiff, dull way that they became bored. Later they read the books of Lytton Strachey and André Maurois, which relighted their interest in history and set them studying. About boys' schools I know little; but am inclined to think that in some ways boys are worse taught than girls.

Someone may say that persons such as myself should not express opinions on subjects which they have not studied closely. If no one expressed opinions except on subjects they had studied closely, how few opinions there would be. Would that be a good thing or a bad thing? A bad thing I think, and I think so because I have observed that the opinion of an intelligent outsider sometimes hits on the head a nail which hitherto has been overlooked.

I choose to think that although uneducated, I am intelligent, and therefore my opinion may be of some value.

Put briefly, I consider that any form of education which fails to interest the pupil is a failure, and that in many cases it fails because the child does not understand the relationship of what it does in school to life outside the school.

Now that our children were away from home and my tea-time hours free, I became an ardent Bridge player; but as I could rarely spare whole afternoons to play what is called "private Bridge," I often played at clubs between tea and dinner time. I, like many other folk, was silly enough to try to pick up Bridge after having one or two lessons in the rudiments of the game. Bridge players, especially those who play at clubs, dislike partners who are picking-up the game. They disliked me and did not hesitate to show it, for, with some notable exceptions, manners at these clubs were a trifle unrestrained. Soon I realised that auction is a game which needs considerable study if one would play it even moderately well; while contract is still more difficult—though to me far more interesting.

I also began to realise that although I was playing for stakes which I could afford to lose, others were not, and in addition to the irritation caused by my mistakes, there was the irritation caused by losing more money than could be spared. I often wondered to what extent the house-keeping in many a home suffered after a run of bad luck at cards. Bridge became an obsession with many women. By three o'clock they would be waiting impatiently to begin to play. They drank their tea while they played, ate a light club dinner, talking Bridge meanwhile, were in the card-room again directly it opened for the evening's sitting, and departed only when its doors closed, which, if they were willing to pay fines, might not be until a late hour.

In those clubs where poker was played, very late hours were kept, and play might end with breakfast at six or even seven o'clock in the morning. Life was further enlivened by betting on horse-racing, and later by the use of automatic gambling machines.

During the War, Bridge clubs became homes from home of women who had little to do, and who were glad to save their strictly-rationed fuel by spending their afternoons at a club. Bridge killed "at homes," and "partnerships" offered an inexpensive means of entertaining friends.

The stakes played at auction varied, at most of these clubs, which might be for women only, or cock-and-hen clubs, from sixpence to ten shillings a hundred, and to-day, after a run of thirty years, Bridge in its present form of contract is as popular as ever.

LIFE'S ENCHANTED CUP

It was in this year of 1913 that I woke one morning feeling bright and gay, which for me is unusual. Generally, I feel serious and desirous of solitude until after breakfast. Suddenly I found that I was talking aloud. "This is going to be a lucky day," I assured myself. I felt no doubt whatsoever about it. This would be a lucky day.

Only when I looked at the newspaper did I realise that it was Derby Day. I did not bet or take any interest in racing, but that day I looked at the list of horses and at once knew that Aboyeur—a rank outsider—would win the Derby.

I asked Charles if on the way to his office he would back my horse to win. "Put on a pound," I said, for I was feeling poor just then, and also knew that a request to put on £5 would have been ill-received. He, who disliked any form of gambling, remarked, "You will only waste your pound." "Never mind," said I, "believe me, it's going to be a lucky day."

About ten-thirty the telephone rang. Could I make it convenient to see the Editor of *The Queen* at two-thirty that afternoon? I could. I returned from Windsor House, as it was then called, the richer by a contract for a salary of £700 a year (afterwards raised to £800) and the position of the Editor of the Household Department, which I held for seventeen years.

In Piccadilly I thought I would celebrate the occasion by buying some fruit at Soloman's. On coming out of the shop I saw men selling early evening papers. My outsider had won the Derby at 100 to 1.

Intuitions do come to me now and then. One, as I have said, came to me in that sale room in Chelsea, another when having tea at Cap Martin, I felt that I must immediately go to Monte Carlo. The feeling was so strong that I asked my hostess to forgive my abrupt departure. Being something of a gambler herself, she understood the urgency of the matter.

Arrived at the Casino I wandered about waiting for a call. But no call came. Being impatient, I began to play and lost all the money I had with me with the exception of one five franc piece and sufficient centimes to pay my tram fare back to Mentone. But believe that my intuition had played me false I would not. Suddenly I knew that I must risk my last five francs *en plein* on number thirteen at the table on my right. Half-an-hour later I was the richer by over £50.

And yet another intuition came to me at Aix les Bains. I had lost nearly all the small sum I had allowed myself for gambling money, and was leaving for home that evening. In the morning I started with friends for a day's motoring. In the afternoon it began to rain; so hard did it rain that we turned back. I had three hours in which to finish packing, dine and get to the train. An intuition came to me then; I packed, I ate, I played, and just caught the train, having won back all I had lost and some £20 extra.

Is it wrong to gamble? I cannot answer that question. It did not seem wrong for me, because I regarded gambling as an amusement, set aside a certain sum as gambling money, and, if I lost, ceased to play. In short, I had control of my gambling, and not my gambling of me. But if gambling is truly an anti-social act, then it was wrong of me to gamble.

At other times, and about serious matters, intuitions have come to me. I have always received them thankfully and have been guided by them.

CHAPTER XIV

Belgian, French, German and English—" And perhaps they will not be there "—We sell our house—The murder of the Austrian Archduke and Duchess—The Suffragettes try to petition the King—Trouble in Ireland—War looms large—War is declared —People fear for their food—Working parties—Prices—The Moratorium—The grocer lends me £3—Yet another home— The Soldiers' and Sailors' Wives Club—Gentle, mousey-looking and middle-aged—The *Lusatania* riots—A war party—War songs—National War Savings—War changes our lives— Munition workers—Canteens—Smart to be shabby—Coal shortage—Begging a lump here and there—The knitting mania— Eat, drink and be merry, for to-morrow . . . ?

IN the spring of 1914 I spent a few weeks in Switzerland, to complete the cure of my damaged lung, and often played Bridge with a Belgian, a Frenchman and a German. As events fell out, it was long before persons of these nationalities were to meet again in amity. After the children had gone back to school, I went on with Winifred Herbert to Mentone and spent happy sunlit days writing, while she painted, in the garden of a charming little hotel in the hills above Mentone, where stocks and carnations and anemones bloomed. There were unusually few English people in Mentone that spring. Almost all the guests at our hotel were Germans. It seemed to me that they were not quite so pleasant as in other days.

I asked the hotel proprietor the reason of his change of clientèle. "I regret it, madam, for I prefer the English," said he, "but one must live." He paused, and then added, "Perhaps your countrymen will not be here next year." His manner was so peculiar that it impressed me. "But perhaps it will be the other way about and we shall be here and the Germans will not," I replied lightly.

In Paris, where I stayed on my way home, there was no gold to be had. Why? I met my Bridge-playing French friend and asked him. He shrugged his shoulders. "One never knows, and it is wise to be prepared," said he.

In the beginning of June, in the middle of a specially gay season, my husband suggested that we should sell our house. He had often been amused by my intuitions, but this time an intuition had come to him. "I don't feel happy about things. Suppose there was a war. It might affect us considerably." I felt rather fretted. Our eldest girl would be coming out in a few months time, and it was a house in which it was easy to entertain in a modest way. In the end, I agreed to sell if we could get our price. During June the sale was concluded, the final payment being made on August 4th, the day on which war was declared. On the 28th of June, the Austrian Archduke Francis Ferdinand and his wife were assassinated at Sarajevo. The murder resulted in a note couched in sharp terms from the Austrian Minister in Belgrade asking for the punishment of all concerned. This was referred to in our newspapers as a very serious note. But we in England had what we thought more serious matters to discuss—the Irish Conference and the fear of civil war. The doings of the Suffragettes was another exciting topic and, according to what kind of mind we had, we felt interested, amused, or infuriated by them. Also it was nearing holiday time and one's summer plans gave one plenty to think of. Towards the end of July some suffragettes tried to present a petition to the King at Buckingham Palace and were arrested. Dear, dear, dear, they might have tried to assassinate His Majesty and been scarcely more reviled!

On July 22nd the papers shocked us with an account of a battle in the streets of Dublin, and also announced that Austria demanded an end of Serbian plotting. "Mobilisation on the Continent: Great activity in diplomatic circles: the King not to go to Goodwood," were some of next day's newspaper headlines. Life became almost as feverish and staccato as the headlines. There was a sense of strain and anxiety, and in better-informed circles talk of the resignation of certain Ministers; but just as Civil War in Ireland was so terrible to contemplate that we felt it could not really happen, so we felt about an European war, and that in spite of the many people who went about saying that Germany had been working up to war for years. Faced with the menace of a great European war, interest in the Irish question and in the Suffragettes lessened. "War looms large," was splashed across a page of one of the great dailies. Then came Sir Edward Grey's warning: "The world must prepare for the greatest catastrophe that has ever befallen the Continent of Europe. The consequences, both direct and indirect, will be incalculable."

On July 29th Austria declared war on Serbia. "Europe an armed camp: May England be involved?" "Fall of prices on Stock Exchange: Financial Condition Grave," the papers reported, and on a back page I noticed a paragraph announcing that the Liverpool Millers' Association had advanced the price of flour one shilling per sack. On Thursday, July 30th, the papers cried, "All Europe Arming: British Fleet puts to sea: Position of extreme gravity." The Prime Minister, Mr. Asquith, assured the House that His Majesty's Government were doing everything in their power to circumscribe the area of possible conflict." The price of flour rose one-and-six and then two shillings per sack, and fifteen Stock Exchange failures were reported. The Bank Rate, however, remained at three per cent., and the papers were well supplied with holiday news and gay fashions.

That year we were wearing rather pretty clothes, the skirts of ankle length, the bodices with Magyar sleeves. These were so easy for the home dressmaker to cut and make that when the first Magyar blouse was illustrated in the *Daily Mail* thousands of applications for the pattern were received. Our hair was waved and brought over the ears, and we wore large becoming hats with wide flat brims.

By Friday, July 31st, the news was so serious that one could give little attention to fashions. "Europe drifting to disaster: Last efforts for peace: The Archbishops of Canterbury and York appeal for the prayers of the nation." Those were the headlines which met our eyes when we opened the morning papers.

On August 1st exports of food from France and Germany were forbidden, and the price of provisions in Germany had risen by seventy-five per cent. Seventy-five per cent. That meant that those who had spent £1 a week on food would now have to spend £1 15s. Is that going to happen to us, we asked ourselves?

The papers were depressing reading for the housewife. The price of bread rose by a halfpenny a four-pound loaf, and it was said that we had only a month's supply of meat if our overseas supplies were stopped.

Women who had money and storage-room hurried to buy a stock of provisions, and a large provision firm reported that eight normal days' business had been done in one day. Fear-stricken people arrived at shops in cars and taxicabs and loaded them with food. Some of the smaller provision shops were sold out. The result of this panic was to push prices still higher and to make ill-feeling between rich and poor.

We had just then taken a house at Hook Heath, near Woking, for the holidays, and the charwoman who was helping us to settle in grumbled angrily that the rich were taking all the food away from the poor.

Charles came home from London saying that there had been remarkable scenes in the City, that the Stock Exchange was to be closed until further notice, and that after the Bank Holiday, gold was to be called in and paper money issued.

On Bank Holiday war was the only topic of conversation.

We had thought of going abroad that summer, but were glad that we had not done so as all the English people then on the Continent were making their way home as fast as they could.

We were thankful that Cecilia had been able to get back safely from her school in Paris, on the 1st August. The girl she was with had so much luggage that it took all their change to pay for it, and although they had notes, no one would change them, so they returned home extremely hungry, having been able to buy but one ham sandwich, which they shared, from the time they left Paris at seven o'clock in the morning until they arrived late in the evening at Victoria. On Bank Holiday a friend came back on a boat from the Hook which carried 780 exhausted, excited passengers instead of the usual 100. She told us of an invalid, scarcely recovered from an operation, who was thankful to travel home in a cattle truck, and reported that travellers from Germany had been turned back at the French frontier and told to proceed as best they could.

We heard, too, that at a meeting of the Cabinet on Sunday, there was complete unity of opinion in regard to intervention; but someone better-informed said that there had been a great diversity of opinion. So pacifist was the Cabinet in general that it was hinted that in the event of intervention some seven or eight resignations might be expected. This was an exaggeration, for when it came to the point, only Mr. Burns, Sir John Simon, and Lord Morley resigned, and when a final decision was taken, only Lord Morley and Mr. Burns kept to their original intention.

It was on this Sunday morning, August 2nd, that it was finally agreed to mobilise the Army and the Fleet, though as a matter of fact, as one learned later, Mr. Winston Churchill had on the previous Saturday night mobilised the Navy in defiance of the decisions of the Cabinet made early on that day.

Everyone we met seemed quite certain that England would win the war—if war there had to be. In three months the whole affair would be over. A retired colonel who came to tea assured me that everything was arranged, and that the organisation was perfect. Yet in spite of that assurance, a week or two later wounded men were loaded into filthy cattle trucks; the dead, the dying, and the wounded were crowded together in ships and in the Casino at Boulogne, hastily converted into a hospital, the stretchers were packed close on the floors, the veranda, and the garden paths, and the cries of men, to whom no attention could be given, were heard throughout the night.

On Sunday, Germany attacked France and violated Belgium, our Army was mobilised, and the Reserves called out. Great Britain declared war against Germany as from 11 p.m. on August 4th.

A few days after war was declared, a neighbour had already organised a working party to make baby clothes for soldiers' and sailors' wives. I wondered why these women should be in greater need of baby clothes then than at any other time, but as social life came to an end almost at once, we liked to meet and to feel that at any rate we were doing something which might help someone, and to discuss our experiences.

There was much talk of food, for prices continued to rise, and women whose husbands had been called up were in many cases obliged at once to cut down their expenses, and to find ways of living more cheaply.

That was the beginning of life in other people's houses, to which, until then, women of the better-off classes had been unaccustomed, and which, as prices rose, and the housing shortage developed, caused such bodily discomfort and mental strain.

I remember that one of our working party begged us not to dismiss any of our servants. She feared that unemployment would cause suffering. Her fears were groundless, for soon there was work for everyone who was capable of working, and before the end of the War the servant shortage had become acute. Dismiss them indeed! We were thankful if anyone would condescend to apply for our situations. We discussed the withdrawal of gold and the moratorium. I did not know the meaning of the word, looked it up in the dictionary and found that it was an emergency measure authorising suspension of the payment of debt for a stated time, which in this case was one month.

I have reason to remember the moratorium, for I found myself after the Bank Holiday with 2s. 9d. in cash. I wanted to go to London but had not the money to buy a ticket. No one would cash a cheque for me; but eventually the grocer lent me £3, which was trusting of him, for we were newcomers to the neighbourhood, who had but taken a furnished house for a few weeks.

At first many people drew quite large sums in gold,

which they locked away ready for an emergency; but a little later an appeal was made to return all gold to the banks, and from then onwards the sovereign and the half-sovereign became rarities, to be replaced by £1 and 10s. notes. The first issue was withdrawn in August, 1915, because it was said they were too easy to forge, and others of different design took their place. I doubt if our younger daughter knows what a sovereign or half-sovereign looks like.

Other remembrances of those early war days are of a hurried visit of a friend of Cecilia's, whose regiment was one of the first to leave for France; and the ceaseless noise of trains running throughout the night, conveying troops to Southampton.

We returned to London in September in order to move into our new home. This house we made as labour-saving as is possible in a many-staired basement house. Now we had two bath-rooms, central heating, a service lift, gas fires in each room but the drawing-room, and telephone bells.

We began life again with three maids, which was an ample staff considering that Cecilia, who disliked the idea of nursing, shortly became an under-cook in an Officers' Hospital in Cadogan Square, where the V.A.D.'s slept four in an attic. This hospital kitchen was not well equipped, and all the dressings had to be brought into the kitchen and burnt in the coke boiler. Our younger child, Denise, returned to a school then at Broadstairs, which when Broadstairs became a favourite target for German bombs, and the school was hit by a bomb which fortunately caused no injury to life, was moved into the country. Her chief remembrance of the War is that on Armistice Day they had eggs for tea, and hers was bad.

I, like most other women, spent all the time I could spare

on war work. Women busied themselves in caring for the wives and families of the fighting men, and for the flood of homeless Belgians which flowed into the country.

At first the wives of our soldiers and sailors were at a loose end, for it was not until some time later that the call for women to take the place of men became so urgent that every woman who could leave her home was fully occupied, and clubs for the wives of soldiers and sailors were started. So little tact had some of the helpers that one, when she took her first turn at Savings Club duty, was found entrenched at the pay table behind little heaps of Keating's powder.

One of my first war activities was to organise a Soldiers' and Sailors' Wives Club in Lambeth, where my sister Margaret had been working for some years. This was held in a large bare hall, furnished with trestle tables, chairs, a jingly piano, and a small stage. The club proved popular. The women knitted socks, and, like the famous Susie of war-time song, "sewed shirts for soldiers." We served tea, bread-and-butter and buns, which we bought from a German bakery round the corner, played games, sang, and listened to the entertainments provided by kindly amateurs. Some of these entertainments were good; others funny, though not always intentionally so, notably that provided by a troupe of five mousey-looking, middle-aged ladies, who sang part songs in mild, murmuring tones to a stumbling accompaniment on our piano, several notes of which were dumb.

I am sorry to say that our soldiers' and sailors' wives forgot their manners on that occasion and laughed loudly at the ladies. This experience of amateur troupes made me realise how very much better is almost any professional performer than the most willing and enthusiastic of amateurs.

Our club endured until after the "Lusitania" riots in

May, 1915, which followed the sinking of that ship when 1,198 men, women, and children perished, a tragedy which was used all over the world for propaganda purposes. A powerful cartoon appeared in the *New York World* depicting the forms of little children rising from the sea, holding out their hands and asking the Kaiser, "Why did you kill *us*?" This event inflamed public opinion bitterly against Germany, and those Germans who, until then, had remained unmolested and in possession of businesses received some rough treatment.

In Lambeth there were a good many German shops and much rioting, some of which began in ill-feeling and continued from the desire to loot. The loot was not confined to articles thrown from the windows of foreign households, as I learned from overheard conversations between some of our ladies, regarding articles of use or ornament which they had acquired. Charles, too, like other men over military age, was a Special Constable, and had a rough time amongst the looters in a poor part of Chelsea, where in the end the Specials had to be augmented by a squad of that body, drawn from another part of London.

In Lambeth, although the treatment of some foreigners was harsh and unjust, the baker's wife from whom we bought bread and buns was protected by her customers. This woman had lived for years in the neighbourhood and had been a good friend to many of her customers in times of distress, giving long credit, and in some cases, gifts of bread, and at that time was expecting her confinement.

As more and more women took the place of men who had been called up, our club had to come to an end, an event celebrated by a river party. We met at Waterloo Station, and not even the Granny *in excelsis* of the Club, then well over eighty, was left behind. Her appearance in a beaded dolman and a bonnet in which rakishly nodded a crimson rose gave quite an air to the assembly. Two of the women carried huge, paper-covered parcels. "What are . . . ?" I began, but received a sharp nudge from Granny and took the hint. We packed into our carriages and sat and sang. Arrived at Hampton we sat by the river waiting until dinner at a nearby hotel was ready, and sang, for singing was one of the most popular war-time amusements. "The roses round the cottage door," "Sister Susie," "Take me in your arms and say you love me," "The long, long trail," and "There's a light shining bright in the window to-night" were our particular favourites. We waved our hands to everyone in trousers who passed by, and when a load of wounded men in hospital uniform was driven past, one of our liveliest members, stout, middle-aged, and the mother of seven, burst into "There's a girl for every soldier." The brake stopped, and its occupants joined in the song.

Eventually the gentlemen departed amidst much blowing of kisses, giggles and haw-haws, and a spirited rendering of "Who's your lady friend?"

Cecilia, who by now had been obliged to take a rest from her hospital work owing to the arches of her feet being affected, was one of the party, her chief employment being to retrieve ladies who strayed away to drink in pubs. At the "good meat dinner" provided for us the paper was removed from the parcels, and two huge bouquets of carnations emerged and were presented to Mrs. MacNair and myself. As a prelude to a long day of pleasure, two of our members had risen at five o'clock that morning to buy the flowers at Covent Garden.

After dinner we went up the river in a launch, bouquets and all, still singing. It was then that the mother of seven told me what a joy it was to sit down to a meal which you had neither cooked nor which would you have to wash up. Being by then an experienced washer-up in canteens, I could believe her.

We returned to Waterloo at eight o'clock, Granny game to the last. Willy nilly, Mrs. MacNair and I, linked arm in arm with our ladies, were compelled to dance down the platform, whilst with all the breath left to us, we bade amused onlookers "Keep the home fires burning."

At this time I had become a member of a society known at United Workers, the Chairman of which was Sir Charles Stewart, then Public Trustee. Sir Theodore Chambers, who afterwards became Controller of the National War Savings Committee was an United Worker, and it was through him that I began to speak for United Workers and later for the National War Savings Association.

By January, 1917, it had become evident that great economy must be made by the nation in its food consumption, and the National War Savings speakers, who then and later carried on valuable food economy propaganda, were instructed to emphasise this point in their appeals. I invited about forty people to come to our house one Sunday afternoon to hear Lady Ferrers, one of the star speakers for the Association, and Sir Theodore Chambers on the subject. Many ladies in the audience responded to Lady Ferrer's invitation to hold food economy meetings.

The first large food economy meeting, organised by the Women's Sub-Committee of the Lord Mayor's Committee for War Savings, of which I was a member, was held at the Adelphi Theatre, the expenses being paid by Lady Mond, now Violet Lady Melchett.

By this time the War had changed our lives completely. All formal entertaining had come to an end. Practically every woman who could spare time to work outside her own home was working. Everywhere there were workrooms, in which hospital necessaries were made, and canteens, not only for soldiers, but for war workers.

Women were now employed in munition works where, in the earlier months of their employment, conditions were so bad that they could not be tolerated. Mr. Lloyd George, then Minister of Munitions, decided that prompt measures must be taken to remedy them. A Departmental Committee was appointed, and on their recommendation a Welfare and Health Department was established, and a panel of trained candidates for welfare posts was created. Amongst these was my youngest sister, Margaret, who spent the war years welfare-working on Tyneside.

In the course of my later duties I visited many of the great ammunition works. In some of these the girls clocked in at seven in the morning and were supposed to remain until seven o'clock in the evening, but in most cases, in order to prevent their leaving the works at the same hour as the men, and the consequent overcrowding of trams and omnibuses, they went out at six-thirty. After they had worked for one hour, they had a ten minutes' respite for refreshments, and then went on until 12 o'clock, when there was an hour's break for dinner. I believe that the law forbade the eating of dinner in the "shops," but many of the girls did eat their dinners there, after wiping their greasy hands with a greasy rag.

At four o'clock, or four-thirty, half-an-hour was granted for tea, after which the women were tired and very little work was done.

When on night work the women came in at six-thirty, and many a supervisor told me that after four o'clock morning tea, very little work was done. The hours were too long.

When women first began to flock into munition work, there were no canteens, no place where the girls could heat the food they brought with them, and conditions in general were bad. Lodgings were difficult to obtain and it happened sometimes that six girls slept in a room by night and another six in the same room by day, so that the beds and the rooms were never properly aired and cleaned. Later on, hostels were built and canteens started.

In all munition factories there was great mingling of classes, from girls of the very roughest type to young ladies well known in Society. It was good for them to make acquaintance with each other. One point which struck me was that the better-class girls, who all their lives had been well fed, were not as hardy as the lower-class girls, who brought both to work and play an extraordinary amount of energy. It was not an uncommon thing for these girls to work all day and to dance practically all night, while the ladies went home exhausted after their day's work.

Munitionettes, as they were called, earned from 25s. to £5 a week. They spent a considerable amount on food and they also spent lavishly on their clothes, and their standard of taste and of cleanliness became noticeably higher. It took some time to popularise trousers, which were necessary for safety when performing some kinds of work. Some of the older women considered trousers indecent, others objected to wearing them because "the fellers would laugh." An elderly woman who had worked a long time in one firm refused to wear the trousered and overalled uniform, which soon became general in engineering shops. An exception was made in her favour, and she continued to wear her skirt and blouse. When, however, the King visited that town and there was a parade of munition workers, she cast away her skirt and put on trousers. "Why," said my sister, "you've got your trousers on, Mrs. ————." "Yes," said Mrs. ————, "I'm a loyal woman I am, and I put 'em on to please the King, and I'll take 'em off again to-morrow."

As the speaking which I did for the National War Savings Association did not absorb all the free time left to me after my journalistic and literary work was completed, I did some canteening. It was amusing to find how, when we did this domestic work, we developed the idiosyncrasies of careless servants. Many of the ladies wasted the gas, and were shockingly extravagant in the way they cut the rinds off the bacon and spread the butter, or, as it was generally known, the "marge." Sometimes the washing-up was none too thorough, and invariably every shift complained that the outgoing shift had not left things properly.

Cecilia and I worked for some time at the Liverpool Street and Cannon Street canteens. She, in addition to suffering from foot trouble, had been obliged to undergo an operation for appendicitis, but was now recovered and began to work in the Air Ministry, where by the time she was twenty, she was in control of eighteen clerks. Like most of her contemporaries, she worked by day and danced by night. It was not then thought necessary that girls should be chaperoned, partly because as a rule their mothers were working hard in canteens and workrooms, and did not wish to sit up late at night, and also because the supply of petrol was so short that cars had to be laid up, and often at night it was impossible to obtain a taxi.

Mothers who were "particular" used to see to it that their girls went to dances with other girls well known to them, and did not walk or drive home with young men alone. Most of the dances were small, champagne was not provided, refreshments were simple, and a pianist took the place of the pre-War band.

To entertain in a lavish manner was considered vulgar, just as it was considered in bad taste, at all events in the day time and out of doors, to dress in any but the quietest clothes. Numbers of women, indeed, belonging to the large number of Women's War Associations which came into being, wore uniform. Clever skits appeared in *Punch* of aristocrats clad in rags and tatters, whilst the new rich flaunted their new finery.

When war was declared, waists were in the normal position, and boots had not been replaced by the smart shoes which are worn to-day. The silk stocking craze did not become general until 1917, when practically every woman was earning, and girls had an unusual amount of pocket money at their disposal. That was the time when, owing to the number of girls of good class who were working in the Ministries in the West End of London, and who lunched in Soho restaurants, that the smart Soho dress shop appeared.

At first the daily newspapers had continued much as before. Advice on "Housekeeping in war time," and Economy Columns, were published, together with articles on "What women can do in war time," which did not seem to be much. *The Queen* Newspaper took the lead in publishing articles on the responsibilities of women. In a fine anonymous article it was pointed out that "the tables that are to-day laden with luxurious food belong to enemies of the commonwealth," and women were asked to save, and to dress plainly, and reminded that before the end of the American Civil War women who had been rich were clothed in dresses contrived out of cotton bags, and it was not the women who clamoured for peace in the end. It may be noted too that before the end of the War the German women were reduced to similar straits and it was not they who clamoured for peace in the end.

As I was responsible for the articles on food and house-keeping in *The Queen*, I was glad to be permitted to take this patriotic attitude, and I spent considerable time in experimenting in the use of cocoa-butter, beans, war-margarine, and war-flour, and, because fuel was now strictly rationed and costly, in such dishes as did not need long cooking.

The sharp rise in the price of food did not cause as much distress as one had at first thought would be the case. The working people were, for the most part, better off than they had been, and could afford to buy even at increased prices, and although the house bills of well-to-do folk were higher, this expenditure was balanced by their lessened expenditure upon other items. People could not go abroad or, indeed, travel much in their own country, they did not entertain, their establishments were reduced, and instead of spending their time paying to be amused, they were now occupied with work which, though unpaid, cost them nothing.

As early as August 7th, 1914, a Cabinet Committee on Food Supplies began to function, and some maximum prices were fixed, such as 4½d. per pound for granulated sugar, 5d. for lump; 1s. 6d. per pound for butter; 8d. for margarine; 9½d. for Colonial cheese, and 1s. 4d. and 1s. 6d. for Continental and British bacon. These prices seemed high to us then; they were nothing to the prices which were to come.

But if the price of ordinary necessities rose, that of the luxury foods fell. That year one could buy English chickens for 2s. 3d. and 2s. 9d.; ducks for 2s. 6d. and 3s.; English peaches for 2s. and 3s. a dozen; hot-house melons

Dorothy C. Peel
1917.

for 1s. 6d. upwards; and pineapples from 1s. It became an economy to feed on luxuries for there was a collapse in luxury trades and in the wine trade.

By the winter of 1914, London had gone back some twenty years as regards lighting, and by the end of the War it was almost as dark in the London streets as it had been in the Middle Ages. When, in the later years of the War, it was my duty to go into parts of London hitherto unknown to me, in order to speak at meetings, I did not enjoy groping about in the dark.

It was on one of these occasions that I asked a man in an omnibus the whereabouts of a certain place in the dock district, and scarcely knew whether to be pleased or alarmed when he offered to accompany me on my quarter of a mile walk from the stopping place of the omnibus to the hall in which I was to speak. Though rough looking, he proved to be a well-read, interesting companion.

It was on a similar occasion, and on a very hot summer night, that a stout, elderly woman, after directing me, remarked "Dearie, *how* your poor feet will ache before you get there." People in poor neighbourhoods are sympathetic and helpful, though I was to discover that many of them, if they do not reply that they are strangers to the locality, have a passion for directing you, even when they know no more where the place you desire to go to is than you do.

By the beginning of 1915 the coal shortage was causing such inconvenience that complaints were made in regard to profiteering, and to hoarding in private cellars. The poor, who buy in hundred or half-hundred-weights, were paying at the rate of 35s. per ton for coal which cost 9s. 9d. at the pit head, and 16s. by the time it reached London. A month later, people who bought by the ton paid 34s. for best coal. These prices, however, were trifling in comparison with what we paid later, and do pay to-day. Only the other day I saw coal being sold in a poor neighbourhood at 2s. 8d. the cwt. During the War I blessed my forethought in having installed central heating and a gas cooker. One furnace, which burned coke, kept the house fairly warm and provided us with plenty of hot water. Indeed, from that time onwards we were often able to offer fuelless friends the hospitality of a hot bath.

It became a fashionable occupation to tear up newspapers and make them into fire-lighters, or crumple them into balls, which helped inferior coal to burn better. Haybox cookery came into fashion, and cooks learned to steam cakes—and oh! how nasty war cakes often were—because they could not be permitted the fuel necessary to heat the oven.

I remember Miss Ella Hepworth Dixon telling me that their house was large and old-fashioned, with a huge kitchen range and no other apparatus for cooking and obtaining hot water. Her mother was ill, there was no coal, and Miss Dixon drove round London in a cab with a laundry basket begging just a few lumps from this friend and that.

The months wore on, and now the income tax was doubled, and because the amusement trade had come to a standstill, musicians and theatrical performers were reduced to serious straits. Rich women organised concerts to which we all went, accompanied by our knitting. Men, women and children knitted, socks, waistcoats, helmets, comforters, mits and body belts. It was said that the trenches were littered with knitting, much of which was used for cleaning accoutrements. In trains and omnibuses and parks, in restaurants and canteens, people knitted. It was soothing to the nerves to knit, and comforting to think that our knitting might save some man something of hardship, for everyone was haunted by the knowledge of what suffering had been, and must be, endured in order to win the War.

At that time night clubs became an outstanding feature of war-time life. Such places had, of course, existed, but never before had they been patronised by women and girls of good reputation. Some mothers, myself amongst them, allowed only an occasional visit to one of the most reputable night clubs. This was no hardship, for there was always plenty of dancing to be had in private houses.

By the winter of 1915, many complaints were made about these clubs. Silly young officers were victimised by women known in criminal slang as "crows," who lured them to some place where they could rook them at cards. Many were the charges of theft and blackmail made to the Provost Marshal by victims of men and women of the underworld.

The unhappiness and restlessness caused by war led to a desire to consult fortune tellers, palmists, crystal gazers, and thought readers reaped a considerable harvest. The less reputable of these people were said to act as agents for blackmailers, and as decoy ducks of keepers of disreputable houses and gambling dens. By the beginning of 1917 so many complaints had been received, that a number of fortune-telling parlours were raided and closed. The style of dancing altered during the war years, and jazz came into fashion; and as the casualty lists lengthened, "Eat, drink and be merry, for to-morrow we die" became the motto of the young, and led to the many war marriages which took place after a few days' acquaintance, and in other cases to temporary connections. The mental strain and the desire to forget led to an increase of drinking, drugging, gambling, dancing, and an utter breakdown of what people of my generation considered to be sexual morality.

CHAPTER XV

Board of Agriculture or Ministry of Food ?—Mrs. Pember Reeves—
" Round about £1 a week "—Furniture suitable to our position
—Voluntary food economy—So little sugar, so little fat and that
horrible cocoa-butter—Some humorous stories—A speaking
campaign—How different some men are—The odd ways of
Chairmen—" Some of 'em 'ad a bit o' muck ready in their
pockets "—" I like to feel a bit between me and them planes,"
said he—The great daylight raid—The airyplanes amused baby
very much—A woman's head came rolling towards him—They
gathered on the kitchen stairs—The raid night novel—Sheltering
in the Tube—Food meetings in theatres—What the children
thought about it—Food economy and patent shoes—A desirably
dowdy appearance—from Plymouth to Newcastle and 176
meetings.

ONE morning in 1917 I received a telephone message
asking me to make an appointment to see Mr.
Prothero (later Lord Ernle), President of the Board
of Agriculture, but before a date for the interview was
decided I was summoned to the Ministry of Food to see the
late Sir Henry Rew, who asked me if I would accept the
position which I afterwards filled in partnership with Mrs.
Pember Reeves.

I do not recollect that any fixed duties were assigned to
us at this interview or at any other time. Public opinion
was in favour of there being women in responsible positions
in the Ministry, and Sir Henry desired that we should begin
our work there as quickly as possible.

It was then the middle of February, and as my publishers allowed me to break my contracts, and I could put
aside all newspaper work with the exception of that which

I did for *The Queen*, I was able to take up my position at the Ministry on March 1st. We were allotted as an office the ballroom of Grosvenor House. In pre-War days many famous pictures, including Gainsborough's Blue Boy, had hung in this apartment, but now the walls were lined with sheets of grey asbestos, and the floor was covered by brown linoleum. Three telephones stood upon the floor. Furniture there was none, and, apparently, there was no means of warming our new quarters.

Looking small and fragile in this vast bare space stood Mrs. Pember Reeves, my Co-Director of Women's Service, that being the title chosen for us, a slight grey-haired woman with brilliant dark eyes, clad in a plain black dress with a white collar. Mrs. Reeves had been born and brought up in New Zealand and had married at the age of 19. After the birth of her two elder children, and feeling "so ignorant," she had returned to college. It was, perhaps, because she had known what it was to study in the intervals of tending children, helped only by a little nursemaid, and having the entire care of the babies at night, that she could sympathise with working mothers and smile at those women who employ nurses, under-nurses, and governesses, yet think that the poor mother should be tied day and night to her children lest her sense of responsibility shall be lessened. Mrs. Reeves had enjoyed considerable experience of official life, when her husband was Minister of Labour and Education in New Zealand, and High Commissioner for New Zealand in London.

It was while living in London that my Co-Director learned something of the conditions under which so many of our working people exist. Money was put at her disposal in order that she should make an investigation into the causes of infant mortality, and thus she obtained the information for her well-known book "Round about a Pound a Week," a chronicle not of slum life but of the lives of many sober, industrious, honest folk.

It is often supposed that women cannot work amicably with other women. This has not been my experience. Twelve difficult, nerve-racking months spent in the Ministry of Food left me richer by the friendship of my Co-Director, and of Mrs. May (now Lady May, O.B.E. wife of Sir George May, Chairman of the present Tariffs Commission), Miss Isabel Bellis and Miss Barratt, all members of our staff.

But to return to our first day in the Ministry. "Well, my dear," remarked Mrs. Reeves, "so here we are." "We are," I agreed, "but there does not seem to be very much else here, does there?" Then, unknowing of the laws which control such matters in Government Departments, we proceeded to explore, bent on discovering furniture for our ballroom. With the help of the head messenger we commandeered a carpet, hat and coat stand, a shaky screen, wash-hand stand, and some tables. We were to learn later that all these articles belonged to the Office of Works and application should have been made to it for furniture of a kind suitable to our position, that, I believe, being decided by the amount of salary received. I do not think that Mrs. Reeves received any salary, while I had agreed to accept only a small "war" salary, so it is possible that we were not entitled even to what furniture we took. However, I doubt if any which might have been granted to us could have been shabbier than that which we had.

We had scarcely possessed ourselves of two chairs and a waste paper basket when the Press arrived. They leant against our grey walls, notebooks in hand, and asked us what we proposed to do. All that we could say was that we proposed to take such steps as might assist the cause of voluntary economy of food. Being good journalists, what we could not tell them our visitors invented. The position as regards the nation's food supply was that Great Britain did not and could not produce as much food as she needed, and home reserves were dangerously low. There was food and to spare in other countries, but to bring it to our shores necessitated the use of ships, and the supply of shipping was becoming shorter. Further, of the available shipping a considerable proportion was needed for the carriage of munitions. It was, therefore, necessary to increase production and reduce consumption. To do the latter, waste caused not only by throwing away food fit for human consumption, but waste occasioned by bad or improper cooking must be reduced to a minimum.

It seemed, then, that we must assist the people to understand, first, why there was a food shortage, and secondly, the best means of meeting it.

It was also our duty to persuade the public to help the Government, for only by the goodwill of the people could the necessary reduction of consumption be attained.

The public, like the Press, did not wait for us to mature our plans. A vast correspondence flowed in upon us and a queue of visitors made it necessary that we should arrange appointments at ten-minute intervals throughout the day. We received invitations to speak at almost every town in the country. Everywhere we met with offers of help, and soon, Food Economy Committees were formed all over the country, and meetings, demonstrations, food economy exhibitions, and food economy shops organised.

The London County Council suggested the use of a travelling demonstrating kitchen as a valuable form of propaganda. A few weeks later I went with Miss Catherine

Gordon, who had the matter in hand, to see one of these demonstrations at the Public Library at Walworth. Oil stoves were used, and they with the other simple apparatus required and the materials for the meals to be cooked, were, together with two demonstrators, packed into a motor-car driven by a girl chauffeur. The travelling kitchen proceeded to any place where it might be required, all the demonstrators then needed, being a room, a table, and an audience. The demonstrators sent out by the L.C.C. and the education authorities knew their audiences, which many of those anxious to help in the good cause did not.

An ordinary pre-War wage for a working man was anything from 25s. to 30s. a week. How many of the ladies who offered to go and talk to the poor could have attempted to house, clothe and feed a family on such a sum? How many could have worked surrounded by a tribe of small children, been kept awake at night by a teething baby, and yet have remained cheerful and uncomplaining?

As the days passed we discovered that there was an enormous demand for war cookery recipes. Women said that war flour made their bread and puddings heavy; they did not know how to use barley and maize; how could they manage with so little sugar and so little fat as were then available, and what were they to do with cocoa-butter? I never did know what to do with cocoa-butter except to bear it. Whatever one did to it it was horrid. We obtained permission to start an experimental kitchen in the Ministry and publish Food Economy leaflets, of which millions were distributed.

On the second day of our Ministry of Food career we discussed the question of communal or public kitchens, national kitchens as they came to be called later. It was evident that conditions as regards food, labour and fuel might become far more difficult than they were at the moment, and such kitchens might be as necessary here as they then were in Germany. The consent of the Food Controller, Lord Devonport, to organise a Ministry of Food experimental public kitchen was obtained. It was opened in the following May by Her Majesty the Queen. Women of the Labour Party were interested in these kitchens, which they thought might ease the life of the working class women and ensure for them and their families better food. The experiment proved that food produced in national kitchens could not be produced as cheaply as by women at home, whose labour is unpaid and who must in any case have some firing to warm the room and to produce hot water.

Later, Mr. Kennedy Jones, well known in the journalistic world, for he had been associated with the Harmsworths in the production of the *Daily Mail* and other Harmsworth newspapers, was appointed Director-General of Food Economy. He was a man of strong personality with a sense of humour, and appeared to be profoundly impatient of official red tape. His manners were as unofficial as his methods. Often have I sat discussing some subject, Mr. Jones with his heels on the mantelpiece, and smoking a strong cigar.

It was K.J., as his friends knew him, who taught the British public some respect for bread. Before the War, bread was so cheap that it was estimated that the nation wasted one out of every twelve months' supply.

For some weeks our activities were hampered because we were not permitted the services of an experienced secretary. The salary which we were allowed to offer was so inadequate that naturally a person such as we required would not accept it. Had we been men in a position of such importance—which indeed was considerable—as we filled,

I have little doubt that we should have been allowed the assistance of an experienced secretary trained in Civil Service routine. Eventually, when our work threatened to overwhelm us, we were allowed to make other arrangements and were fortunate in securing, through Mrs. Hoster's agency, Miss Isabel Bellis as private secretary, and Miss Barratt as organising secretary.

There was no monotony about our work in Grosvenor House, and it had its humours. Changes were frequent both of staff and of rooms, and often one would hear snatches of conversations, such as: "Where is so-and-so's secretary now?" "Oh, he is in the Duchess's bathroom." Or, "Fats have moved, haven't they?" "Yes, they are up in the nurseries." "Where have Public Meals got to?" "They used to be in Number Nine, but exchange says Fish is there now," and so forth.

Some of the hundreds of orders which were issued afforded mirth. One concerned poultry food, and ran as follows :—Scheme (B). "Other birds, being hen birds, hatched since January 1st, 1916, and not receiving rations under Scheme (A) will be able to obtain certificates entitling their owners to purchase up to an amount per head per day (which will be less than two ounces per day) to be fixed from time to time, according to the quality of food stuffs available."

Sometimes, too, one smiled at the strange manner in which duties were allotted to members of the staff. It appeared that if you were an expert in one subject, that seemed the best possible reason for not allowing you to deal with it. On going to a certain section one of our secretaries found a gentleman of her acquaintance. "But what are you doing here?" she asked, "I thought you were the greatest living authority on fish." "Precisely," was the bland

reply, "and that is why I am controlling mangel-wurzels."
Life was even brighter in other Ministries—notably so, it is
said, in the Air Ministry—while according to the accounts
of a friend who worked in the Separation Allowance Department of the Ministry of Pensions, some of the letters
received cheered the staff considerably. Our friend declared
that the following examples were genuine :

"You have changed my little boy into a little girl. Will
it make any difference?"

"My Bill has been put in charge of a spittoon. Will
I get any more pay?"

"I am glad to tell you that my husband has now been
repotted dead."

"I have not received any pay since my husband was confined in a constipation camp in Germany."

"If I don't get my husband's money soon, I shall be
compelled to go on the streets and lead an imortal life."

"In accordance with instructions on ring paper I have
given birth to twins enclosed in envelope."

"I have been in bed with the doctor for three days. He
doesn't seem to do me any good. If you don't send my
money soon I shall have to go to another one."

Lord Devonport, the first Food Controller, resigned his
position on May 30th, 1917. Circumstances made his task
harder, possibly, than that of his successors. During his
term of office people were excited with regard to profiteering,
alarmed, and not without good reason, by the submarine
menace, and yet for the most part ignorant of the difficulties
which beset the Government in their task of obtaining food
at controlled prices. "Give us enough food at a moderate
price and get on with winning the War," they demanded.
To get on with the winning of the War necessitated the
possession of vast sums of money, vast quantities of coal and

munitions, vast numbers of men, and vast numbers of ships. To produce food at home required the services of men needed in the Army; to bring it from overseas required tonnage which could ill be spared. To subsidise food was a costly process, and to reduce prices discouraged production.

Lord Devonport was blamed in some quarters because he recommended a Voluntary Economy Campaign. He should have been praised, for it was a wise act. When he was appointed in the early part of 1917, the country was not ready for rations, but needed education concerning the national food supply and its relation to the conduct of the War. The economy campaign brought about some decrease in consumption, and that in spite of the failure of the potato crop, which made it harder to lessen the consumption of cereals, and all the more so that the shortage came at a time when fruit and green vegetables were scarce and dear.

The fact, too, that for the first time in their lives many working class people earned wages which enabled them to buy as much food as they desired did not tend to lower consumption. Hitherto if they had gone short it was because they could not afford to buy. Now, when they could afford to buy, they were asked not to buy, and did not always understand the reason for restricting their purchases.

Approached in a sympathetic spirit, working people, as one knew would be the case, showed themselves no less ready to make sacrifices for the sake of their country than did persons of any other class. I found the fatigue of constant travelling and speaking very great. Often I had to start at seven o'clock in the morning to get to the station. Taxis were unobtainable and I had to travel as best I could by Tube, Underground, or omnibus, carrying my suit-case. Arriving again at a London terminus, often between eleven and twelve o'clock at night, neither porters nor cabs could be found.

My husband would come with me to the station and meet me on my return whenever his own ever-increasing work made it possible for him to do so, but as in addition to carrying out munition work for the Admiralty, he was a Special Constable, and on Saturdays and Sundays one of the workers at the canteen for Scottish soldiers, at St. Columba's, Pont Street, it was not always possible for him to do so.

The habit which railway companies contracted of altering the times of trains, or taking them off without warning, added another horror to travelling. I arrived at St. Pancras one day to find that my train which had been put on by ten minutes, had gone, and that there was not another train from there or from any other station which would get me to Sheffield in time for my meeting. So I took the next train to Doncaster and persuaded a taxi to drive me the twenty miles to Sheffield. There had been a blizzard and the roads were deep in snow, and neither I nor the chauffeur enjoyed the trip; frequently the car skidded in such a fashion that we expected to end our days in the ditch. I nervously ate a war-cum-railway-buffet bun, hoped for the best, and arrived at the Cutler's Hall punctually.

On another occasion, after addressing a meeting in Battersea, I had to catch a train for Liverpool. My husband had managed to get off in time to go to the station and to keep a seat for me. He had also obtained a dinner basket, for on very few trains then was there a restaurant car. Two or three seconds before the train started, a naval lieutenant precipitated himself into the carriage, calling to all and sundry to bring him a dinner basket, but not one was to be had. About an hour later our train broke down, and we were held up for two hours until another engine could be procured. My travelling companion fretted at the delay. So upset did he appear to be at the idea of not reaching Liverpool at the time fixed, that I ventured to ask what dire consequences would befall should he arrive there a few hours later, or even not until the next morning.

"Well, it really wouldn't matter much," he admitted; so I suggested that he should cease from troubling, and, as he could not obtain a dinner basket for himself, share mine. I did not wish to share my dinner with him, for I was hungry, and the *pièce de résistance*—a chicken leg—was small and skinny. While dining off this dainty, a fossilised roll and a wilted tomato, we came to the conclusion that we could probably catch a train at Crewe which would get us to our destination that night; but as we neared Crewe it became evident that it would be a toss-up whether or no we could catch the train. Judge, then, of my amazement when, as we drew into the station, that young man flung open the door, snatched his suit-case, leapt from the carriage, and made for the Liverpool train! Running was not one of my accomplishments, especially when encumbered by a suit-case, and I arrived on the platform panting, to behold the train dwindling in the distance. It was late and dark, bitterly cold and raining fast. I made my way to the nearest hotel and there I found the night porter drinking tea and eating bread and "marge." I asked him if he could procure some tea for me. He regretted that everything was locked up, but, moved to pity by my cold and wearied appearance, he offered to get another cup if I would not mind sharing his meal. So we sat in the office and discussed trade unionism. How different some men are from others, are they not?

I had many amusing experiences during my speaking tours. One occurred at a certain south country meeting organised by the mayoress. The local Member, who was a brewer, had not interested himself in the affair, and at first professed himself unable to bestow the light of his presence upon it. When, however, it appeared that the audience would be large, and it was found necessary to engage the local cinema, he discovered that his engagements would permit him to say a few words. I had been sent by the Ministry to ask the audience to make voluntary economy in food. The Member greeted me with kindly condescension, and then began his few words. He spoke for three-quarters of an hour, assured his audience that they would be on compulsory rations in a week or two's time, inferred that he enjoyed the innermost confidence of Lord Devonport, and summed up by saying that this being the case he thought the food question would be settled without any necessity for voluntary effort on the part of anyone. "And now, ladies and gentlemen," he ended, "I am sure that our friend Mrs. Peel will be kind enough to give us a few recipes for rice pudding." He had put me into a difficult position, but he found himself in one still more difficult when at question time the audience showed itself solid for war-time prohibition.

At another meeting the Member took not the slightest interest in the food question, but delivered an impassioned harangue on the shortcomings of the Foreign Office. "We will not forget," he cried, "we will not forget! When the War is over it will be your duty—your patriotic duty—to make your resentment felt." In the front row, gazing at him entranced, sat a remarkably stupid-looking woman with her mouth wide open, and by her side, a small boy afflicted with a violent squint and dressed in a velveteen suit, striped socks and a man-of-war cap. I pictured them to myself at the Foreign Office making their resentment felt.

At the time when potatoes were extremely plentiful, and the Food Controller was anxious that they should be used largely in order to lessen the consumption of cereals, one Member, a dear old gentleman much beloved in his constituency, but somewhat muddled as to what it was that the Food Controller did wish us to eat, rose, and with tears in his eyes implored the audience to refrain from eating potatoes. Some of my audiences were difficult. I arrived at Portsmouth Town Hall to find His Worship the Mayor in a fret. He had been warned that the audience would be a rampageous one—packed with pacifists—and he doubted if a lady's voice could fill the large Town Hall. I assured him that I was accustomed to speak in large halls and to difficult meetings, but it was a worried gentleman in robes and chain who introduced me to the meeting.

So many people came that numbers had to be turned away, but in the end, all went well. I had sympathy with genuine pacifists, and when the hecklers understood this, we settled down amicably to discuss the best ways of meeting food shortage. It was a much comforted Mr. Mayor with whom I ate a war tea in his parlour when the meeting had come to a harmonious end.

At Deal I faced another hostile audience. Fortunately, the moment I set eyes upon them I saw that there was no need to ask for food economy here. Most of the faces which looked up at me were those of hard-worked and underfed folk. I changed my tactics; I asked them to eat as well as they could, to keep themselves in health to help their country. Would they help the cause of food economy by influencing others who had more to spend, and so form a right public opinion?

After the meeting an old man came up to me and shook my hand. "That was right what you said. Folk liked that and they'll do their best, they will. And," his old eyes twinkled, "I don't mind telling you some of 'em 'ad a bit o' muck ready in their pockets for you, so 'twas lucky you said what you did say." For that meeting I stayed with some kind people near by. For some reason which I have forgotten, I jogged off to the hall alone in an ancient fly driven by an ancient man. The roads were slippery and I feared for the horse. Presently there came a droning sound; the driver stopped, clambered from the box and opened the door of the fly, "If you've no objection ma'am, I'll come inside, I like to feel a bit between me and them planes," said he. "But how about your horse?" I asked. "Oh, 'e'll stay still. If 'twere the last trump, 'e wouldn't move," so there we sat while the droning became louder and louder and then fainter and fainter. The planes were on their way to London, where they did a considerable amount of damage.

Other people liked to feel a bit between themselves and "them planes." One woman friend always sat under the billiard table when there was a raid. My husband told me that many people who arrived at South Kensington Tube Station to shelter, refused to go below and were quite content to stay upstairs where, had they realised it, the only "bit" above them was a glass roof.

The raid which made the most impression on Londoners was, perhaps, the daylight raid of June 13th, 1917. I had been away speaking the previous day, and had not been able to get back to London until after midnight, so it was later than usual the next morning when I started for the Ministry. My husband, who was on early Special Constable duty, returned just as I was starting, to tell me that an air raid warning was out. These warnings often did not come to anything, so I decided to make a start. We walked to the Oratory, and there I got into an omnibus. Presently I observed that the conductor was clinging to the staircase and peering up into the sky, and that the people on the pavement were staring too. One man, walking head in air, fell into the gutter. "What is happening?" I asked the conductor. "Look out there and you'll soon see," he replied, and, looking, I saw a cloud of aeroplanes. Then the guns began. There appeared to be about thirty large black planes travelling slowly, and a larger number of smaller planes flying faster. Some of them seemed to drop out of the clouds and began firing at the larger planes, which continued in formation, led by one well ahead of the main body.

Arrived at the Hyde Park Hotel I thought I had better take cover. Knowing that Hyde Park House was then used as a department of the Admiralty, I ran into it and made for the stairs leading to the basement. By this time the noise was deafening. The basement was packed with women clerks, some of them crying hysterically. One seized my arm, "Oh, I am going to be killed, I am going to be killed," she moaned, pinching me so violently that, what with pain and excitement, I so far forgot my manners as to reply, "If you pinch me like that I hope you will." She stood staring at me with her mouth open, the picture of idiocy. A girl nearby who had also been crying, remarked quietly, "You are not very sympathetic." "I am sorry," I apologised, "but she pinched very hard."

After the guns ceased I nerved myself to go out into the street again, expecting to see it strewn with dead and dying people, for I imagined that the noise we heard had been caused by bombs. It was completely deserted, except for a butcher's boy on a tricycle and a dreary-looking woman who had been selling flags, and began to try to sell them again. "Won't you buy a flag?" she asked. So I bought a flag, and as neither cabs nor omnibuses were to be seen, I started to walk across the park to the Ministry.

Charles told me afterwards that in Yeoman's Row, a turning out of Brompton Road, he had found a laundry van with a frightened woman clinging to the reins of a frightened horse. She assured him that showers of bombs had been falling in Knightsbridge, whereas what she had heard was the firing of anti-aircraft guns in Hyde Park. Charles found it impossible to keep the Yeoman's Row people in their houses. They would come out into the street, bringing their children with them. One woman stood with her baby in her arms, pointing up and saying, "Look at the airyplanes, baby, look at the airyplanes." The airyplanes amused baby very much.

On the occasion when a bomb fell in Piccadilly, a man was horrified to see a woman's head rolling towards him. It came to a stop almost at his feet, when he discovered it to be the head of one of the dummies from Swan and Edgar's window. My eldest daughter had gone to the theatre with a party on the night of this raid. They returned by Tube, and, as it was hot and stuffy, alighted at Piccadilly, intending to walk home. Just as they arrived at street level, crowds of frightened people poured in, so they turned and went back into the Tube just before the bomb fell.

She had another narrow escape when a bomb fell on the Embankment, close to Cleopatra's Needle. She was then working in the Air Ministry, and, becoming tired of waiting for a raid which was long in coming, walked along the Embankment towards Charing Cross, and had just got into a taxi when a bomb exploded, wrecking a tram car and killing and injuring several people.

Her third escape was when she had planned to return from Ireland (where she had been to recoup after an operation for appendicitis), in the "Leinster." Suddenly she felt that she could not do so, thus upsetting all the arrangements which had been made to provide an escort and to meet her at Euston. She could give no explanation for this capricious change of plans. She merely felt that she could not travel by that boat and telegraphed to us that she would come the next day. The "Leinster" was torpedoed.

Perhaps the most horrible result of a raid was when a bomb fell upon the printing works of Messrs. Odhams, in Long Acre. A number of people, of whom many were children, were accustomed to shelter in the basement. The floors above gave way, and the great printing machines fell on to the crowd below. An eye-witness described how in the Police Station nearby he saw terrified, sobbing children being washed clean of the blood which was smeared and spattered over them.

In spite of the danger of these raids, most of those who endured them remained calm. Housewives would gather their family and servants together, generally on the kitchen stairs, which was then advised as the safest place, and read aloud some particularly exciting novel which was kept ready for raid nights, or they would knit or sew and sing.

A friend who lived in Knightsbridge used to take refuge in the deep basement of Harrods, where concerts were organised, one of the star performers being a young man who played beautifully on a toothcomb.

I had one experience of sheltering in the Tube. I had gone with Miss Bellis to India House, Kingsway, to transact some business, and on our arrival we were informed by the commissionaire that a raid warning had just come through. We thought there would probably be time to get home, but our taxi-man said he didn't like raids, "'e couldn't drive straight in 'em and 'e'd go right 'ome," so we made for the

Holborn Tube Station, imagining that as it was only the first warning that had been given, the general public would not have realised that a raid was impending.

We were mistaken. I shall never forget the sight at Holborn Station. The girl who was working the lift kept her head but was quite powerless to control the mob, and Miss Bellis and I stood by her and helped as much as we could. One woman was screaming loudly, having already frightened her three children into hysterics. I spoke to her sharply and annoyed her so thoroughly that in order to abuse me she stopped screaming, which was something to be thankful for. All the platforms, stairs, and passages were packed with people, and already family parties with pillows and wraps and food were arranging themselves for a lengthy picnic.

Miss Bellis said that she would come home with me, and by the time we arrived at Brompton Road Station the raid had begun. We both felt, however, that the dangers of the raid plus fresh air would be preferable to the Tube, and made a run for it, our house being only a few seconds walk from the station.

Although raids did not frighten me, I admit they made me extremely cross.

One of the largest meetings I addressed was at Torquay, and some of the most interesting were at Newcastle. At the Town Hall meeting the Mayor was my Chairman, but that did not prevent him from expressing his decidedly adverse opinion of the ways of the Food Ministry. I enjoyed some good-humoured heckling and met some of my audience again the next day when I did a tour of ten-minute speeches in the munition works and public houses of Tyneside. Some of the meetings took place in the canteens of munition works during the dinner hour, and an exhausting task it was to make oneself heard amongst the clatter of the service.

I had to do some outdoor speaking and also spoke in between the turns at music halls and cinemas, which was not easy, as what one had to say had to be condensed into a few words.

Broadstairs, Ramsgate, Folkestone had suffered terribly from air raids, as also had Margate, where I had an enormous audience, and in the Mayor the best Chairman any speaker could desire. He was indeed the exact opposite of a well-known politician who took the Chair at a town hall meeting at a great industrial city. This important gentleman did not trouble to say how do you do to me, and had spoken for over half an hour when someone called out, "We came to hear Mrs. Peel," at which there was a little burst of clapping. My Chairman glared angrily, looked at the agenda and remarked, "I see that—er—Mrs.—er—er—Peel is going to speak to you. I don't know who she is, or why she is here. Perhaps she will tell you." He then sat down, crossed his legs, and appeared to go to sleep.

Some of the most interesting London meetings were held in theatres—His Majesty's, the Adelphi, Drury Lane, and the Coronet, at Notting Hill, where Sir Herbert Samuel was a Chairman who would have made any meeting a success.

It was at Drury Lane that Sir Harry Lauder and I were co-speakers, and a fine and moving speech he made. When he first came on, the audience, which was composed entirely of domestic servants, began to laugh. They were so accustomed to laugh at this comedian that they laughed as a matter of course. With what skill did he still that laughter and bring them to hushed attention, and then to tears!

Photo. L.N.A.

THE THREE FOOD CONTROLLERS

Of the many other speakers I heard during that time, Mr. Lloyd George was the finest; he had a happy choice of words. I remember that in a black moment he implored, "Be the comrades of your soldiers. . . . If we do all we can, we shall never be able to requite our men for their agony; if we do less than all, we shall dishonour their sacrifices."

It is too soon yet to know if we have dishonoured their sacrifices. It is a matter which only subsequent events can decide.

In London I addressed the children of a number of Council Schools, and that was not too easy a task, for the Board of Education had to be satisfied, the teachers, many of whom were Socialists, placated, and the children interested. Our idea, or rather Mrs. Reeves's idea, was to interest the children, and through them the parents. So the pupils were encouraged to write essays on what they had heard. The two best were chosen by the head teacher of each school, forwarded to the Ministry, and returned stamped with the Ministry of Food stamp and a letter of appreciation. One little boy of nine was quite clear as to what part he should play. "If," he wrote, "I *here* of any people grumbling about not enough food I shall tell them not to be always grumbling. Many people have less to eat than you." Another boy had evidently considered the difficulties of the situation and was full of sympathy for Lord Rhondda who had then succeeded Lord Devonport as Food Controller; "Lord Rhondda's position is no enviable one; his work is most difficult, for he has to provide for rich as well as poor, and some peace fads poison his ideas and tasks in abundance." Another youth preferred to consider the faults of others rather than dwell upon what he himself must do, and remarked, "In many rich households waste of a most disgusting kind is carried on"—a fact only too true, though in fairness to the upper classes it must be said that well-to-do people effected a great reduction in their food consumption long before rationing became compulsory. The submarine menace was a point which interested all the boys, and one, writing of a sailor in the Mercantile Marine, who had been torpedoed no less than three times, and had yet signed on for a fourth voyage, remarked with brevity and truth, "And I call that plucky."

Another young person ended her essay with a postscript, "Ladies who come talking food economy shouldn't wear patent shoes." The connection was not clear; but the criticism of the pernickety brat caused me to discard my comfortable old shoes and buy at a cheap shop in Edgware Road a dreary-looking pair which cost more than my patent leathers had cost at a fashionable shop in pre-War days. Another critic wrote to say that ladies shouldn't talk about food economy "dressed to the nines." I generally wore a blue serge dress and did not think I looked dressed up, but, ever willing to oblige, I borrowed Miss Bellis's penknife, ripped off its white collar and cuffs, removed the trimming from my hat, put it on wrong way round, and so, with my expensive, new and deplorable shoes, achieved a sufficiently dowdy appearance.

During the 313 working days of that miserable, anxious twelve months between March, 1917, and March, 1918, I travelled about England from Plymouth to Newcastle, addressed 176 meetings—more than one every other day—spent a week in France studying mass feeding, attended numerous conferences, wrote thousands of letters, interviewed hundreds of people, "fed" the Press, and prepared leaflets for the use of the speakers and recipes for the use of war foods which were issued in millions, prepared new speeches to suit the ever changing conditions created by a World War, and not infrequently drafted replies to questions asked in the House.

Mrs. Reeves was working equally hard, and she, poor soul, worked while enduring the heart-breaking grief of the loss of her only son, an officer in the Royal Flying Corps. What courage, what endurance that woman had.

CHAPTER XVI

Southampton Dockyard—I am sent to France—To the War in a Pullman—Boulogne in war time—In Paris—At the Citroën Works—Perfect organization—2,700 to *déjeuner*—The Renault Restaurant—Introducing oatmeal porridge—From Paris to the Front—Where the Uhlans came—Tragedy and Comedy—A large pink pig—They looked like pantomime rats—A treeless desert—In the town of Ham—Like a deserted theatre—Stones and dust and weeds and rusted wire—And so back to Paris.

IT was when speaking at Southampton that I was asked by the Mayor to visit the Dockyard and see under what wretched conditions the men were working. There was not enough accommodation for all the workers in the existing canteens, and on the cold, wet day of my visit, men, many of them elderly or old, were standing out in the rain, munching their bits of food. They had pieces of newspaper over their backs, and leant against the walls of the canteens, which inside were dirty and comfortless. On my return to London, I set to work to see if things could be bettered, for the matter was serious, dissatisfaction with conditions being so great that there was fear of a strike.

I trudged from the Admiralty to the War Office, and from there to the Ministry of Shipping, which was a wooden building in the drained lake of St. James's Park. I also approached the L. & S.W. Railway, for all these organisations were, it seemed, concerned with the Dockyard.

To persuade into action three Government Departments and a Railway Company was beyond my poor powers to achieve. Had I had then even as much worldly wisdom as I now possess, I should have realised that there were less direct methods which might have been employed with better results.

I spoke of the provision of canteens to Mr. Ulick Wintour, then Permanent Secretary at the Ministry of Food, with the result that a week or two later I was sent to France in the company of Miss Kate Manley and Mr. Herman Senn in order to study French methods of mass feeding.

We started from Charing Cross for Paris on a fine autumn day, travelling in the officers' leave train in a luxurious Pullman car. But comfortable seats and an excellent lunch did little to lighten the depression of those whose leave was ended and who were returning to the squalid horrors of war. In spite of the fact that many of our fellow-travellers were mere boys going out for the first time, it was a quiet and depressing journey. For once the weather was kind to me, and we had a smooth crossing, but, nevertheless, everyone was ordered to wear a life-belt for, accompanied as we were by two destroyers and an aeroplane, even so it was not impossible that we might be the target of a German submarine.

Arriving at Boulogne, we found that we had missed the train for Paris, and, rather than wait several hours and then travel by night, we arranged to stay in Boulogne, and to go on to Paris by the Sunday midday train.

Boulogne had become a town full of khaki-clad British soldiers, brightened here and there by the grey-blue of the French, the red fez of the Algerian, and the blue of the Portuguese uniform. The hotels were crowded, but, owing to the blandishments of the Base commandant's chauffeur, fortune favoured us, and that night we ate our dinner in the dining-room of the Hôtel Meurice, two women in a room full of men.

Suddenly the lights went out. An air raid warning had come through, but although the dining-room was roofed with glass, the waiters produced candles and continued to serve the dinner.

After a good night's rest in excellent French beds, and a breakfast of coffee and an ample supply of rolls and butter, a great treat to us, we went out. It was Sunday, and the shops were shut, but from a small girl in a black alpaca pinafore we were able to buy two large baskets of grapes and, thus laden, made our way to the Casino, now a British hospital. On the verandah were rows of beds, their occupants shaded by brightly-coloured Japanese umbrellas. The beautiful airy wards looking out over the sea were full of men who had fought and suffered, and some who would suffer as long as they lived. A beautiful fair Australian boy had his left arm fractured, his right arm and left leg amputated, a wound in his thigh, and his reply to our words of sympathy was: "Well, it's a man's life and I am glad to have lived it." Would that gladness endure throughout a crippled life?

Our days in France were to be so few that we had to hurry away to lunch and to catch the train to Paris, but sitting in the restaurant on the quay, how could one have appetite to eat?

There had been a great battle; trains full of wounded were coming in, and ambulance waggons began to crawl past, bearing their loads of mangled men. Silently we made our way back to the hotel to collect our luggage, then noticed that everyone was staring skywards. A raiding plane was on its homeward way, but it dropped no bombs, and we were in no danger except from the falling shrapnel of the French guns. While the noise was at its worst, we took shelter in a doorway, then, fearful of missing our train, made a dash for the hotel, pausing to pick up two pieces of shrapnel by the way.

Stopping often, we travelled past the great hospital at Etaples and on through the peaceful country, and always there were soldiers. Silhouetted against the sunset sky, fishing industriously with a stick and a piece of string, was the familiar figure of Tommy, his tunic unbuttoned, his cap on the back of his head. At almost every station women were collecting money for the wounded.

At Amiens men from the front joined the train on their way for a few days' leave in Paris, and at last we arrived at the Gare du Nord, to wait three-quarters of an hour while our porter hunted for a taxi.

In Paris we missed the familiar khaki. Here, there was a mass of blue, and only occasionally did we see a British soldier, though the figures of Australian, South African, New Zealand, and American soldiers were not infrequent.

The morning after our arrival we presented our letter of introduction at the Ministry of Commerce, a dignified building in the official quarter on the south side of the river, shut off from the street by high gates and a courtyard.

In Paris, Government messengers are clothed in full evening dress. We were ushered by an old man so attired into a brocade-hung room, the windows of which opened into a well-kept garden. The curtains in this room were of rose-coloured brocade, the chandeliers of cut glass, and one or two pieces of Empire furniture were placed against the walls, a beautiful antique Empire table taking up the centre of the floor.

A coquettish girl wearing a short-sleeved sailor jumper, a bangle, and her hair cut across her forehead in a straight fringe, came to assure us that M. Clementel would not keep us waiting long, and shortly afterwards we were ushered into the room of Captain Gallard, his secretary, and there for a few moments had the pleasure of an interview with the Minister himself—a handsome, grey-haired man with charming manners.

Through the kindness of M. Clementel, we received an invitation from M. André Citroën of the Quai de Javal to lunch with him at the munition works which bore his name. Messrs. Henri and Hugh Citroën employed something like nine thousand hands, their works were modern, they made vast profits, and it was possible, therefore, to do everything to increase the health and comfort of their employees.

At the time we visited the Citroën works, the restaurant was under the control of a manager and *maître d'hôtel*, and M. Hugh Citroën also interested himself in its arrangement.

The restaurant, store rooms, and kitchen were all gathered together in one enormous glass-roofed building. At one end were the entrance doors and turnstiles; at the other end the kitchen and store rooms. Over part of the kitchens was built a platform served by lifts from the kitchen, and on this platform dined the executive, the salaried staff and the clerks. Precisely the same meal at the same price as that provided for the work-people was served. At twelve o'clock some 2,700 diners sat down together on the platform and in the hall.

It was unusual for men and women to dine together in canteens, and when the Citroën restaurant was first opened, and it was proposed to make this arrangement, the suggestion met with adverse criticism. It was prophesied that it would be impossible to keep order; but the prophets who had so prophesied spake falsely. It was pleasant to see parties consisting of father and mother, with their grown-up boys and girls, relatives and friends enjoying each other's society in the one-and-a-half hours interval which was granted them for the chief meal of the day.

The menu the day we were there consisted of hors d'œuvre, roast veal, bread, cheese or dessert. Supplementary portions could be bought if desired, also biscuits to eat with the dessert, which on that occasion consisted of a pear. Wine was an extra, and most of the workers drank coffee which also was an extra.

Owing to the extraordinarily good organisation the 2,700 diners were served in less than one hour.

The restaurant itself was divided into ten sections, each complete in itself and marked by a distinctive colour. The tables were placed in the centre of the great hall, and up and down either side the entire length of the restaurant were serving counters fitted with electric hot plates. The cold food plates were also set out ready on the counters.

Each table seated twenty persons and each dish contained ample portions for five. The tables with chairs to match of a highly polished wood were set neatly, each worker having his table napkin, which was rolled and replaced in its numbered ring in a numbered receptacle provided for the purpose. The cutlery and glass was of good appearance, and it was interesting to see how neatly the workers consumed their meal.

The waitresses and all the serving staff were becomingly dressed in uniform, and were on duty from eight to five-thirty. In all 120 servants were employed. There was a male *chef* and one or two male helpers, but for the most part the staff consisted of women.

The kitchen equipment was extraordinarily simple, and yet the *chef* produced a meal far better cooked than is usual in this country, where kitchen equipment is generally more costly and elaborate. The kitchen was square and on either side were store rooms, a pastry-making room, still-room, and vegetable room, while the end nearest the restaurant was given up to service. It was there that the electric trolleys were loaded. These trolleys ran on wheels, and on each of them was a V-shaped erection of shelves. They were driven by girls who fetched the required number of hot plates and dishes for each section, returning with the dirty plates to the washing-up room.

In addition to the restaurant, there was a recreation room, and a crêche for the babies of nursing mothers. For the workers there was an infirmary in which a doctor and nine nurses were employed. Four to five hundred patients passed through their hands each day. We watched a nurse dressing a cut hand, and in the dental clinic saw the dentist and his two assistants in spotless overalls stopping teeth.

The way in which the wages were paid was interesting, each worker presenting himself with his note at one of a row of hatchways marked with the figure corresponding with the figure on his note, the note being immediately exchanged for the sum due to him.

Our last visit was to the cinematograph, conference and entertainment hall, where on the film we saw re-acted all that we had witnessed during the day.

We also visited the works of Messrs. Renault, where some 25,000 hands were employed, 8,000 of whom were women and 200 children. I believe the restaurant system adopted at the Renault works was originally organised by M. Duval, whose restaurants are a feature of Paris life. Then it was under the management of a co-operative society, controlled by a committee of the workers, on which committee a member of the firm was nominated to serve.

Unlike the restaurant at the Citroën works, the Renault restaurant was divided into three :—

A restaurant for the staff, where meals were served *à la carte;* also a special dining-room for those who wished for lunch at a fixed price of 3.50 francs, with coffee and wine included.

A restaurant for the employees, where the men were charged 1.50 francs and the women 1.20 francs. The bill of fare consisted of hors d'œuvre, meat, vegetable, cheese or dessert.

A canteen where meals brought by the workpeople could be re-heated, and this was used by whole families.

As M. Renault said, "We extend hospitality to them." There was no charge for this hospitality, the great object being to make it unnecessary for the employees to patronise places where they would be expected and encouraged to drink.

Some 6,000 persons were served each day, including 2,500 who brought their own meals to be re-heated.

The midday meal was the only meal served, but weak, cold coffee with bread was distributed during the day at a charge of a halfpenny. Tea was not popular, and the management had not thought of trying to popularise barley water. They were, however, introducing oatmeal porridge. Some time later I received a letter from one of the interpreters with the French Army saying that he wished for several recipes for porridge as it was such a good dish. "It is a pity French people do not know of it," he remarked.

For the workers on night shift a cup of soup was provided for one penny, and meals brought could be re-heated.

It is supposed that French people live on soup, but in reality they do not like it at midday, and neither at Renault's nor Citroën's was it served, except in Renault's works during the night, when one penny was charged for a quarter litre.

Puddings were rarely served, and none of the large steamers in our canteens and kitchens were provided.

Renault's staff restaurant consisted of a central kitchen and two dining-rooms on either side—one for men and one for women, furnished with comfortable chairs and tables with table cloths. The furniture was made by the firm and the washing was done by the firm also. In the dining-room there was a special counter for fruit and cheese very prettily set out. A hot plate ran the whole length of the service hatchways.

There was a flat roof to this building, and we were told that it was proposed to make a roof-garden, and to arrange billiard and writing-rooms.

At Renault's the meals were distributed by volunteer workers who were allowed to leave their work ten minutes earlier than others, and obtained their meal free of charge in lieu of payment.

It is perhaps no wonder that the cooking in such restaurants was better than that generally found in similar places in England, for the *chef* in No. 1 restaurant was paid £26 per month with board, lodging and washing in addition.

Undoubtedly if we judged by these and other canteens which we visited in the environs of Paris, and in Paris itself, the standard of cooking and service was higher than ours. The French have a better taste in food than we have, and do not suffer bad food and service patiently. We are apt to put up with anything that is given to us. Lunching at the restaurant of a well-known stores not long ago, I gave my order. The waitress brought a dish which I had not ordered. I pointed out the mistake, "I can change it, madam," she replied with surface politeness, but her manner said, "Of all the pernickety fools I have ever met, you take the cake." Messrs. Lyons have done much to improve the service of inexpensive meals, and their latest Corner House is a miracle of space, time, labour- and waste-saving planning.

Had we seen no more than I have here described while in France, our visit would have been a cherished memory, but I can never be sufficiently grateful to M. Clementel for arranging that we should visit some of the devastated country captured by the Germans in 1914, recaptured, again entered by the Germans, and then once more in French possession.

It was decided that Miss Manley and I should leave Paris at eight-thirty, by car, travelling via Senlis and Compiègne to Noyon, Ham and Jussy, approaching within seven or eight miles of the front lines, and returning to Paris that night—a drive of about 175 miles.

It was a damp, cool morning on which we drove through the streets of Paris, but in that city, where business begins earlier than in London, everyone was astir. Country people were coming into the markets, and our military chauffeur, who drove as the taximen of Paris drive, with a considerable addition of soldierly dash, early made me feel that I must put away all fear for my personal safety; he would drive as he would drive, and therefore the sooner I ceased to worry about it, the better.

I have to trust chiefly to memory for the details of our day's sight-seeing, for travelling at so great a pace the notes which I endeavoured to make proved for the most part illegible. I remember that we drove along wide paved roads, and as we came to Meaux the rain was ceasing, but the sky was still grey and misty. Here, M. Faidides, who accompanied us, reminded us of the army of General Gallieni, which in September, 1914, dashed out from Paris in motor cars, omnibuses and taxi cabs—eight men crammed into one cab—those men who fought the Battle of the Marne, who saved France and saved England.

Out to our left lay the battle field of the Marne. Keeping to the north and slightly to the east along straight, paved avenues, we passed a huge aerodrome, coming presently to the village of Loevre, which was full of soldiers in grey-blue uniform, standing about in the grey-paved street. Along a tree-bordered road we drove until, turning sharply round a corner, we entered a village of buff-washed houses on which were pasted great placards in blue lettering, and there, gathered round the inn, was another party of grey-blue clad soldiers. Later we passed the forest of Chantilly, beautiful in its autumn tints. It was into this forest that the Ulhans penetrated in the black days of September, 1914.

Passing a hospital, we came to Senlis, once a peaceful cathedral city, girdled by a Roman wall. We stopped the car and walked through some of its streets. I looked through a gate of delicate wrought ironwork into what had once been a garden, and was now a wilderness of stones, crumbled bricks and plaster. The side walls of the house still stood, but the front of the dwelling had fallen to the ground, leaving exposed to view the inner part of the house. It was as if some mischievous giant child had torn away the front from its gigantic doll's house. In one room a wall, covered with a gay, rose-patterned paper, stained and torn, still supported a gilt-framed picture.

As ever in life, tragedy and comedy go hand in hand. Our chauffeur suddenly put on the brakes, and the car bucked. From a side turning there advanced into the main road a strange little equipage something like a bathing machine, driven by an old man in black broadcloth, who wore a child's straw sailor hat with ribbons dangling down his back—yes, with ribbons dangling down his back. As he turned the corner, the doors of the bathing machine opened, and out fell a large, pink pig, which, nothing abashed, began to rootle in the gutter. His attention arrested by the shouts of the chauffeur and the hoots of the motor horn, the old man checked his old horse, clambered down from his machine, seized the pig by its hind legs, and, trundling it as if it had been a wheelbarrow, disappeared within the gates of a courtyard.

From this time onward we saw but four animals, one a cow with a string round its neck, led by an old peasant woman to graze along the roadside, another a goat which had clambered on to the wall bordering a street leading up to a little church set high above the red roofs and grey houses of a village spared, why I do not know, by the destroying hand of the enemy, and a pair of cream-coloured oxen working near Compiègne.

Compiègne, it was said, had been selected as the Kaiser's headquarters when his victorious army should enter Paris, and for that reason it had been spared. Over the wooden bridge we drove, through the forest, and once, by the roadside, a strange sight met our eyes—a group of what looked like huge pantomime rats—men in gas masks, drilling.

After that we met no civilian traffic, only grey-blue motor lorries travelling to and fro between Paris and the front. At intervals we passed gangs of German prisoners looking well fed and clothed, Chinese, neat in khaki blouses, breeches and puttees, and Algerian and Portuguese labourers.

Now we were in a fruit country, with great apple orchards and avenues of apple-trees, and then soon there were neither apple orchards nor avenues. Everywhere the trees had been felled and left to lie in cross-stitch pattern upon the roads. The bridges, too, had been destroyed to delay the advance of the French. By then the trees had been cleared away, but the stumps rose nakedly from the weed-choked borders of the road.

There were now no more villages, nothing but heaps of stones and plaster crumbled to dust. In the fields of that beautiful agricultural country, so rich before the War, now gashed by trenches and pock-marked by shells, weeds flourished, and amongst them coiled the rusted remains of wire entanglements.

To a little wood we came, amongst the trees of which were graves, and mounting guard over this lonely burying place the figure of Christ upon the Cross.

Just before we entered Noyon I looked out of the car and saw before us an enormous hole in the road. Whether the chauffeur saw it or whether by this time holes in roads were matters of little moment to him I do not know, but putting on speed he took the chasm at a leap, which caused me to bound from my seat and return to it with a jerk of the neck which I felt for many a day.

At Ham we stopped for lunch. The chief hotel of the town had been used by the German officers as their mess, and a few months earlier instead of two English ladies, one French gentleman, a French soldier, and a chauffeur, the dining-room had been filled with German officers waited upon by the very girl who now waited upon us.

After lunch we walked to the old castle of Ham—once the prison of Napoleon III—now in ruins. In the street of Ham we stopped to buy picture postcards in true tripper fashion. We talked with the old man and his married daughter who kept the little stationer's shop. "No, the Germans were not cruel; severe yes, but not cruel, not, that is to say, if we obeyed. The children? Yes, they had been sent away for the most part, but the others," the old man shrugged his shoulders, "it was their home, where else could they go?"

When the Germans left they had not destroyed the houses of Ham, but they had spoiled or taken with them much of their contents. This old man and his daughter were philosophical, but they bore upon their faces the tale of the anxious months through which they had lived.

Then, our chauffeur refreshed, we drove off again even faster than before, through Chauny to Blerancourt and Jussy, and there again left the car and stood by the canal. A temporary bridge had been built across it, and along its shell-torn banks fluttered shabby remnants of painted camouflage like the wings and flies in a deserted theatre. We stood there in the silence of desolation, broken only by distant thudding of the guns, and at each thud a jagged piece of the wall nearby trembled, and now and then a morsel of plaster fell.

It seemed as if the world had turned to stones and dust and weeds and rusted wire. Away to the right was what had once been a railway station. An engine lay toppled over on its side, the metal rails curled fiercely yet helplessly about it as though they had once had life and had died writhing in some fierce fire. Then the rain came down again and the sky turned to a leaden grey. And so we came back to Compiègne.

Later the rain ceased once more, and as the light began to fade and the last streaks of the setting sun lit the sky, the wet, paved road rose in front of us like a band of steel; the purr of the engine deepened and almost in a moment the great car had eaten up that mile of hilly road and was throbbing on through the fast-falling dusk to Paris.

217

CHAPTER XVII

The end of voluntary rationing—Tea with Lord Northcliffe—He asks
me to go to America with the American Mission—The *Daily
Mail* Food Bureau—£20 a week to stick up envelopes—I edit
the Woman's Page—The summer and autumn of 1918—The
Armistice—A wheezy old gramophone played "God Save the
King"—"Have we won the War?" roared the crowd—
"Yes, we've won the War"—One of the grimmest tragedies
of Peace—Lord Northcliffe and *The Times*—"They were born
in the Ark and they are still in the Ark"—Nagger in Chief—
When all the people turned up and nothing happened—The
interests of women, *vide* the *Daily Mail*—Writing leaders—
The 1920 Husband Hunt—There are drawbacks to being a
woman—Not a normal woman—Tea at Printing House Square
—"I am sorry. I am very sorry," said Lord Northcliffe and
tears were running down his face—I walked down Wimpole
Street thinking that my day was done—The Insulin treatment
for diabetes was discovered.

WHEN it became known that compulsory rationing
would be enforced I felt that my work in the
Ministry of Food should end, and I asked permission of Lord Rhondda to resign my appointment. This he
refused, saying that changes would be made and my services
might be required. So I did as I was bid and for some
weeks waited to see what would happen.

In the meantime I had tea one afternoon with Lord
Northcliffe at Crewe House, then the Ministry of Information. I told him that I hoped soon to leave the Ministry of
Food. "Then you can work for me," said he. "I wish you
to go to America with the American Mission and I shall
send you on a speaking tour." I asked him to let me think
over this invitation or, as it perhaps might more truly be
termed, command.

I felt dreadfully exhausted by the strain of the past year's work, but I longed to go to America.

Again I asked to be released from the Ministry of Food and again Lord Rhondda was kind enough to wish me to remain and desired me to see Colonel Weigall, now Sir Archibald Weigall, who was then President of the newly-appointed Food Survey Board. Colonel Weigall informed me that if my desire to leave the Ministry was explained by the considerable financial loss which I suffered by being there, Lord Rhondda wished to make a suitable arrangement. That was not the reason although, naturally, as we had to earn all but a very small part of our income, provide for two children, help to support an aunt and save for our old age, I could not be entirely indifferent to money. The reason was, as I have said, that I could not see that there could be any further use for the kind of service I was best fitted to give.

Owing to the circumstances of my life, I had become accustomed to act on my own responsibility and to act quickly. I was not a good under-dog, and did not intend to try to learn how to be a good under-dog. I felt that I could do what we used to call "war work" quite as well outside the Ministry of Food as in it. From one cause and another, some of which could not be avoided, for conditions changed from day to day, there was a lack of organisation and co-ordination in the Ministry which made my work more difficult and fatiguing than it need have been. I felt at times that I had strayed into the Alice in Wonderland croquet party; if one found the mallet, the hoop had disappeared; when one captured the ball, the mallet was no longer there. So again I asked if I might be allowed to depart.

Lord Rhondda now accepted my resignation and

wrote me a charming and complimentary letter of fare-well.

I discussed with my husband Lord Northcliffe's invitation to go to America. He begged me not to go, declaring that in my fatigued state I could not endure the voyage and the constant train journeys, especially as I was at all times a bad traveller; he pointed out too that our ship might be torpedoed and that I ought not to leave the children, the younger of whom was then but eleven. So in the end, though it cost me one of the worst heartbreaks of my life, I gave up the idea and went to Crewe House to acquaint Lord Northcliffe of my decision. He was sitting in his large arm-chair, one leg doubled under him, a favourite attitude, drinking a cup of some compound brought to him by an attentive woman secretary. "Very well," said he; "if you won't go to America then you can come to the *Daily Mail*. I want you to organise the *Daily Mail* Food Bureau." I did not feel any special desire to do this and told him that I must rest before I undertook any new work. "I can't wait," he replied. "The thing has got to be done at once and you have got to do it. I shall send someone to see you at your house to-night to discuss terms. You can have practically what you want." I was so tired that I felt unable to argue the matter further. It was less trouble to do as I was told.

After dinner, that charming writer, Mr. Percy Izzard, appeared, though why Mr. Izzard should have been chosen to discuss terms with me I do not know. But that was the way Lord Northcliffe did things. As that surprising man had said that I could ask practically any terms that I liked, and as I did not want the job, I thought that I would ask such terms as would not be accepted, so suggested a salary of £1,000 a year and stipulated that I must be allowed to retain the Editorship of the Household Department of *The Queen* and that I should not be required to keep fixed hours. It must be left to me to do my work in the way in which I thought fit, and, as I did not want an agreement, if the work was not well done the arrangement could be terminated at once. To my surprise, these terms were accepted. Indeed, the terms were better, for I was paid at the rate of £20 a week, and Lord Northcliffe insisted that any work which I might do outside my department should be paid extra. The organisation of the Food Bureau interested me. Letters poured in, not only from people in England, but from prisoners in the German War Camps. These men were not supposed to receive English newspapers. It was evident that they received the *Daily Mail* with considerable regularity. It was evident, too, that sometimes they managed to get uncensored letters through. They asked for help to cook their scanty rations in such ways as would make them palatable and nourishing. One man wrote asking for recipes. "They have made me cook of the Officers' Mess," he explained; "God help them." In a very short time it was necessary to employ three young girls in addition to my assistant, Mrs. Mabel Wijey, and a typist. When applying for the assistance of these girls, I was amused to be told by one of the *Daily Mail* grandees that with good organisation I could manage without any further help. He began to explain to me a quick method of moistening the gum on envelopes and fastening them. "You see," he said, "we must not lose sight of economy." I agreed meekly, thinking that it was scarcely economical to pay me £20 a week to stick up envelopes. Basket after basket full of letters was brought into our office, and soon the entire time of the three little girls was taken up opening the letters and putting the replies into the envelopes. I found that the best way to keep up with this enormous correspondence was to write a short article suggesting ways of using war foods, and saying that recipes could be obtained on application. Suitable recipes were roneo-ed by the hundred and were ready for the demand which invariably followed. In addition to these, many correspondents needed special replies. Before I had done with that Food Bureau, the number of letters replied to was in the millions. When the War ended, I told Lord Northcliffe that I thought the Food Bureau work would dwindle and that at last the time had come for me to rest. "Nonsense," he replied, "I intend to begin the Woman's Page again" (this had been discontinued shortly after war broke out), "and I wish you to edit it. You will have plenty of time to make your preparations. Collect a staff and be ready to begin. I will give you several days' notice before I require the page. I don't know what you are earning," (I think he knew very well) "but I suppose it is something pretty good, so go on earning it." So I went on earning it, but I was not given time to collect a staff before Sir Andrew Caird, whom Lord Northcliffe used to speak of as "that black dog of mine," came to tell me that the Woman's Page would be required for that night's paper, which means in journalistic parlance, the paper that was to be on your breakfast table the next morning. My former experience of newspapers stood me in good stead. By dint of telephone messages, telegrams, and my own pen, the Woman's Page with its due quota of illustrations by that famous line artist Bessie Ascough, appeared next day.

Lord Northcliffe, desiring to be extremely kind to me, now made my position difficult. He invited me to take possession of his own magnificent room, which he had ceased to use, preferring his room at *The Times* or a sitting-room at Fleetway House. His room at Carmelite House was a gloomy apartment, panelled in mahogany, handsomely furnished in the taste of its day. On the writing-table was a bust of Napoleon, on a large easel a crayon portrait of Lady Northcliffe. Fortunately, there was an ante-room attached to this magnificent apartment, and I took possession of that. "The Chief," as he was known to his staff, desired that I should attend the Editorial Conferences, which took place at four o'clock in the room of Mr. Thomas Marlowe, the Editor-in-Chief, a good-looking, grey-haired Irishman, who put on his hat with an air and used his keen blue eyes to advantage. As an example of the strange way in which things happened in the *Daily Mail* office, when I first arrived to work there I received a message from Mr. Marlowe to say that he would like to see me. "And how did you come here?" he enquired. I explained that Lord Northcliffe had desired my company. It seemed strange that an Editor-in-Chief should know nothing of the appointment of a member of his staff. Mr. Marlowe was a man of great parts and I left the *Daily Mail* full of admiration for him.

As the dreary summer of 1918, much of which I spent at Carmelite House, drew to a close, one began to feel as if the War would go on for ever. The streets were dark, the clothing of the people was dark, for although few now wore mourning for their dead, gay colours were not seen, and the shops stocked little but black and grey material.

Although the fear of starvation was over, food was still scarce and so dear that all but the very rich were obliged to put a strict limit to consumption. Inadequate nourishment and lack of warmth were weakening the stamina of the people. A specially severe type of influenza raged. Added to the long War Casualty lists were the names of those who had died of influenza or pneumonia, into which this type of influenza often developed.

Then, when it seemed as if the misery of the world was too great to be endured longer, there came rumours of peace. Just as in August 1914 few of us could believe that a European war could happen, so now we could scarcely believe that peace could come. I was at the *Daily Mail* when the news came through on the telephone. We opened the window wide and could hear cheering and immediately somewhere near a wheezy old gramophone began to play "God Save the King." I longed to go into the street but could not, for whatever happens, newspapers must go to press. I was correcting proofs and my eyes kept filling with tears, tears for those to whom peace had come too late to save some one dearly loved. By the time my work was over, it was five o'clock and raining heavily, and there was no other way to get back to Alexander Square than by walking. Amongst all that I saw, one scene stands out. I went through the Temple which was deserted, and up one of those little streets which lead to Charing Cross, and there under an archway were two old women in jet-trimmed bonnets and capes, dancing stiffly to the strains of a barrel organ—an out-moded organ with one long wooden leg, played by an ancient, bearded man who might have been Father Time himself.

That night in Trafalgar Square there was dancing and singing, flags were waved, confetti thrown. "Have we won the War?" roared the crowd. "Yes, we've won the War," came in answering roar. A song new to us was heard. "What shall we be when we aren't what we are?" chanted those soldier men. It foretold one of the grimmest tragedies of peace—unemployment.

Lord Northcliffe was one of the most interesting men I have ever met. I had experience of him as a host, as a guest in my own house, as an important public man with whom I discussed affairs, and as an employer. Always he was autocratic. On one occasion he lunched with us, or rather I should say with me, as my husband was too busy to get home for that meal. The great man arrived at five minutes to one. By one o'clock I saw him look at the clock. By five minutes past one he was becoming restive. "I was asked to luncheon at one o'clock." "I am so sorry, but it really was a quarter past one." One of the other guests arrived as I finished speaking. It was Mr. Ulick Wintour, the Permanent Secretary in the Food Ministry. Close on his heels came Lord Tamworth, and after a short interval the late Dr. Marion Phillips, then chief woman organiser of the Labour Party, Mrs. Llewellyn Roberts, and lastly my daughter in her V.A.D. uniform. I had not known that Lord Northcliffe was condemned to a strict diet and by the evil chance of things I had provided scarcely anything that he could eat. He bore this well, but at 2 o'clock when we were drinking our coffee, he said grimly, "It is time we were at work. I will take you down to the *Daily Mail* with me."

During the drive I asked him to what he attributed his success in life. "I was fortunate enough to have a wonderful mother who taught me never to be ashamed of changing my mind. In a changing world, how can your mind remain unchanged?" His certainly did not; sometimes one found its changings hard to bear.

On other occasions, he told me some of his experiences of the great men of the day. It seemed to me that he was extremely indiscreet, but I doubt if he cared whether he was or not. He said what he chose to say, and perhaps he trusted me not to repeat what he told me.

Lord Northcliffe began the day early, and by the time most well-to-do folk were thinking of getting up he had been at work for some hours. One morning as I was break-fasting comfortably in bed, my telephone rang and a voice remarked, "It's the Chief speaking. Would you do me a kindness and come down to *The Times* at three this afternoon. I intend to introduce fashion drawings in *The Times* and no one in that place can write a caption. All the ancient men there think the end of the world is coming. They say, 'What! put pictures of women who look as if they were in the family way into *The Times*!' I tell them that it is the correct silhouette, but it's quite useless. They were born in the Ark and they are still in the Ark."

How well I remember that room in Printing House Square, the large arm-chair, the writing-table strewn with fashion sketches, the Chief now good-tempered and joking, and the faces of two of the "ancient men."

For his profession Lord Northcliffe had a passionate love. Quite apart from the wealth which his newspapers brought him, he loved them and he was anxious to improve conditions for journalists, and had procured for them, as far as possible, a five-day week, for he realised, from his own early experiences, that work on a daily paper is high tension work, and that good journalists must be quick witted and highly strung. In one of the daily messages which were sent to all members of the staff, which they were bidden not to keep, but which he knew they did keep, he stressed the necessity for shorter hours. "Having been a sub-editor myself, I know and no one better, that it is impossible that a man should do such work six nights a week and do it well."

He christened himself the Nagger-in-Chief, and nag he did with a will. On the other hand, he did not hesitate to compliment those who he thought had done well, and while he would pay liberally for what he thought was worth paying for, he was no more averse than anyone else to getting something for nothing.

In one communiqué he complained that use was not made of the books that were sent for review, which should be combed for stories before being sent to reviewers. "The result is that other morning papers are getting capital little news articles or fourth-page articles for nothing." In another he scolded the editor of the picture page, who, he said, was too fond of printing such scenes as "Man with Pipe" and "Man with Turnip." "The Picture man, like the News man," said he, "should always remember how important is the element of surprise in journalism. As an American editor said: A dog biting a man is no news, but a man biting a dog is considerable news."

On yet another occasion he told how, when he was recovering from an operation in a nursing-home, he had asked his night nurse, who was a very intelligent woman and had travelled a great deal, what she thought the most interesting thing in the paper that morning, and she had replied, "The story of the wedding where all the people turned up and nothing happened!" This was the type of intelligent woman which the *Daily Mail* people then understood. They expected women to be interested solely in knitting jumpers, in caring for their complexions, in looking after babies, in cooking, in a "good" murder and in silly stories about weddings. It had, however, dawned on Lord Northcliffe that the women who had come out of their homes during the War to work as nurses, Waacs, Wrens, munition girls, to take their place in banks and offices, and Ministries, would not return unchanged by such experiences. It was for this reason that on several occasions, he asked why more use was not made of my services. After one curt communiqué on that subject, Mr. Marlowe asked me if I could write in

Bourgeois, which was the size of type used for the leaders. I thought that at least I could try, and from that time on did write an occasional leader, as well as news stories and literary page articles, in addition to attending to my own work.

I thought then of Mrs. Pember Reeves, who once said laughingly, "You think you can do everything." But that was not true. I did not think I could do everything, but I did think that it was worth while to try to do what I was given a chance to do, to find, as someone said—but who I do not know—that those who do most make the most mistakes! Still, if one is frightened of failing one is not likely to succeed.

On more than one occasion I was glad I had said that I thought that I could write in Bourgeois, especially when a leader had to be written about the employment of Women Police. Mr. Marlowe saw no reason for the existence of such persons and asked what I thought. He listened to what I had to say, considered it, and, being a man with an open mind, bade me write that leader from my own point of view, which was that there should be police women, because they are better fitted to perform certain duties connected with women and children than are men.

The four o'clock conferences which I was obliged to attend were sadly boring, consisting chiefly of a low-toned duet between the News Editor and the Foreign Editor. It was seldom that the opinion of any other member of the staff was expressed. Had I been encouraged to offer an opinion I might have saved the *Mail* from annoying women by an article which appeared on the 29th February (Leap Year) entitled "The 1920 Husband Hunt." It did not seem to occur to anyone that women are not complimented by the suggestion that it is necessary for them to hunt for husbands;

they are still sufficiently old-fashioned to prefer husbands to hunt for them.

Does it seem that I was a conceited woman? Indeed I was not, but I had been put into the position I held by Lord Northcliffe because he considered that my intelligence and my experience were worth paying highly for, and it irked me not to be allowed to earn my salary. But, as I have said, the Chief made my position none too easy, and my own impatience and lack of tact did not improve it.

There is no doubt that it is more difficult to be a working woman than a working man: that is, in any post of importance. A man is expected to know his job and to do it. A woman must first prove that she knows her job, and then do it unless her opinion clashes with that of a man, when it is taken for granted that the man must know best and the woman should give way.

I wished to be treated as a person doing a job, instead of which some people were kind to the poor woman, some people were jealous of the damned woman, and some people thought the tiresome woman had better go home and make way for a man. On one occasion an important member of the staff with whom I had been told to converse remarked, "Oh yes! we all know that you are the blue-eyed girl to-day, and what you say goes." This description as applied to an ill, tired woman, then nearly fifty, made me smile.

After one of the many afternoon conferences, during which I sat dumb, Mr. Marlowe asked, "Feeling snubbed, Mrs. Peel?"

For once I behaved with tact, said nothing and smiled a nice, diffident, womanly smile.

No, I had not felt snubbed, but a trifle amused that all these men who were engaged in producing a paper, the success of which depended on the good will of women—for it is women who spend the greater part of men's earnings and so make advertisements pay, and without advertisements no paper can live—should think the opinion of a woman of so little importance.

I said this to a man I liked—the night editor, Mr. Beattie. He replied, "Yes, but we can't take you as representing the normal woman—you are an exceptional woman." I was not. I loved my husband, I loved my children, I loved my home and was deeply interested in household matters. I loved pretty clothes, was never happier than when sitting in a garden sewing a seam. I was terrified of mice and always wanted to cry when baffled and annoyed. I seldom did cry, but oh! how I wanted to! And then Mr. Beattie said I was not a normal woman!

As Lord Northcliffe became more and more ill, his communiqués were sometimes so worded that it was difficult for the persons concerned to endure his criticisms of their work, especially as a typewritten copy was put up in the Newsroom and could be read by the typists and office boys.

Eventually this great man became so deranged that shortly before his death his papers passed into the control of other directors. Before this happened, and after I had been in Lord Northcliffe's employ for some two years, I was asked to sign a contract. This I refused to do. I was trying to make up my fatigued mind to abandon my job, and eventually decided to do so.

The Chief was annoyed; but when I explained to him that I was too ill to continue work which must of necessity be exhausting, he became sympathetic and insisted that I should take a six weeks' holiday on the Riviera on full pay. Such kindly generosities as these were part of his complex character.

Just before Lord Northcliffe left England for the last

voyage he was ever to undertake, I went to have tea with him in his room at Printing House Square. He seemed low, worried and irritable. We discussed various newspaper matters and then passed on to other affairs. He told me the history of his quarrel with Mr. Lloyd George and a great deal of gossip about Mr. Winston Churchill, then invited me to come down to the Board Room where some men were waiting to show him a cinematograph. The performance was remarkably bad, and Lord Northcliffe lost his temper. He seemed so ill and upset that I persuaded him to come upstairs to his own room again. At the door he paused and looked towards the abashed and disappointed operators. "I am sorry, I am very sorry; I should not have spoken like that," he said, and tears were running down his face.

It was the last time I saw the man who had been a kind friend to me. His understanding of newspaper work amounted to genius and, according to his lights, he was a great patriot.

Shortly before I left the *Daily Mail* I had become so ill that I determined to consult a well-known woman doctor. She told me that I had diabetes which must have been affecting me for the last few years and had been intensified by war food and my exhausting work at the Ministry of Food.

I had walked up Wimpole Street thinking I should need to take a rest before regaining my health. I walked down Wimpole Street thinking that my day was done.

I have been granted an observant eye, but as I had walked up Wimpole Street nothing I saw appeared to be of any importance. There was the street, there were taxis and cars, a policeman, a milkman, and a yellow cat. As I walked down Wimpole Street, the yellow cat was still there, the milkman was not, there were other taxis, a child in a perambulator was screaming, and to the west there was a red glare in the darkening sky. Now everything seemed of intense importance. It might not be for very long that I should see such sights, and so they became precious to me.

A year or so later, by which time I had become very ill and was in a nursing-home, the Insulin treatment for diabetes was discovered.

CHAPTER XVIII

A wedding with cakes and cream—Mr. and Mrs. Walter Page, Cabbages and Carnations—In a nursing-home—Dreams—In Bavaria —What German ladies said about the War—In Germany, Italy and France—The housing question—How some of us live—The baby in the chest of drawers—Why did they not use the bath? Ah! Why!—Women's Pioneer Housing—The Peckham Health Centre—A thrilling experiment—Stowe Palace becomes a Public School—The domestic servant problem—She threatened to shoot me *dead*—In Venice—The tragedy of Domo d'Ossola—I see Sir Henry Wilson murdered—The General Strike—People who make revolutions—" A Hundred Wonderful Years "—" How We lived then "—Husband and wife in partnership—" The Stream of Time."

IT was in 1919 while I was working at the *Daily Mail*, that Cecilia married Major Harry Straker, R.A. It was a pretty spring-like wedding, with nine bridesmaids in leaf-green dresses, carrying sheaves of tulips, and took place on the first day after it again became possible to obtain sufficient sugar and other nice things to enable the *chef* at the Rembrandt Hotel, where the reception was held, to exercise his culinary skill to the full.

Tea was served at small tables and those who in normal times would have taken little notice of what they ate exclaimed with pleasure at the sight of iced cakes and cream, and sat down to enjoy a solid meal. After becoming accustomed to go out to tea carrying one's own portion of sugar, and feeling that it was scarcely mannerly to eat other people's restricted allowance of butter, it was pleasant to feast unashamed. Not that I was permitted to feast, for my diet was that of the diabetic, and many a day was I condemned to

233

loathsome meals of cabbage, or, scarcely less unpleasant, of milk and soda water.

When cabbage appeared for breakfast, luncheon, tea and dinner, I thought of Mr. Walter Page, the American Ambassador during the War, who said that the English had quantities of vegetables—all of them cabbage.

When looking through old diaries and papers I came upon some yellowed carnations which I had kept as a memento of a day when I had tea with Mr. and Mrs. Page, in Mr. Page's sitting-room, and Mrs. Page had given me a posy from a great bundle of carnations which had just arrived from the country, and which she was then arranging.

Mr. Page looked fragile and worn, as indeed he well might, for, as he revealed in the book which he published later, how hard and anxious had been his task of promoting a right spirit between his own country and ours.

After I resigned my position at the *Daily Mail* I enjoyed the six weeks' holiday which kind Lord Northcliffe gave me, first at St. Raphael and then at Monte Carlo. On this occasion Mrs. Barrington Crake and I had decided to adventure in an aeroplane which made half-hour flights from Cannes. On the day fixed I was not well enough to go out. That day the aeroplane crashed.

Somewhat recovered after my holiday, I came home and managed by the help of my admirable secretary, Miss Threlfall (now Mrs. Harold Smith) who was with me for nine years, to continue my work for *The Queen*, to complete a poorish novel, "Tony Sant," and a number of articles. I prided myself that during my journalistic career I have never let an editor down. If I promised an article, it was delivered punctually. Once I wrote an article when still dazed by the effect of morphia; on other occasions I have written propped up in bed almost stupefied by inhalations of nitrate of amyl.

About this time I was in a nursing-home and spent the greater part of one night, because I was in too much pain to sleep, writing an article for a new edition of the "Encyclopædia Britannica." I fully expected that it would be returned, for honestly, I scarcely knew what it was about, but a good spirit guided my pen, and in due course a proof arrived.

When ill or unhappy if one can force oneself to work, much of one's pain, mental or physical, may be worked out of one. A friend when showing me her garden, said "I have dug sorrow into this garden, and it has been translated into flowers." A young friend who reads this book as I write it, and criticises it, says "All that sounds rather sloppy and Sunday schoolish," then, after a pause she adds, "But I daresay it's true." Reflections which sound Sunday schoolish sometimes are true.

The mention of the nursing-home reminds me of a dream which I dreamed there. I dreamed that one night I could not sleep, so got up and looked out of the window, up Queen's Gate towards Kensington Gardens. It was a still, misty night; the leaves of the trees scarcely stirred, and the houses looked grey and solid and essentially like Queen's Gate houses. One could imagine that rich stockbrokers lived in all of them. Then in the distance appeared two small figures. The mist cleared, a clear white light shone, the trees woke up and looked so alive that one felt that they might begin to walk, but the houses became thin, like stage scenery, and faded from solid prominence into a wavering background. As the figures came nearer I saw that they were grey apes walking upright, very precisely, even mincingly. They wore shiny, curly-brimmed top-hats, white gloves, tail coats, and carried canes with silver knobs. The taller of the two had an eyeglass attached to a black ribbon fixed in one eye. They were talking vivaciously, and every gesture showed a polished courtesy. Suddenly there was the noise of a car being driven at high speed; it stopped at the door, two men carrying bags sprang out and up the steps. At the first appearance of these human beings, the monkeys dropped their walking-sticks and, shrieking and gibbering, fled up the nearest tree. Their top-hats fell off and came rolling down the pavement and disappeared. The light faded to the normal grey hue of early morning, the houses became solid; humanity regained possession of the world, and nurse stood by my bedside saying, "Would you like a cup of tea?"

I recall a dream scene on the Leas at Folkestone. A chattering, laughing crowd, of which I was one, a clear space of grass, and down it, galloping one after the other, five large grey donkeys harnessed to five tiny shining broughams, driven by violently excited, red-cheeked little boys, dressed as mutes, and in each carriage sitting stiffly, a corpse, in its grave clothes. As the procession passed such horror overtook the spectators that one by one we turned to stone. It was exquisite torture, that of petrifying flesh and blood.

And another dream. I was acting in theatricals and one of a chorus which wore Greek robes. The dress rehearsal ends and the stage manager exclaims at the dirty hems of our dresses. A grim woman appears with a washing-basket, our dresses slip off us as if they are alive, and lie down in the basket. The woman casts a glance of malign amusement at us. . . . We are dressing for the performance and suddenly we chill and stiffen, despair ages and whitens every face. It was not our dresses but our souls that the washer woman took away and now has brought back in her accursed basket. Alas! not one of them was marked. Never again shall we know which soul belongs to which of us. There is a scene of horror and despair as the souls, which now look cold, damp and semi-transparent, come crawling over us trying to find their way through our mouths into our shuddering bodies.

What does the psycho-analyst make of these dreams?

Why should they sear my memory as no event of my real life has done? But to return to realities again. In 1921 I took our younger daughter, Denise, to Bavaria. We wished to visit Cecilia, whose husband was then on the Commission of Control, engaged in the disarming of Germany. His centre being Munich, he, Cecilia and their baby son had settled for the hot weather at the Hotel Kaiserin Elizabeth, at Feldafing, on the Starnberger See, where we joined them.

During our stay at Feldafing we decided to have some German lessons, and made the acquaintance of a highly cultured and interesting woman who in happier times had been the governess of various princesses. Although she was in receipt of several pensions, these had become practically valueless, and I fear life was very difficult for her. It was a pleasure to us to invite her from time to time to luncheon. Through her introductions I was received in several German households. The ladies I visited gave me vivid descriptions of their life during the War, they showed me kitchens denuded of all their cherished copper pots and pans, which had been taken from them to be used for munitions, and told me of the long, cold winters when hardly any fuel or artificial light was procurable. Families sat in the dark trying to keep cold, restless, underfed children happy until it was bedtime. As one of my hostesses truly said, "One could not put the little ones to bed at five o'clock on a winter's afternoon and expect them to sleep until daylight at eight or eight-thirty next morning."

These long hours of darkness to people whose minds were filled with grief or with the fear of grief to come, were a misery almost too great to be endured.

The German ladies whom I met were convinced that we had forced Germany to go to war, and the Hochgeboren, who had suffered at the hands of the "reds," felt bitter towards us because they thought that by destroying their arms we were in some way playing into the hands of the Communists.

My hostesses had no knowledge of the way in which we had lived during the War, and they learned with surprise that fuel and light had been rationed, that we had been obliged to eat war bread, that at one time and in some places, our meat ration had been reduced to half a pound per head per week, and that the consumption of sugar, butter, tea and flour had been reduced.

Our conversations always ended, however, with the reflection that the suffering of the English had never, in any way, been commensurate with that of themselves, which was true.

During the last part of the War, the people in Berlin had neither tea, cocoa, bacon, ham, fresh or dried fruit, vegetables or cereals other than bread, and milk was reserved for invalids and children under six. The butter allowance was less than two ounces a week, and that of margarine one ounce. Six ounces of sugar or treacle was the weekly allowance. Jam and coffee were made of "substitutes," and sometimes there would be one egg per week and sometimes only one per fortnight. The price of clothing rose to excessive heights; 30s. a yard was charged for an ordinary make of serge, and clothes were rationed, and if new garments were bought, the old ones had to be surrendered. Linen became so scarce that a man visiting Berlin directly after peace was made found on his bed in an hotel de luxe, in lieu of sheets, a pair of old cretonne curtains.

That summer I was in Germany and in Italy and in France. If we had all spoken Esperanto and been blindfolded, one would scarcely have known if one was in any of those three countries or in England. The conversation of the women was everywhere almost identical, and amongst the upper classes the one common complaint was that servants were scarcely to be had, that the wages of the few who remained were exorbitant, and that their manners and morals had changed greatly for the worse. But indeed, if it came to that, why any of us should have expected that war should result in happiness and content, I do not know. Still, it was remarkable that everywhere the domestic servant went back to service with reluctance.

During the early years of that unpeaceful time which followed the making of peace, my chief activities, outside those of my own profession, consisted of sitting on committees. Two of these, if I remember rightly, were Ministry of Reconstruction Committees; one to enquire into the housing of the working classes and to advise on the fitting of the working class flat or house, the other to enquire into the conditions of domestic service.

That housing committee did some good work because it was composed of women who had practical knowledge of housework as well as of women who had knowledge of what apparatus was already on the market, and in what way it might be improved were the manufacturer convinced that his market was waiting for him.

I also served on other housing committees; one which was concerned with Welwyn Garden City. I had the pleasure of meeting pioneer housing reformers such as Mr. Ebenezer Howard, Dame Henrietta Barnett, Captain

Richard Reiss, Lady Emmott, who must have chaired more committees than any other woman yet born, and whose clear head and charm of manner enable her, without wounding their susceptibilities, to keep her flocks from wandering and make her invaluable at the job; and that group of women who are so admirably carrying out Miss Octavia Hill's theories of estate management, which briefly, consist not only in collecting rents but in making the rent collector a friend of the tenant, and thus improving such property as is capable of improvement and preventing new property from degenerating into slums.

When studying housing problems I did not confine my attention to inspecting new or improved property, but visited slum property, both in London and other large cities, and in small country towns where it is sometimes quite as bad as in large cities.

Once, companioned by a woman sanitary inspector, I visited a family of seven who lived in one room and a slip of a kitchen in a tall tenement house, with one W.C. and one water-tap, both in the basement. It was situated in a peculiarly dreary part of north London. The husband and all but two of the children were out. The elder of the two left at home, a precocious little girl of five, showered her attentions upon me. Presently, assuming an air of mystery, "Would you like to see our baby?" she whispered. I looked round the room. So far I had seen no signs of a baby. "Yes," I replied, "Where is the baby?" The little girl cast a furtive glance at her mother, who was talking with the "Sanitary Lady," as she was known. "He's in the chest of drawers," she replied, and with her finger to her lip and still with an eye on her mother, began tip-toeing towards that piece of furniture, one of the few which the squalid room contained. The idea of the baby being shut up in the chest of drawers horrified me; surely the poor little thing would be smothered. Just at that moment the mother looked up, saw her interfering daughter about to pull open the drawer, shrieked at her to desist, and burst into tears. The baby had been dead for two days and was destined to remain in the chest of drawers two days longer before the funeral would take place with all the pomp and circumstance beloved of the very poor.

Another family which I visited lived in an odd little house consisting of one bedroom, one ground-floor room, and a basement kitchen opening into a high-walled yard, more like a tank than a yard, and from which almost all light was obscured by surrounding buildings which pressed right up against it. In these quarters lived a respectable hard-working man, a kind, good hard-working mother and seven children. There had been nine, but the eldest boy had been killed in the War ("Oh, he was a good lad to me," sighed the mother) and the eldest girl, aged seventeen, was out in service.

In the bedroom the bugs were crawling on the walls and dropping on to the beds. "We have tried everything," our hostess explained, "but as fast as we get 'em down, they come in fresh from houses on either side."

Father, mother and the two youngest children slept in this room. Three girls slept in the ground-floor room and the two boys in the kitchen. The mother took in washing. It was a hot June day when we visited her, and the kitchen was an inferno of heat, and thick with steam. The children were just coming home for their dinner, which they would eat there. All the clothes had to be dried in the house, for if hung in the yard, they became black with smuts. At twelve-thirty on this summer morning, gas was burning in the kitchen for the only window was a mere slip just above the pavement and obscured by dirt. It could not be opened except after everyone had gone to bed, for while any children were about, and they played in the streets until late at night in that neighbourhood, they would lie on their stomachs and throw dust and stones and garbage into the kitchen.

The "Sanitary Lady" told me that the children of this family were sickly, but admirably brought up, and that every week on her afternoon out the eldest girl came to lend her mother a hand with the ironing and to bring a few sweets for the little ones.

And yet, when thousands of our population are condemned to live in homes such as these, a rightly-taught birth control is by many considered to be a deplorable interference with the laws of nature. When visiting a new housing estate on the outskirts of an important provincial city, I was told that the authorities had been disheartened to find how little use was made of the baths. I asked if I might see a bath. It was in the kitchen-scullery, a room already too small for its legitimate purpose, and this made it necessary to place a flap table over it. On this were various articles for which no other place could be found, and which had to be placed on the floor and the flap fastened back before the Town Clerk could proudly display the bath with its cold-water tap. "How is the hot water procured?" I asked. When hot water was needed the copper had to be lighted and the hot water carried from it to the bath.

Something peculiar about the bath then struck me. There was no waste pipe, so the dirty water had to be bailed out and emptied down the sink.

In another block of houses elsewhere the housewife was condemned to make a tour of her ground floor in the course of preparing a meal. The larder was placed by the front door opposite the living-room. The kitchen-scullery was so small that meals had to be served in the living-room which therefore had to be warmed. As but one fire could be afforded the cooking had to be done in the living-room grate but preparations and washing-up took place in the scullery where all utensils must be kept.

The housing of our working-class population is a scandal, and for various reasons a difficult one to put an end to, especially as the cost of building new flats and houses for small-wage workers is prohibitive. Still, it cannot be beyond the power of man to achieve cheap, suitable building material. Indeed it seems likely that such a material may soon be put upon the market.

With decent housing there comes the desire for a more decent standard of life. Decent housing could scarcely fail to lessen drinking still further, for at present the ''public'' is a refuge from the squalid, overcrowded home. As public houses are dividend-earning concerns, and the Government benefits hugely by the sale of drink, those who use them must pay for their welcome by consuming drink, and so far too large a proportion of the weekly wage is spent on beer.

I was not content to study the housing conditions of the working class and the middle class at home but obtained a considerable amount of information regarding new houses and flats then being built in America and on the Continent.

At this time I often spoke on housing, and recall, with a smile, a meeting at the London County Council Hall. When coming away I heard two women, who were walking in front of me, discussing me. "She's a lazy woman, she is," said one, "wants everything just so. Do her good to go down on her hands and knees and do a bit of scrubbing."

The younger women do, however, realise that it is not work that any sensible person objects to, but unnecessary work, which eats up energy and absorbs time which might be better spent in performing other duties, or in relaxation.

About that time various people worked out interesting charts which showed how much unnecessary walking, reaching up and stooping down ill-planned houses entailed, and the *Daily Mail*, by means of the Ideal Home Exhibitions, did much to educate the public by showing them well-planned houses and the latest apparatus, with the result that to-day many new working- and middle-class homes are admirably planned and fitted, and it is beginning to be realised that it is not only labour which is paid for in direct wages, but also the labour of the woman in the home, which is paid for indirectly by the wage received by her husband, that is of importance to the nation. Indeed, it is of more importance to the nation than the labour of any other persons, for the wife must produce and tend the next generation at the same time that she fulfils her exacting task of cleaning, cooking and washing.

The demand for labour-saving homes was further increased by economic depression which caused educated women to become their own cooks and housemaids, and to learn from personal experience how far hard and dirty domestic work might be eliminated from the day's domestic programme.

A further activity with which I was connected was Women's Pioneer Housing, Ltd. The post-War housing shortage caused much hardship amongst professional women who could not afford the increased rents demanded for rooms, and in many cases were obliged to leave those in which they had lived for a considerable time and come to regard as "home." It was then that Miss A. E. Browning conceived the idea of converting large houses of which, owing to the cost of upkeep and the difficulty of obtaining servants, there were many to be had at a moderate price, into one-, two- or three-room flatlets, to be let at rents which professional women could afford to pay. In spite of many initial difficulties, sufficient money was raised to complete the first house, with the help of a subsidy from the Ministry of Reconstruction. Women's Pioneer Housing, Ltd., now owns forty-five large houses containing over 300 flatlets, pays six per cent. on its share capital (to which figure a Public Utility Company is limited), makes full provision for depreciation, upkeep and unforeseen expenses, and is steadily extending its activities. When it became impossible for me to attend the fortnightly meetings, my husband took my place on the Committee of Management.

It is odd that a company such as this should not attract the average investor, whereas he is always willing to entrust his capital to the promoters of "wild-cat" schemes. What those who give largely in charity often fail to see is that it might be more charitable to invest in a sound, well-directed company, such as Women's Pioneer Housing, which helps to keep workers healthy and able to work, than to assist them when they have been harassed into incompetence.

It is because schemes for the prevention of injury to humanity, rather than those for patching it up when the injury is done, appeal to us, that Charles and I became connected with an important social adventure—the Peckham Pioneer Health Centre. We visited the centre, we talked to its members, we talked to those who were running it, and became members of the Committee of Management.

The Pioneer Health Centre started its active campaign in 1926. A small house was taken in the densely populated district of Peckham. A medical officer, a social secretary, and a housekeeper were installed, and families living in the neighbourhood were invited to join a Family Club on the payment of a small weekly sum. In return, each member of the family received a periodical medical and dental overhaul; a parent's clinic, ante-natal, post-natal, infant-welfare clinics, and a children's afternoon nursery were established.

The service offered was purely advisory and was given in the hours convenient to the members, so that there was no loss of working time, which was of great importance to them. For the first time in any country of the world, an opportunity was thus afforded to doctors of observing the conditions of health, and detecting disease in its early stages.

The results were startling. Ninety per cent. of the members over twenty-five years of age (mostly wage earners of £2 10s. to £3 15s. per week) were found to be suffering from some disease of disability, and a large proportion of those under this age were victims of physical and mental devitalisation.

Yet the experiment was enormously encouraging. Beginning with one family, who brought others, the centre quickly filled to capacity. This ready response showed that the wage-earning family is able and willing to pay for direction about health. Detected at an early stage, their ailments could be cured. The experiment proves beyond doubt that if facilities for the preservation and development of health are open to the artisan population, they are eager to take advantage of the service for themselves and their families; they cannot pay for the buildings and equipment, but they can, and will, pay for their maintenance.

Since then, friends have given land in Peckham and designs for the building have been passed. A nucleus of trained workers is waiting to join this centre. We now lack nothing but enough money to put up a building sufficiently large to serve two thousand families. With those numbers the centre would be self-supporting.

This scheme has aroused interest all over the world, and had it not been launched at a time of unequalled economic depression, it would probably have been in running order by now.

Perhaps some of those who read these words will be interested, in which case they have but to write to the Organising Secretary, The Pioneer Health Centre, 6 Gower Street, W.C.1., who will answer all their questions.

How much I wish that such centres existed to be used not only by working-class people but by everyone. What doubts and fears and mistakes and muddles I might have been saved in the days when I was doing my incompetent best to bring up a family, had such a centre existed!

Another interesting job which came my way was to become one of the committee whose task it was to advise on the reconstruction of Stowe Palace, which was destined to become a public school. Stowe was not an easy house to remake, for, when it was built for the then Duke of Buckingham and Chandos, the English aristocracy were in the full pride of their wealth and power, and if a hundred servants were needed, a hundred servants there could be. A footman might have to walk a quarter of a mile from the kitchen, where all the water was heated, to carry the canfuls of hot water needed for the bath, and, of course, another quarter of a mile back again, but what did that matter? All the domestic premises, other than the servants' dormitories and rooms of the superior staff, were in a basement, and the food and equipment needed for the great parties which took place in the dining-hall, which could accommodate three hundred persons, had to be carried up and down a not too conveniently-planned staircase.

I had at one time or another visited several schools for boys and girls and had formed the opinion that never will the epidemics of measles, mumps, and other diseases which sweep through these scholastic establishments be reduced until the dormitory accommodation is greater so that the beds need not be placed so close together. In the days when our children were young, school food often was not as good as it should have been, not I think—if the War years are excepted—because there was not sufficient of it, but because it was badly chosen and badly cooked. It was seldom thought necessary to employ a housekeeper who had been trained for her post. Although since then the servant shortage has caused great inconvenience, it has had some good results, one being the employment of educated women who have been well trained to act as caterers and cooks in schools.

Our Stowe Ladies' Committee consisted of Lady Gisborough (another of our numerous cousins), Dean Janet Lane Claypon, formerly Warden of King's College for Women, Mrs. Norrie, C.B.E., and myself. I was asked to prepare a motion plan of the domestic premises and a work plan for the staff. If these still exist, they might be of interest years hence to students of social and domestic history. In the course of this work I had the pleasure of meeting Mr. Roxburgh, who was appointed to the head-mastership of Stowe, and who has since made it so successful.

One of the interesting enquiries held by the Ministry of Reconstruction was on the domestic service problem, which was then acute. During the War, men-servants, if suitable, became soldiers, and the younger women joined the Women's Armies or took positions as clerks in various ministries. They became booking clerks on the railways, they drove tradesmen's vans, cleaned windows, undertook, in fact, practically any work abandoned by the men who had been called up. The women who had been servants, and who went into the women's armies and lived in hostels, found life there more amusing than it had been in private service, and when the War ended were exceeding loath to return to it, while the young girls then leaving school were determined that they would not become servants. The position was serious for the would-be employer, and likely to become serious for the working girl who wished to enter already overcrowded occupations, thereby adding to the number of the unemployed. It was felt that matters might be adjusted if the good will of all concerned could be secured, and that effort to do so must be made.

The task of those ladies who chaired committees which were formed with the object of bringing employer and employee together was not an enviable one, for feeling ran very high, and the tone taken by some of the newspapers did little to soothe disgruntled employers or employees.

A reform which seems to me to be necessary if domestic service is to become a satisfactory profession is that girls should be trained for it, and not allowed to "pick up" their work as best they may, for this "picking up" process is extraordinarily trying to all concerned. The relationship of a servant who lives in is always more difficult than that of a person who works only for stated hours of the day and then leaves the place of employment, and when added to this, a girl, young and perhaps rather heedless, must be taught her work, and in the course of her tuition breaks and spoils articles which the employer must make good, considerable tact and good feeling on both sides are needed to preserve a pleasant relationship. Did the servant come to her work trained, much nerve strain would be avoided. On the other hand it is equally important that the mistress should be trained, for servants often have to bear with employers who are inconsiderate, more often owing to ignorance than to ill will.

At a time when I was concerned in endeavouring to better matters, both for mistress and maid, I received an anonymous letter from a lady who was kind enough to warn me that she intended to shoot me dead—with three dashes under dead. As, however, she did not say where or when the shooting would take place, her warning was of little use to me. I am glad she repented, as from her letter I judged her to be an excitable woman who might merely have mangled me and not shot me dead with three dashes.

I may add that I have had my full share of domestic trouble—some of it entirely my own fault—and I know few kinds of trouble which are more irritating. I have tried to learn from my mistakes and not to allow annoyance, even when just, to betray me into wrong action, and I have not always succeeded. On the other hand I have received much kindness and admirable service from those who have worked for me, and I never cease to be grateful for it.

The years between 1920 and 1930 were not occupied entirely with committee work. I went abroad once or twice and for the first time to Venice—a Venice of trippers and noisy, puffing steamers, and yet a place of such beauty as one can never forget. I re-create a day of sunlit calm, an opalescent sky, a gently rippling opalescent sea, the high curved prow of the gondola curtseying gently to its movement. A wall rises starkly from the sea, from behind it, black against the sky, rear spear-like cypress trees. By some steps a gondola floats, two nuns and some white-clad children carrying wreaths disembark. . . . The dead of Venice have a lovely place in which to lie.

I went to Switzerland again with Winifred Herbert, and from there once more to Italy. There was an accident and we did not reach Domo d'Ossola until late in the evening, and then had to wait an hour for the Milan train. We entered the station restaurant and ordered a meal. As we sat waiting until it should be ready there came to us the sound of weeping. Oh, that weeping! I hear it now. When the waitress returned I asked her what had happened —was there anything we could do? She burst into tears. Alas! alas! but an hour since, the little son of the house had fallen down the stairs and had broken his neck, and he but nine years old and the only child of his mother. And now his mother cooked our spaghetti and wept.

Later, in response to our messages of sympathy, she came into the restaurant, a stout, dark woman no longer young. Between storms of tears she told us of her boy, so clever, so handsome, so loving. Her husband no longer loved her as a wife; it was but as the mother of his son that he loved her. He was away on his affairs and as yet he did not know. His heart would break as her heart had already broken. And when he knew, there would be for her nothing, neither the love of her child's father nor of her child.

Of yet another tragedy I was a witness. I was driving to Victoria to catch a train, when I heard what I thought was the back-fire of a car. I heard the noise again and again. It was the noise of revolver shots. My taxi stopped opposite 36 Eaton Place, for on the steps lay the figure of a man in uniform. It was Field Marshal Sir Henry Wilson who had just then come home after unveiling a memorial to Captain Fryatt at Liverpool Street Station.[1] The first shot missed him and he turned round and made as if to draw his sword, then came another shot and he fell. Lady Wilson, hearing the shooting, rushed out and helped to carry him in.

[1] Sir Henry Wilson was murdered on the 22nd of June, 1922.

The two murderers made off down Eaton Terrace, Chester Terrace, South Eaton Place, where Cecilia was then living, and so into Ebury Street where they were captured, after having wounded two policemen. They were chased by a number of people and unarmed constables, but kept them off by firing their revolvers. Both paid with their lives for a cruel action which could in no way further the Irish cause.

I was obliged to continue my journey, but it was a white-faced, shaken woman who arrived at her destination.

.   .   .   .   .   .

Looking back on the post-War years I think that they might well come to be known as the Age of Discontent.

This discontent boiled up in the Great Strike of 1926, when we saw in the streets convoys of food supplies under the protection of armed soldiers and armoured cars; when Hyde Park became a food depôt from which the public was excluded; when newspapers shrank to one-page leaflets and those of us who had wireless sets invited others who had not to gather and listen to the news. Then we, like most other people, used our car to take workers to and from their work, and the few omnibuses which ran had boarded-up windows and engines protected by an entanglement of barbed wire.

Young men from the universities drove these omnibuses or took the place of drivers and stokers on the trains, and women turned to as they had done in the War and made themselves useful wherever they could.

It says much for the common sense and good feeling of the nation that the strike which began on May 4th and ended on Wednesday, May 12th, was, for the most part, a good-humoured and disciplined strike. On one of the strike days I went in the late afternoon to play Bridge at a certain club. I happened to know that an elderly woman who was then on duty in the cloak room lived at Camberwell. "How did you get here?" I asked. "I had to walk ma'am. Perhaps I'll be lucky in getting a lift home." I asked her if she would care to come and stay with us while the trouble lasted. One of the club members overheard this conversation. "Oh, I suppose you are one of those Reds yourself," she said in scathing tones. "The working classes want a lesson. Those damned strikers ought to be shot."

The cloak-room attendant watched her as she walked indignantly away and then she looked at me. "Those are the people who make revolutions," she said.

In November, 1928, our younger daughter married Mr. (Patrick) D. Pole Welman. As he was in the West Indies and could not obtain leave, Sir Frederick and Lady James were kind enough to take Denise out to Grenada with them to stay at Government House, and from there she was married. How kind it was of them to do that, and how grateful to them we were and are.

By then I had ceased to write novels and was occupying myself with historical books. The first of these was suggested by the conversation of a very old lady. What a mine of memories she possessed. I christened this unborn book "A Hundred Wonderful Years," and began reading up the period. The success of this venture encouraged me to write another book of similar character. I had for one reason and another needed information about life during the War years and found that by 1929 memories were becoming vague, and that much of the material I required was not to be found in libraries or in the War Museum. So, while my own memory was to be depended upon, I wrote "How We Lived Then," which it pleases me to find is approved by school children, who thrill to learn of all their parents and grandparents did and endured. If it incites in even a few of them a loathing of war, I have done something worth doing.

About this time my husband became very ill, an illness which lasted for nearly two years, and as, by then, it was impossible for him to resume his former work, so just as he had used a shoe horn when a spoon was not available, he adopted another profession. The social histories which appear under my name are really written in partnership with him, though he will not allow his name to appear upon them.

When he was well enough to live in London again, we moved to yet another house, this time of a still more labour-saving kind. Settled in our new home we then set to work on another book, "The Stream of Time," which necessitated a considerable amount of grubbing in libraries. This book, as an old village friend used to say, has been "blessed to us" by the number of appreciative letters received from people all over the English-speaking world. I now undertook to write "The Home Life of the People" section for "Early Victorian England," shortly to be published by the Clarendon Press, and edited by Mr. G. M. Young, one of the most inspiring editors for whom it has been my pleasant lot to work.

It is by no means easy to reconstruct in detail the domestic life of the poor during this period.

Those friends to all students, Mr. and Mrs. Hammond, know more about the subject than any other historians, but even when we had combed their books and all the well-known libraries, we needed still more information. Then it was that I asked the help of the editors of *The Sunday Times* and *The Observer*, who kindly published letters appealing to individuals who might be interested, and so obtained a number of personal recollections, and of little books and pamphlets written for the use of the poor, which contained invaluable information.

I then undertook an article entitled "Pageant of Women," for the 160th birthday of the *Morning Post*. This had to be done in a hurry, and necessitated an extensive course of reading and an intensive style of writing to compress the necessary information into 3,000 words. I propose to use this article as the foundation of a book to be called by the same title.

If I had not the nine lives of the proverbial cat I should not be proposing to write any more books, for while correcting proofs of "The Stream of Time," I fell ill with Angina, and sat propped up in a bed strewn with slip-proof, while I refreshed my failing energies with inhalations of nitrate of amyl.

Well, probably it was better for me to think about proof sheets than about Angina.

CHAPTER XIX

Sixty years of change—Weaving the world together—The downfall of the aristocracy of Birth and Wealth—Education, Insurance and Amenities—Dishonesty—Well-to-do squalor—Bad manners —Changes in the life of the educated classes—Less ceremony— Bed-and-breakfast houses—Birth control—A new standard of morality—Men in my youth—Women become citizens—How changes come—What lies before us ?—How strange are human beings—Reflections—Beautiful places, interesting people and Parties—Why fear old age or death ?—Age brings freedom— If I had my life to live over again ?

SO far in this book I have begun at the beginning and worked on to the end. Now I shall begin at the end and look back to the beginning, for the changes which have taken place in the sixty years of which I write are extra-ordinarily interesting and worthy to be further stressed.

The inventions which have made the greatest changes in the lives of people of my generation are those which have been the means of weaving the world together. To-day every civilised country knows in the course of a few hours what is happening in any other civilised country, and nationalism has had, perforce, to give way to international-ism.

Another change which has come about in my lifetime is the decline of the aristocracy of birth and of wealth, and the rise of the aristocracy of brains and personality.

There is now no place to which a working man of small means cannot attain. We have already had a Labour Government. Our present Prime Minister, Mr. Ramsay Macdonald, was educated at a Board School and was a pupil teacher before he became a journalist, and Mr. J. H. Thomas was an engine driver.

Russia is in the hands of the people; Mussolini, who is the son of a blacksmith, is in power in Italy and at the moment Hitler, an ex-house decorator, controls the fortunes of Germany. Of all the Kings and Princes who attended or sent representatives to the Coronation of King George V, how many remain in the position which they then held?

In this country, one now finds the great houses of the aristocracy used as schools, as institutions; the gardens have become market gardens; the shootings are let to syndicates. Heavy taxation, the rise in wages, and now the economic depression, make it impossible for more than a few very rich persons to live in anything approaching the manner in which they lived when I was a child and young married woman.

But those are not the only reasons of the changes which have come about. The spread of education is another cause.

Two years before this book begins, in 1870, it became compulsory that every child should receive some education, though he might be partially excused attendance at school at 11 years of age. Mr. Clynes, the third Food Controller, worked as a half-timer in an Oldham Mill and at twelve years old was doing a man's work in the same mills—the fees for his night school he saved out of his earnings. To-day the leaving age is fourteen and free places and scholarships provide that ladder from the gutter to the University which Professor Huxley desired.

As the masses became better instructed the newspapers catered for them, and with this newspaper knowledge, added to what they saw for themselves—and as transport became easier, they saw more and more—their influence was extended.

Until the post-War blight of a vast unemployment fell upon us, the position of the working classes had been steadily improving. They were not only better educated but better fed and better clothed, although by no means always better housed, than they had been during my youth.

Sickness Insurance, Unemployment Benefit, Old Age Pensions and Widows' Pensions have made a vast difference to their lives, as has also the coming of the bicycle, the motor omnibus, and the cheap excursion train, as well as such amenities as public libraries, public baths, an increased number of playing-fields, the cinema and the wireless.

Yet although for the last sixty-three years it has been almost impossible for a child to escape from attending school until he is fourteen, I do not think that the improvement in the mental standard of the people has kept pace with that of the standard of material prosperity. Study the crowds which pour out of London public-houses at closing time. One finds roughness, vulgarity of speech, silly shrieking laughter. Study the mental fare offered by the majority of the cinemas. Does one gain the impression that the cinema trade is catering for persons of much intelligence?

It is sad, too, that during the War and to a great extent to-day, there is a low standard of honesty amongst boys and girls. They will "nick" any article that takes their fancy. These children probably are hypnotised by a word; "nicking" sounds so far less serious than thieving, though it means precisely the same thing. In some large establishments, with the working of which I was familiar, it was the custom to dismiss a thief, but to take no proceedings against him. Whether this is any kindness to the transgressor I doubt.

Two experiences of my own show how little nine years of education may do to effect refinement of conduct. When moving into our present house I employed a charwoman

whose miserable appearance excited pity. I saw to it that
she had milk to drink and tried to persuade her to have her
teeth put in proper order. One afternoon her sixteen-year-
old daughter appeared "to help mother," in reality to see
what our house was like. She was dressed in a smart coat
with a fur collar, a modish little hat, silk stockings, patent
leather shoes, carried a *chic* handbag and umbrella, and was
liberally powdered and lipsticked. Her clothes might have
been worn by any young girl, but her face was not only
common but vulgar, and further disfigured by two large
strips of sticking plaster. I learned afterwards that my
poverty-stricken looking charwoman was the wife of a man
who earned £4 a week and perquisites; their son earned £2
a week, two daughters 16s. and 18s. a week respec-
tively. The mother took in washing and went out to
"oblige" and earned roughly 22s. a week and some of her
food. The collective wage of the family was £8 16s. a week
in money and something in kind, and the whole family,
including two more children still at school, lived together in
two rooms and a kitchen.

They had a piano, which none of them could play, and
an expensive wireless set, both bought on the hire purchase
system. They proposed to buy a motor car on the same
system.

The young lady who came to "help" her mother sat and
watched her mother work. The sticking plaster covered
wounds inflicted by the finger-nails of another young lady,
the two girls having fought in the street for the possession
of a "boy" coveted by both, amidst the cheers and cat calls
of the assembled neighbours. This information, needless to
say, I obtained from an outside source—my cook—who lost
patience when I suggested that our charlady might be the
better for some good strong soup.

Another experience of a low mental standard occurred a few days before this book was finished. Having occasion to engage a new maid I was told that a young girl was waiting to see me. I went downstairs, entered the room, and bade her good morning. The young girl was lolling back in an armchair; she continued to loll and made no reply to my salutation. "Good-morning," I said again. The young girl still lolled and said nothing. I felt my temper rising, but I subdued it. "Don't you think it would be pleasant if you stood up and said good morning to *me?*" I suggested.

"I see no necessity to do so," replied the young girl in a loud, sharp voice.

You could have knocked me down with the proverbial feather. At last I recovered sufficiently to remark that I thought our interview might end and to bid her another good morning. Now what maggot had that girl in her brain? Did she wish to infer, "I am as good as you?" I have no objection to her being as good as me, in fact I should like her to be considerably better. But in what way does such an exhibition of bad manners and unfriendliness help her or anyone else to achieve anything?

I am sorry now that I did not still further strangle my wrath, loll in another chair and in the course of a little friendly conversation try to elucidate her point of view.

Yet another change is that which has taken place in the social and domestic life of what we used to call the Upper Classes, but to which most of us now refer, rightly or wrongly, as the Educated Class. Apropos of that, since we are altering our labels, it is time that we ceased to talk about the Working Classes, because nowadays there is scarcely a man who does not work, if he can find work, and it would seem in the near future that the working classes may work shorter hours and have more leisure than those who do the kind of work which is now performed by those who are almost as wrongly described as Black Coated Workers.

London is a striking witness to the changes which have taken place in the life of the educated classes. With few exceptions great houses have become clubs, institutions, offices; their former owners can no longer afford their up-keep. The roomy houses in which Victorian and Edwardian families lived have been divided into upper and lower parts, reconstructed to form flats, or turned into boarding houses, private hotels or hostels. Young people of good position live in reconstructed mews and many girls who would in pre-War days have married into a nice little house, and kept a nice little household, live in a minute flat or upper part and afford, perhaps, a nurse, and themselves act as cook and house parlourmaid, with or without the assistance of a "daily." In my youth there were charwomen but the "daily" is a new invention.

When after the War various persons of experience suggested that the servant shortage might be met by employing daily workers who lived in hostels, the idea was not approved. Now, because rents and rates are high, and the accommodation in flats and upper parts restricted, employers are thankful for daily service.

The way in which educated women have become skilled cooks or house-parlourmaids with very little teaching other than that obtained from books is rather surprising. I have been assured, time after time, that it takes at least six months to train a girl to be a fair plain cook. Well, to use a homely saying, "the proof of the pudding is in the eating."

At the moment I know a woman whose husband fills a high position who, to meet a shrunken income, has become her family's cook. Another, the wife of a man whose family forty years ago lived in a palace, has done likewise and yet another, brought up in affluence, cooks and does all the housework, with the help of a young nurse, and none of them makes any to-do about it.

Another noticeable change in our social life is the reduction of ceremony. The telephone and the Bridge table have killed note-writing and calling, and the "here to-day and gone to-morrow" attitude towards life, which is the outcome of the War, and of the unstable economic position which makes it impossible to know what the income may be from month to month, causes a restlessness which shows itself in the informal "throwing" of parties, rather than the carefully planned giving of elaborate parties such as were a feature of my young day.

The cheap motor car has also had a great effect on social life. Faced with the choice of a solid house, a nursery and children to put in it, or the possession of a car, the car wins the day, and in order to afford it, the house becomes a bed-and-breakfast dwelling, which may be run with little trouble or expense. This brings us to another change of extreme importance. When I was a child the average "nice" married woman knew nothing about birth control. Although my father and mother were badly off and had no desire for a large family, they had nine children. When I married, young people were practising birth control by methods which could not be depended upon and which were only whispered about. To-day people discuss birth control with the same freedom as they discuss the latest novel or an earthquake in Japan and it is practised in all strata of society, except, perhaps, in the one in which it is most needed, that is, amongst the poorest and most degraded of the community.

It would appear that there is yet much to learn with regard to the results of birth control and many persons, even outside the Catholic Church, still resent any mention of it.

As a matter of fact it is economic pressure rather than lack of religious, or shall we say ethical, feeling which causes people to remain childless or to produce but one or two children.

Morality has always been affected by geographical and by economic conditions, as was plainly shown during the War, when the "fallen" girl, and her bastard child, both by ourselves and by the Germans, were translated into the "unmarried mother" and the "War baby" because of the fear that without the illegitimate child, the population might be too seriously depleted.

To-day the standard of sexual morality is very different from that which obtained when I was a young woman. All through the latter part of the nineteenth century, the idea of an equal standard of morality for men and women had been growing, but what thinking people then desired was that the standard for both should be stricter. During the early years of the twentieth century the tendency was to permit a looser standard. Then came the War. Men knowing their lives to be uncertain, girls seeing men mown down by the thousand, felt impelled to mate while they could, and the fact that it was no longer probable that this mating should result in the birth of a child made it possible for them to think that they were doing no harm to anyone by indulging in a temporary union.

It must be left to wiser persons than myself to pronounce an opinion on so complex a subject, but there is this to be said, that some persons of experience, whose duties bring them in close touch with the young, find that the pendulum is beginning to swing back, not because young people regard a certain amount of promiscuity as anti-social, but because they are beginning to find that a union which is merely physical is of so little value. I, brought up in the strict

263

standard of sexual morality of my class and time, although I have an open mind to other ideas, remain convinced that physical union, unless it is combined with mental union, is worthless and that paid prostitution is hideous and as degrading to the purchaser as to the purchased.

Here again, one of the young people who do me the kindness to read this book as I write it and to criticise it, suggests that physical union should be put in its proper place as being of very little importance. Is that so? I have an idea that increased scientific knowledge now suggests that the act of physical union may have greater mental and physical effects upon the subsequent life history of those concerned than is yet realised by the world at large.

The restlessness from which the young do undoubtedly suffer to-day, though in some degree caused by past events, is also caused by the present world upheaval, and by fear of the future; fear that there will be another war and one far more terrible than that which we endured and from which our children and grandchildren now suffer. "What is the use," young men and women say, "of planning for the future when in a few years' time we shall all be dead, killed by poison gas?" How do they know there will be another war? Why be so ready to believe that the horrible will happen? Some people die a thousand deaths before they ever come to die and most of us fail to realise that if the peoples of the civilised world truly desired peace, peace there would be.

But whatever standard of morality there may be, is it much worse than that of my young day, when every young man was expected to be a rake and it was not thought surprising if the rakishness did not end with youth and the virtue of one section of society was purchased by the degradation of another?

Then the average Englishman divided women into three categories: mothers and wives; the latter when young might beguile and when elderly were useful: persons of the female gender at whom he never troubled to look but who ministered to his needs and therefore were valuable: and those whom, with Victorian reticence, we will term "others."

Mothers and wives should stay in the home, those who ministered should naturally be in such places as their duties required them to be, and "others" should exist only when wanted.

For the greater part of their grown-up lives, the men I knew preferred to be with other men. Even at parties they liked to collect in groups and especially was this noticeable in the country. In my youth men stayed almost all the evening after dinner in the dining-room. Now since nothing is as it used to be, a fact which worries many people greatly and does not worry me at all, men do mix more with women, and even find it possible to talk with them on any subject. I look back on men who flirted, who chatted, who paid compliments, but on few who conversed with women on terms of equality.

Yet another change which I have seen come to pass is the raising of women from the status of infants and imbeciles to that of citizens and the opening to them of the doors of the House of Commons. I was in the House of Lords on the occasion of the last Debate on Woman Suffrage. It was amusing. One after another gentlemen rose to record their dislike of the situation. Twenty-seven years before in the House of Commons women had been spoken of as persons "the majority of whom were not bread winners, and who had not to bear the burden and did not understand the responsibilities of life." Still My Lords referred to women as "irresponsible persons." Even at the age of 30, which women must then have attained to be granted the vote, it did not seem that life might have taught them a sense of responsibility. However, the general public felt that they had been so useful during the War that they might be given a vote, much in the same fashion as a biscuit is given to a little dog when it has done its tricks nicely. So in 1918 women over thirty became citizens, and my Lords sat down and sighed that the Country was going to the Dogs.[1] And even now whose dogs and what dogs those are I do not know, but I incline to think that the Country was not going but had then already gone to the dogs. Were they by chance the dogs of war?

It may be thought that I am a feminist. I am not. I am merely one of those sane people who think that, as "male and female created He them," the best brains of both sexes are needed to conduct the world's affairs, and that as children are obliged to have mothers as well as fathers, and to be influenced, both before and after birth, by those mothers, it is as well that they should be intelligent persons.

In the days when Women's Suffrage was a burning question, sometimes I suggested this point of view. It was seldom approved. Another idea I have sometimes ventured to suggest is that in sports which involve cruelty, it is not only the animal which suffers. Those who find amusement in giving pain are sinning against their own natures. But history teaches that there is in humanity a passionate dislike of change except in dress and that changes of thought, as a rule, come slowly.

When it was fashionable to burn offenders at a stake, there were always plenty of people to insist that it was the right and proper action to take. When it was fashionable to

---

[1] In 1928 the vote was granted to women of 21 on equal terms with men.

hang, draw and quarter them, well, why not? A messy business, but still. . . .

Many of his contemporaries thought anti-slavery Wilberforce a fanatic and Mrs. Elizabeth Fry, with her worryings about prisoners, a bore. When Lord Erskine, then Lord High Chancellor, introduced into the House of Lords a Bill for preventing "wanton and malicious cruelty to animals," his efforts were met with catcalls and derision. Later on in 1824, when a Society for the Prevention of Cruelty to Animals was started, the House of Commons was vastly entertained by the idea. It was not so much entertained as shocked at the idea of a Society for the Protection of Children.

When women wished to go to college and to enjoy what was termed higher education, they must do nothing of the kind. When they wanted the vote, why should they have the vote? They had never had a vote before.

A hundred years hence we may perhaps have come to the conclusion that we might, for a change, practise the Christian Religion instead of merely preaching it. On the other hand, we may be honest enough to admit that we have not yet practised Christianity as Christ taught it, that we do not intend to try to do so, and therefore we will not call ourselves Christians. We will be instead, the kind of people whom Mr. Aldous Huxley describes in his "Brave New World," a well-named book, for it would indeed require one to be very brave to live in it.

Personally I have a feeling (how feminine that is!) that the pendulum will swing back and the teaching of a great teacher, whose thought was so in advance of all the time we yet know, that we have never yet truly understood it, will again dominate the world. But I may be wrong. I often am. Yes, indeed, I often am. Who knows what lies before us? We see what we can see but we do not know what we may come to see.

Yet another change which I note is in the young people. They seem so hard, so cocksure, so take-it-or-leave-it as compared with the girls and young men of mid-Victorian and Edwardian times. They tell me that they do not like sloppiness and sentimentality. Neither do I, but I do like sentiment. Without sentiment I doubt if life would be worth living, and I have yet to be convinced that life can be of any use to anyone if it is not ruled by love, for it is the mental effort born of love that makes life beautiful.

"Oh, darling pet," says my young friend (we are all darlings and pets nowadays at half an hour's notice). "How Victorian that sounds," but again she pauses and again she adds, "but perhaps it is true." There she sits on the floor, hugging her slim silk-stockinged legs, for everyone must be slim nowadays, and her pretty nose is powdered, her eyes touched up with mascara, her mouth reddened, her nails varnished, her hair short and curly and on it a new hat which, although I still love new fashions, makes me laugh. Put that hat on a St. Bernard dog, a cow, a leopard, and it would cease to be a dignified animal and become a figure of fun. Why should it not have the same effect on a woman? It does. I laugh at her; I love her; I wonder if her clothes express her, because if so. . . .

But then how strange are human beings. The man or woman who will fret before the looking-glass over the set of a hat, the tying of a tie, who will think it a matter of real importance to wear the right thing, however comic the right thing may be, will give life itself for an ideal.

.   .   .   .   .   .

And now I wish to look back at my own life. How grateful I am that I have been so placed as to lack temptation to commit such crimes as bring one to the scaffold or to the prison and how fully I realise that the wrong I have done was as wrong for me to do as any other wrong which carries with it a heavy penalty, may have been for those others to do.

I am glad that I now feel no bitterness towards the only two people who I think ever deliberately tried to injure me. Probably they did what they did because they looked at the matters in question from different points of view from any which I could see and thus felt their conduct to be justified.

Such things, in greater or less degree, have to happen to us all and the use of them is to increase experience, but I would like here and now to make apology for my own mis-doings. I also like to proclaim my thankfulness for all the love and friendship I have received throughout my life.

When does old age begin? I do not know, and what does it matter? If three score years and ten is the limit of my life I have six more years to live. But now I have Angina, perhaps I shall not live to the full span of man's life here; again, perhaps I may, and longer. And what does it matter either way?

Why are so many people afraid of old age and death? If I am old—my children say that I am not and that age is a matter of the mind and not of the body—well then, I like being old.

I disliked parting with my twenties and detested parting with my thirties; after that I did not care how old I was. Age brings freedom. It is delightful to know that no one will fall in love with me again and that I shall never have to fall in love. Falling in love is part of one's education, but for the most part a restless, teasing experience.

Having children has its delights, but they are nothing to the delights of friendship with grown-up children, to whom you have ceased to be a policeman, while a lover is not to be compared with a husband who, after thirty-eight years of married life, is one's best friend.

When one is old one is able to regard other peoples' opinion of one's doings with unconcern. If only I can convince myself that I have acted rightly (and sometimes I cannot) I am little concerned with what others think.

When I was young and even middle-aged I suffered agonies of shyness and hid those agonies behind what, I fear, was sometimes an aggressive manner. I suffered from too little education and too much upbringing of the kind then thought desirable for nice young girls, and when I was placed in a position of authority never could I quite rid myself of the feeling that I ought to apologise for being where I was. And yet, being there, I resented the attitude of men who took it for granted that any woman should knuckle under to any man. That attitude caused me to bounce, and when I had bounced I felt a fool, as indeed I was.

Often I wonder what I would do if I had my life to live over again. I would be well educated. I would be brought up to believe that I could do what I ought to do. I would be made to understand that I was loved. When I was a child I did not feel that I was loved or that I loved anyone—except Jenny the nursery dog and Aunt Charlotte. My mother I respected but only when I grew older did I love her and then I loved her very much, as she deserved that I should.

I would be taught self-control rather than self-repression and with self-control would come greater patience than I ever possessed and so greater kindness, though indeed I never had an unkind heart.

I often regret that one cannot live backwards and in one's doing time have even as much understanding as one comes to have in one's thinking time, and certainly, if I could live my life again, I would not suffer so much bodily pain. My life has been, and still is, a struggle against illness. With greater knowledge I might have been spared at least some suffering.

I am thankful for all the beauty I have enjoyed. Venice now belongs to me and so does Lake Garda, whose waters I see from a green bluff where blue flowers and olive trees grow. All the loveliness I have seen belongs to me and much that I have not seen except with my mind, conveyed to it through the medium of books. I give thanks over and over again to those who write good books, for books give one the world and all therein.

I like to think of all the interesting people I have met. I have a good memory for faces and for words so that their society is mine to enjoy again at will.

Then the parties I have been to—how enjoyable many of them were. I enjoy going to them again: Ascot, the Derby, Goodwood. Once at Goodwood as I stood outside the regimental luncheon tent of a soldier friend a beautiful woman came up to him and asked if he would be kind and give her something to eat. It was the famous Georgiana, Lady Dudley. What caprice caused her to do that—she so lovely and so sought after?

I recall days at Cowes, and see once more the ex-Kaiser in all the glory of his white uniform and great eagle ornamented helmet. Why did he wear that at Cowes? I forget.

Garden parties, one at Stowe Palace, which then belonged to Lady Kinloss, another at Newlands when Princess Pless was Miss Cornwallis West and Constance, Duchess of Westminster a schoolgirl; parties at which one saw other beauties of King Edward's reign, the Duchess of Leinster, Lady Helen Vincent (now Lady D'Abernon), of whom it was said that the cabmen of Athens fought for the privilege of driving this re-incarnation of Helen of Troy, Frances,

Lady Warwick, Mrs. Langtry, Mrs. Luke Wheeler, Miss Mary Anderson, Miss Julia Neilson, Mrs. Patrick Campbell.

My mind goes back to balls; hunt balls, military balls, the simple War dances to which Cecilia went, the post-War balls to which Denise went and which took place in private houses or at Claridges or the Ritz or that house in Chesham Place which used to be the Russian Embassy and also at a house in Audley Square, which was a fashionable dance house one season. It is amusing too to think of oneself at a reception at Lancaster House, now the London Museum, and used by the Government as an entertainment house, or at the Royal Academy at a gathering of learned men with rows of medals and wives who, like hen birds, look less gorgeous than their mates, or to a party at Speaker's House where the portraits of dead and gone Speakers look down upon the company.

I like to go again to dinners at the Carlton, the Berkeley, the Savoy, the Cavalry Club, the "In and Out," the Bachelor's; to grand dinner parties where the doors were thrown open and grand butlers announced "His Excellency the — Ambassador," and to all the little dinner parties which were such fun. I like, too, to re-live some women's luncheon parties, with good conversation and then an afternoon of Bridge . . . a card party in Sir Bernard Partridge's great studio, . . . a children's party at Bridgewater House in the late Lord's day, . . . celebrity parties given by Lady Astor in the house in St. James's Square, where the flowers are more beautifully done than in any other house I know. What a welcome to find a great double cherry tree blooming in the hall.

How delightful, too, a party in Kensington Palace Gardens when we supped in the garden on a still June night, so still that the candles scarcely flickered, and then Paul Robeson sang.

I think too, of Drawing-rooms and Courts, Royal Garden Parties, an Investiture, and for a change a "red" party in a tumble-down house in Soho.

I can go to all these parties again. . . . I can lunch at that little inn in the hills above Monte Carlo. I can, once more, be young and in love . . . and again a little child walking with dear Jenny the nursery dog amongst the white lilies at Wyesham.

.   .   .   .   .   .

Truly I have drunk of life from an Enchanted Cup, but, unlike that of which Byron wrote, the draught has not sparkled only near the brim. I have a hope that even from its last few drops the sparkle will not fade.

273

INDEX

ABOYEUR'S Derby, 160
Abraham's sacrifice, effect of a picture of, 7, 40
Achilles statue, the, 95, 96
Adam Bede (George Eliot), 39
Admiralty, the, 204
Admirers, the pleasure of having, 43, 45, 57
"Advice to a Mother" and "Advice to a Wife" (Chavasse), 41
Aeroplane, a, a stampede to, 98
Aeroplane accident, author's escape by absence from, 234
Age of consent, the, raising of, 144-5
Age of Discontent, the, 252
Air raids, behaviour during, 195 *sqq.*; the worst, 195, 198
Air Ministry, Cecilia Peel's work in, 176, 197; life in, 189
Aix-les-Bains, a "cure" at, 138; a useful intuition at, 161
Albury Church on Sundays, 38
Albury Vicarage, the grandparents at, 33 *sqq.*; interior of, 34, the kitchen at, 36-7; a last visit to, 51
Alfonso, King, 150
Algiers, 145
Alice, the treasure, 87-8, 93, 94; marriage of, 111
America, a speaking tour in, proposed by Lord Northcliffe, 218, 220

American Civil War, women's dresses in, 177
Amiens, 207
Ammunition works, and the munitionettes, 174 *sqq.*
Amphitryon dining club, the, 96
Anderson, Mary, 272
Antipodeans, childish ideas of, 11
Antiseptic surgery, pioneers of, 140
Antwerp, 69
Architects, and domestic interiors, 125
Aria, Mrs., 66, 94
Ark, the, 46
Armistice Day, a child's memory of, 169; scenes on, 224
Army and Navy Stores, 55
Artists, and the squirearchy, 75, 76
Ascot, 271
Ascough, Bessie, dress illustrations by, 222
Asquith, Rt. Hon. H. H., at the outset of the War, 164
Asthma, 32-3
Astor, Viscountess, celebrity parties of, 272
Athenian cabmen and Lady Helen Vincent, 271
Audley Square, fashionable dances in, 272
Auralie, the French maid, 53, 54, 55
Austrian Note to Serbia, the, 163
Author's own life, a look back at, 268 *sqq.*

Authorship, Bennett on, 65-6

Avenue d'Iéna, Paris, the staff at, 117

Aylesbury, the Girls' Borstal at, 156

BABIES, slum-born, 84; unrecognised till born, 49-50

Baccarat, 77

"Ballad of a Nun" (Davidson), 104

Balls, the author's first, and others, 45, 47-8, 77; Fancy Dress at Covent Garden, 118; memories of, 272; in the Season, 100

Bancroft, Sir Squire, and the cocotte, 120

Bandoline, 6

Bank Holidays, the founder of, 53

Barker, Lilian, and the Girls' Borstal, 156

Barnett, Dame Henrietta, 239

Barratt, Miss, 184, 188

Bastide, La, Villa, 119

Bathing dresses, Victorian, 99

Baths, hot, in bedrooms, 37, 77; in workmen's dwellings, 242

Bathrooms, 77

Battersea Park, bicycling in, 97

Bavaria, a visit to, 237

Bayliff family, the scandal in, 52-3

Bayliff, Aubrey, and the Lane relics, 52

Captain R. L. (father), 5, 6, 23, 28, 42, 45, 56; anxieties of, 11; lessons given by, to his children, 11, 12, 13, 15, 26, 39, 41; in uniform, and as a bear, 5-6; failing health and death of, 62, 63

Charlotte Mary Augusta (Carli), 3, 4, 8, 12, 13, 14, 24, 29, 33, 43, 45, 48, 57, 59, 73, 83, 85, 88; confirmation dress

of, 14; lessons with her father, 11; studies of, in drawing, 11, 29, 42, and illustrations by, earnings from, 62

Hugh, 3, 4, 8, 11, 13; goes to British Columbia, 57, 83; a wedding present from, 68

Margaret, 30, 34, 48, 57, 63, 83, 84, 85; birth of 10-11; work of, before and during the War, 170, 174

Mary Lane, 35 and the Lane relics, 51

Mrs. T. T. Lane (grandmother), 34 sqq., 51, 53, 54; death of, 56

Mrs. R. L. (author's mother) 4, 5, 8, 9, 13, 14, 15, 16, 24, 25, 28, 42, 45, 46, 68, 70, 80, 270; babies of, and their deaths, 3, 4, 14, the ninth, 10-11; dress of, memories of, 6; individuality of, suddenly recognised, 23; visits of, to the poor, 20; taste of, 30; illness and death of, 84-5

Rev. T. T. Lane (grandfather) 33 sqq., 53-54; and evening family prayers, 51; muscular Christianity of, 37; death of 56

Richard (Dick), 3, 4, 5, 6, 7, 11, 12, 13, 14, 18, 22, 24, 37, 57, 69, 78; and the sea-serpent, and the plague, 12

Beale, Dorothea, 31, 153

Beardsley, Aubrey, "period" of, 104; book on (Burdett), 105

Bearing-reins, 95

Beattie, —, on the author as "not a normal woman," 230

Beaulieu, 119

INDEX

Beauties, Edwardian, 271-2

Beautiful women, the three loveliest seen by the author, 120, 121

Beauty, gratitude, for, 271

Becker, Lydia, 153

Bedroom fires, 77-8

Beerbohm, Max, 104

Belgian refugees, care of, 170

Bellingham, —, the gardener, 5, 9, 13, 20

Bella, 13

Bellis, Isabel, 184, 188, 199, 202

Bengough, Mrs., 69

Bennett, Arnold, 105; editorship of, of *Woman*, 62, 64-5; help from, 112; on learning to write, 64-5, and on authorship, 66

Benson, Theodora, book by, 137

Berkeley, the, dinners at, 272

Berlin, night life of, 118; war conditions in, 238-9

Betting, at Bridge Clubs, 159

Betty the witch and the burning of her books, 38

Bible, the, verses from, wisdom of teaching, 41

Bicycle, the, 258; "penny-farthing" model, 29

Bicycling by women, 62, 97

Birch, Lady Susan, 131

Birth and wealth, aristocracy of, decline of, 256, 257

Birth control, past and present attitudes to, 262-3

Black and White, 66

Blackwell, Dr. Elizabeth, 153

Blerancourt, 217

Blood sports, effect of, on sportsmen, 266

Blue Ribbon movement, the, 50

"Blueness", drawbacks of, 31

Board of Education, 201

Books, making friends of, 39-40, 271

Books sent for review, Lord Northcliffe on, 227

Boots, ladies', 17, 18, buttoned, 47; shoes replacing, 177

Borstal Institutions, 155-6; the Girls', at Aylesbury, 156; the life sentenced prisoner at, 156-7

Boulogne in war time, 205-6; arrival at, of wounded, 206; the Casino, as a British hospital, 167, 216

Bourgeois, writing in, 227-8

Brains and personality, aristocracy of, the rise of 256-7

"Brave New World" (A. Huxley), 267

Bread, pre-War waste of, 187; price of, rise of in August, 1914, 165

Bridge Clubs, 158; during the War, 159

Bridge-playing experiences, 77, 101, 158-9, 162, 272

Bright, Jacob, 73-4

Bright, John, a quotation from, 74

Bright plush mills, 73

Bristol, Art School of, 29, 42; orchestral concerts at, 42

British Columbia, Hugh Bayliff in, 57, 83

Broadstairs, a bomb on a school at, 169

Brompton Square, a new home in, 123, 125-6; former reputation of, 125; a suffrage debate at, 128

Brontës, the, 80

Brown, Miss, and some hat-shop clients, 129, 130, 131

Browning, Miss E. A., and Women'sPioneerHousing, Ltd., 244

Brynkinalt, a first experience at, of Society, 59-60

INDEX

Buckingham and Chandos, Duke of, Stowe Palace built for, 247

Burglar, an unfortunate but courteous, 137

Burdett, Osbert, on the Victorian Convention, 105

Burghwallis Rectory, life at, 85

Burns, Rt. Hon. John, resignation of, in Aug. 1914, 167

'Bus horses, falls of, 93

Buss, Miss, 153

Bustles, 47

Butler, Josephine, work of, 106, 153

Byron, Lord, 273

Café de Paris, the Tzigane band at, 117-18

Caird, Sir Andrew, 222

Cakes and cream, a post-War pleasure, 233

Cambridge, F.-M., the Duke of, 100

Campbell, Mrs. Patrick, 272

Campbell-Bannerman, Sir Henry, and a Women's Suffrage Deputation, 151

Campsall Hall, 69

Canada, sunstroke in, 5

Canteen work, during the War, 173, 176

Card-leaving, 98

Card party, a, 272

Careers open to talent, 256-7

Carlton, the, dinners at, 272

Carmelite House, Lord Northcliffe's room in, 222-3

Carson, Lord, 121

Cause, The (Ray Strachey), 31, 154

Cavalry Club, dinners at, 272

Cavendish-Bentinck sale, needlework panels from, 124-5

Celebrity parties of Lady Astor, 272

Celibacy, male, views on, in the '90's, 106, 264

Ceremony, post-War reduction of, 262

Chairmen, varieties of, 193-4, 199, 200

Chambers, Sir Theodore, 173

Change, dislike of, and slow coming of, 266

Changes in sixty years and their causes, 256 sqq.

Chantilly, the Uhlans at, in 1914, 214

Chaperons, 47, 100, the downfall of, 97

Charity Organisation Society, the, 28

Charles I, silver bowl, a, 52

Charwoman, a, her daughter and her means, 259

Chasseurs Alpins, tribute of, to beauty, 119

Chauny, 217

Chavasse, Dr., books by, 41

Chawbacons and Yokels, 75

Cheese scoop, the, 20, 21

Chelsea, life in, 111, 116, 123; looting in, 171

Cheltenham High School, 31

Chesham Place, balls in, 272

Cheyne, Sir William Watson, an operation by, 139-40

Childhood, memories of, 3 sqq.

Childish maladies and mishaps, 22-3

Children, grown-up, friendship with, 269

Victimised, 144, 145, 156

Children's Commonwealth, the, 143-4

Christianity, as yet never practised, 267

Church-going, 13, 38

Churchill, Lady Randolph, 121

Churchill, Rt. Hon. W., 231; and the mobilisation of the Fleet, 167

INDEX

Cinemas, mental fare provided by, 258; speaking in, 200

Ciro's, lunches at, 120

Citroën, MM. André, Henri and Hugh, 208; munition works of, visited, 208 *sqq.*

Clarendon, Earl of, 52

Clarendon Press, the, 254

Claridge's, balls at, 272

Clarke, Sir Stanley, 100

Claypon, Dean Janet Lane, 248

Clementel, M., 207, 208, 213

Clements, the butler, 127-8

Clerical neckwear, 33

Clifton, life at, and removal from, 11, 27, 30, 56, 57, 69

Clifton College, 30; the author's brothers at, 24, 29

Clifton High School, 31

Cliveden, week-end parties at, 96

Clothes, costly, the passion for, ill-effects of, 134

Club member, a, as unintentional "maker of revolutions," 253

Clynes, Rt. Hon., J. R., rise of, 257

Coal, shortage of, and some substitutes, 179, 180

Coal mines, going down, 75

Cocoa-butter, 178, 186

Coke, General Talbot, death of, 129

Coke, Mrs. Talbot, writings of, and papers owned by, 61-2, 64, 86

Collars, high and boned 36, 47

Colleges for Women, opposition to, 31-2, 128

Coming back from the Continent in 1914, 166

Commission of Control on Disarming Germany, 237

Communal, public or national kitchens, 186-7

Compiègne, 213, 215, 217

Concerts, knitting at, 180

Constable, Messrs., 112

Constantinople, 68

Control, struggles for, 30

Cooking and housework, soon learnt by educated women, 261-2

Corner House, the latest, 213

Corniche Road, the, 119

Cornwallis Crescent, Clifton, life at, 27 *sqq.*

Correspondents, characteristics of, 116

Cottage interiors in the '70's, 20

Council Schools, speaking to children in, on Food Economy, 201-2

"Countess Kate" (Yonge), 40

Country Clubs, non-existent in the '90's, 97

Country-house visits, 59, 77-8

Country life and husbandry, 76

Court dress and trains, 107, 109, one worn by Queen Mary, 110

Courtfield, a party at, 16

Courts, Drawing-rooms superseded by, 109, 110; memories of, 273

Covent Garden, fancy dress balls at, 118

Cowes, the ex-Kaiser at, 271

Crake, Mrs. Barrington (*née* Woodroffe), 63, 234

Cremer, —, M.P., on Women's suffrage, 151

Crewe House, 218, 220

Cricket, village type, 38

Crompton, Messrs., 94

"Crows," 181

Cruelty to Animals, 7, 25, 40, 68, 76-7, 95, 98, 121, 266, 267

Cubitt, Mrs. Cyril (*née* Crake), 63

"DAILY," the, 261

Daily Mail, the, 105, 187; the author's work on, 220 *sqq.*;

the magyar blouse pattern in, 165; editorial conferences of, 223, 228, 229; picture page of, 227; Woman's Page in, resumed under the author, 222

Daily Mail Food Bureau organisation of, by the author, 113, 220; vast correspondence involved, 221-2; letters received at, on housekeeping, 115-16

Daily Mail Ideal Homes Exhibitions, 224

"Daisy Chain, The" (Yonge), 39

Dance rules in the '80's, 47, 58

Dancing, changed style of, 181

Dancing Bear, a, 6, 7

Davenport, a, 7

"David Garrick," in London, 55

Davidson, John, poem by, 104

Davies, Emily, and Girton College, and her book on this, 31, 151-2, 153

Davis, Jimmy, 66

Day of Judgment, the, 46

Deal, a hostile audience at, 194

Decolletage, 47

"De Profundis" (Wilde), 103

de Lauzun, the Misses, 55

Demi-mondaines, famous, 120

Derby, the, 271; a successful day in 1913, 160

Despard, Mrs., 153

Devereux, Mrs. Roy, 66

Devonport, 1st Viscount, Food Controller, 187, 193, 201; resignation of, 189; and Voluntary Economy Campaign, 190

Dewsbury, 69; life in rooms at, 71 *sqq.*; old furniture finds at, 124; a tea at, 79-80; farewell to, 86

Diabetes, insulin treatment for, 28

Dinners and dinner parties, bad service at, 78; during the season, 99-100; memories of, 272; precedence at, 77; at the Vicarage, 35

Director of Women's Service in the Ministry of Food, author's work as, 113

Dissenters, the, 38

Divorce, Queen Victoria's view on, 101

Dixon, Ella Hepworth, 104; hunt of, for coal, 180

Domestic departments, control of, by the author in various papers, knowledge derived, from, 113 *sqq.*

Domestic servant, a, bad manners of, 260

Domestic service, the flight from, 168, 239, 248 *sqq.*; training for, on both sides essential, 249-50

Domestic troubles, the author's now share of, 249

Domo d'Ossola, a tragedy at, 251

Doncaster, 69, 73

Doré, Gustave, picture by, 46

Douglas, Lord Alfred, 103

Dowson, Ernest, 104

Doward House, a Christmas party at, and a visit to, 17 *sqq.*; interior of, 18, 19; the storeroom at, 19

Dragon tree at Ecod, 91

Drawing lessons, 32

Drawing-room Teas, 109

Drawing-rooms of private houses, 7, 79-80

Drawing-rooms, Victorian, and after, 107 *sqq.*; memories of, 273

Dreams, some curious, 235 *sqq.*

Dress, decency in, or custom, 98-9 of Government messengers in Paris, 207

INDEX

Dress of Men in the '90's, 94-5; of sportsmen, 18; of villagers, 38

Dress and hair-dressing of Women and Girls; Author's at a first ball, 43, 48, at a coming-out ball, 57, Wedding, 68, when speaking on Food Economy, 202; Bathing, 99; Charwoman's daughter, post-War, 259; Confirmation, 14; Court, 107 *sqq.*, adapted for balls, 57; Dinner, 98; Evening, present day, 99; French sleeveless, in 1910, 98, street toilets, 117; Gardening, 18; German tourists', 119-20; of Grown up girls, 46-7; of Middle-aged and old ladies, 18, 34, 35; of Mothers' and girls' in the '90's, 100; of Munitionettes, trousers disliked, 175-6; in the '90's, 95-6; in 1914, 165; for Operation, 141; of Present-day girls', 268; remembered, of relations, Aunt and Mother, 6, 17; of schoolgirls', 30, for parties, 33, 36; of Villagers, 38; in War time, 98, 177-8, 223; of Women bicyclists, 62, 97; of Women skiers, 142-3

Dress of Schoolboys, 22

Drunkenness, 38; in relation to bad housing, 38, 83, 84, 243

Dudley, Georgiana, Countess of, 271

Duke, a, wish to marry, 50

Duke and Duchess, the, a call by, 9-10, 20

Dust, pre-tarmac, 96-7

Duty calls, the time for, 96

Duval, M. and his restaurants, 210

EARLHAM, 69

"Early Victorian England," section of, on "The Home Life of the People" (author), forthcoming, 254

Earning by girls, in the '80's, and '90's, oddness of, 62

Earning, author's capacity for, 67; reliance on justified, 123

Easter parties and Easter eggs, 36

Eaton Place, 36, the tragedy at, 251

Ecod, Teneriffe, a stay at, 89 *sqq.*

Educated class, the, social and domestic life of, changes in, 260 *sqq.*

Education, failures in, 158; in the '70's, 31-2; spread of, changes due to, 257-8; slight effect of, on refinement of conduct, 258 *sqq.*

Edward VII, Coronation of, 126-7; Court and Courts of, 109, splendour of, 149; reign of, 149, beauties of, 271-2; death and funeral of, 149-50

Egerton Terrace, 125

Eggs, waste of, 115

Elderly people, society of, enjoyment of, 59

Electric engineering career of C. S. Peel, 69, 88

Electric lighting, interior, 77, 88, 125

Ellen, the "general" and her infant, 86-7

Ellesmere House, a children's party at, 272

Eliot, George, books by, 39

Elsie, Lily, and the Merry Widow hat, 132

Emmott, Lady, the ideal Chairman, 240
Empire Music Hall, the promenade in, 118-19
"Encyclopædia Britannica," an article for, written in pain, 235
End of the world, the, 3
English gardens, beauty of, 146-7
English prisoners in German War Camps, letters from, 221
Enjoying one's self, 58
Entertaining in the '90's, 95 *sqq.*, present day, 262
Ernle, Lord, 182
Erskine, Lord Chancellor, 267
Étaples, hospital at, 207
Eve and the serpent, 46
Evening party, an, at Dewsbury, 80
Evening receptions, 100
Eye troubles, 32, 33, 48

"FACADE" (Theodora Benson), quoted, 137
Factory life, 75
Faidides, M., 213
Falling in love, 42-3, 58, 269
Family Prayers, 51
Farm Street, 16
Fast girls, 59
Fawcett, Dame Millicent, 128; leadership of, 152-3
Philippa, "above the Senior Wrangler," 128
Professor Henry, 128
Fear, present-day, effects of, 264
Feldafing, War conditions in, 237-8
Fellow-traveller, an ex-barmaid as, 81-2
Ferrers, Lady, and Food Economy Meetings, 173
Fetter Lane, being accosted in by men, 105-6
Fiction, good, 39, 65

Fish-wife dresses, 36
Firr, Tom, 35
Fleet, the, mobilisation of in 1914, 164, 167
Fleetway House, Lord Northcliffe's room at, 223
Flour, price of, rise of, in July, 1914, 164
Fly, the hired, 33
Folkestone, 56, 57, 171; a doubtful acquaintance at, 58-9
Food, allowances for, 115; and clothes in Paris, learning about, 118; giving of, to the poor, 21; mishaps with, 16-17; unattractive, troubles over, 25
Food Economy campaign, 155 *sqq.*; Children's Essays on, 201-2; the Director-General of, 187; meetings on, 173
Food panic in August, 1914, 165-6
Food prices, rise of, before and during the War, 113, 164, 165, 168, 178-9; lowering of, in 1933, 113
Fortune-tellers, War-time harvest of, 181
Fothergill, Jessie, 73
France, devastated region of, visited, 213 *sqq.*; a study of mass feeding in, 202, 205 *sqq.*
Francis Ferdinand, Archduke, and his wife, assassination of, 163
Frank, Bacon, 69
Frankau, Gilbert, 66
Julia, 66
Frederick, Empress, court of, 119
Freeling, Ethel, *see* Hornsby, Ethel
Lady, 53, 83
Sir Sandford and Lady and their family, three generations of friendship with, 63

INDEX

Fry, Elizabeth, 267
Fryatt, Captain, memorial to, 251
Fuel, rationing of, and prices of, 178, 179-80
Furniss, Harry, 66
Furze, Charles, 61

GAIETY-GIRL, a celebrated, 92
Gallard, Captain, 208
Gallieni, General, motor advance of, 213-214
Gambling, the ethics of, 161
Games at Wyesham, 11
Garda, Lake, beauty of, 271
"Garden of Allah, The" (Hichens), 66
Garden parties, memories of, 271, 273; Royal, 109-10
Garrett Anderson, Mrs. (née Elizabeth Garrett), 153
Gaskell, Mrs., book by, 39
George V, H.M., Courts and Garden Parties of, 109-10; a munitionette's concession to, 175-6; and Queen Mary, Coronation of, 150, 257; the Suffragettes and, 163
German ladies on the War, 238
German prisoners in France, 215
Gibraltar, 8
Girl friends, deaths of, by drowning, 29
Girlhood, difficulties of, 47; discomforts of, 39, 56, 58, Queen Victoria on, 58; occupations in, 49, 50, 51
Girls, fighting in the street, 259
Girls in Society, restrictions on, 95
Girls' schools, conversation at, 32
Girton College, 31, 152
Gisbrough, Lady, 248
Gladstone, W. E., 60, 73
Gloves, tight, 47
Glyn of Gaunts, Lady, 48

Glyn, Mrs. Elinor, famous book by, 67
Gold coins, withdrawal of, 169
Golf in the '90's, 97
God, teaching about to a child, 25
Goodwood, an incident at, 271
Gordon, Catherine, 185-6
Gordon, Lady Duff, 67
Gorringes', a visit to alone, the thrill of, 55
Governessing, 32
Grammar, ignorance of, 64-5
Grant-Duff, Sir E. Mountstuart, wife and family, 63
Great houses, post-War utilisation of, 247
Great Strike, the, of 1926, 252-3
"Green Carnation, The" (Hichens), 66
"Green Dragon," the, 22
Grenada, Denise Peel's wedding in, 253
Greville, Hon. Sidney, 100
Greycoat Gardens, a flat in, 86 sqq. 111; housekeeping in per head, 88
Grosvenor House, Women's Service in the Ministry of Food at, 183, 188
Grosvenor Place, 61, 79
Grundy, Mrs. and her origin, 99
Guardian, The, 35
Guests at the wrong house, 127-8

HAM, a visit to, 213, 216-17
Hamilton (Emma), Lady, a modern replica of, 120, 121
Hammond, J. L. and Barbara, books by, 254
Hannah, the parlourmaid, 28
Happy-go-lucky and small uncertain means, 86
Hardie ,Keir, and Women's suffrage, 150
Hardinge, Lady, a good customer, 131

INDEX

Hardy, Thomas, 105
Harmsworth newspapers, 187
Harrod's basement in air raids, 198
Hart Dyke, Canon Percival, 48
 Mabel, 48-9
 Maud, 49, 50
 Mrs. (Aunt Markey) and the censoring of novels, 49; and the crazy footman, 50-1
Hat-shop venture, the, 129-138; a novel about, 135
Hatfield, balls at, 35
Hat pins, 47
Hats, children's, 36; modern girl's, 268; when author was married, 68
Hay, Alys, 100
Hay-time and harvest, women's field-work at, 38
Hearth and Home, contributors to, 66; domestic department of, controlled by the author, 113; editorship of and of *Woman* and *Myra's Journal*, 129; letters received at, on House-keeping allowances, 115; writing for, 64, 105; article entitled "10s. a Head for House books," 111-12, Dress pages in, done by the author, 94
Hector, the roan, 17, 22
"Heir of Redcliffe, The" (Yonge), 39
Herbert, Winifred, 142, 162, 250
Hereford, Dick's school at, 14
Hichens, Robert, books by, 66
Highbrow attitude to other phases of life, 75-6
Higher education of women, the desire for, and the opposition thereto, 31-2, 125, 267

Hill, Octavia, and house property management, 240
Historical books, writing of, 253 *sqq.*
Hitler, Adolf, rise of, 257
Holloway Prison, Lady Constance Lytton in, 152; men waiting outside, type of, 155; visits to, 154-5, 156
Homburg, cures at, and habitués of, 100
"Home Life, The, of the People" (author) forthcoming, 254
Homes for "fallen" girls, 136
Honesty, low standard of, 258; teaching of, 16, 25
Hook Heath, a house at, 166
Hornsby, Ethel, the hat-shop venture with, 129 *sqq.*
Horses, author's love of, 19, 81; terror of at motors and bicycles, 97
Hoster, Mrs., 188
Hôtel de Paris, Monte Carlo, dinners at, 120; coffee at, 121
Houblon, Archer, 36
House of Commons, Women Members of, 265
House Decoration, Mrs. Talbot Coke's articles on, 62, 64; tastes in, 71-2, 79, 80
Household books at Brompton Square, 126-7; the bug-a-boo of, 28
Housekeeping at 10s. per head in the '90's and early 20th century, 112-13; war time advice on, in the *Dailies*, 177
House lighting by paraffin lamps, 37, later by electricity, 77, 88, 125
Housewives and house-keepers, honour due to, 116; work of, national value of, 244

INDEX

Housing, work on Committees on, and speaking on, 239, 240 *sqq.*

"How We Lived Then" (author), 253

Howard, Ebenezer, 239

Humane killer, the, 37

"Hundred Wonderful years, A" (author), 253

Hunt balls, then and now, 48, 77

Hurlingham, 97; pigeon shooting and polo at, 98

Huxley, Aldous, book by, 267

Huxley, Professor, and the educational ladder, 257

Hyde, Anne, wife of James II, 52

Hyman, Mademoiselle, 41-2

IDEALS, devotion to, of the unlikely, 268

Illegitimacy, 263

Illness, life struggle against, of the author, 271

Illnesses experienced, Angina, 255; Asthma, 32-3, Diabetes, 230 *sqq.*; Gall-stones, an operation and then Pneumonia, 138 *sqq.*; Influenza, 69; Measles, 58

Imported meat, the butchers' scorn of, 29

"In and Out" Club, dinners at, 272

Income Tax at 3d. in the £, 21, at 1s. in the £, 126; doubled, in war time, 180

Industrial Revolution, the, 75

Infant mortality, causes of, investigation into, 183

Infirmaries, "fallen" girls in, 136

Influenza, 69; the 1918 epidemic of, 223-4

Injustice, resentment at, 16

Innocence, and ignorance, 56

Insulin treatment and the price of sweetbreads, 28-9

Interesting people, memories of, 271

Intuitions, 124, 160-1

Investiture, an 273

Ireland, civil war in, fear of, 163, 164

Irish Conference, the, 163

Izzard, Percy, 220

"JACKANAPES" (Orr Ewing), 40

Jackson, Mrs. Huth (*née* Tiny Grant-Duff), 63

James, the rabbit, 22-3, 30

James II, relics of, 52

James, Sir Frederick and Lady, 253

Jane, the nurserymaid, 3

Jawker and the piglets, 37

Jazz, the coming of, 181

Jenkins, and his cough, 45

Jenny, the nursery dog, 9, 22-3, 270, 273; death of, 25

Jewish writers, 66

Jex-Blake, Sophia, 153

Johnson, Lionel, 104

Jolly, of Bath, Messrs., 16, 36

Jones, Kennedy, 187

Journalism and Journalists, Lord Northcliffe's love for, 226; successful, the element of surprise in, 227

Journalistic career, the author's, her special pride in, 234-5

Jubilee of 1897, 116

Jussy, 213, 217

KENSINGTON Palace Gardens, a garden supper in, 272-3

Kent coast towns, air raid damage at, 200

Kentish, Ethel, *see* Hornsby, Ethel

King's College for Women, 248

Kings and Princes, throneless, 257

Kinloss, Lady, 271

Kipling, Rudyard, 105

INDEX

Kitchen management, studies of, and writings on, 111-12

Kitchens, experimental, of the ministry of Food, 187; travelling, of the L.C.C., 185-6

K. J., *see* Jones, Kennedy

Knitting, in war time, 180

LABOUR PARTY, women of and public kitchens, 187

Labour Government, a, 256

Labour-saving appliances, changing views on, 243-4

Lady, The, domestic department of, controlled by author, 113; letters received at, on Household allowances, 115

Ladysmith, siege of, 105

Lambeth, attacks on Germans in, 171

Lancaster House, a reception at, 272

Lane, Dorothy, 52

Lane, Jane, and Charles II, 52, 53

Langtry, Mrs. (Lady de Bathe), 61, 121, 272

Lauder, Sir Harry, on Food Economy, 200

Laughter at horrible things, 102

Lawn tennis in a top hat, 36

Lawrence, Mr. and Mrs. Pethick, 153

Leader-writing, by the author, 227-8, 229

Lear's " Book of Nonsense," 40

Leeson, Dr., 69

Le Gallienne, Richard, 66, 104

"Leila on the Island" and "Leila at Home," 40

Leinster, the beautiful Duchess of, 271

"Leinster," the, torpedoing of, 198

Liberal house, a, a visit to, 73-4

"Life of Lord Carson" (Marjoribanks), 102

Lister, Lord, and antisepsis, 140

Liverpool Street Station, the Fryatt memorial at, 251

Living among richer folk, 59

Lloyd George, Rt. Hon. David, and the impoverishment of the land-owners, 114; and the munition workers, 174; quarrel of Lord Northcliffe with, 231; as Speaker, 201

Local Chairmen, M.P.'s and others and the author's speeches on Food Economy, 192 *sqq.*

Loevre, 214

London, compensations of, 146; darkness in, in 1914, 179; dwellings in, of the educated classes, changes in, 261; fog and frost in, 92-3; in the 'nineties, the parade in, of vice, 105 *sqq*; public house crowds of, manners of, 258; sightseeing and theatre-going in, 54-5; slum property in, visits to, 240 *sqq.*

London County Council, travelling kitchen of, 185-6

London Museum, the, 272

L. & S.W. Railway, now S.R., 204

Loving and being loved, in childhood, 270

Lowe, Miss, editress of *The Queen Newspaper*, 63-4

Lubbock, Sir John (later 1st Baron Avebury), 53

Lucile, Madame (Mrs. Wallace), now Lady Duff Gordon, 67

Lucy, the masseuse, tragedy of, 147-8

INDEX

Luncheon parties, women's, memories of, 272

"Lusitania" the, sinking of, London riots after, 170-1

Luxury foods, fall in price of, in 1914, 178-9

Lying, 25, 26

Lyons, Messrs., Catering of, for a Royal Garden Party, 110; providers of inexpensive meals, 212-13

Lytton, Lady Constance, 152

MACDONALD, Rt. Hon. J. Ramsay, rise of, 256-7

McLaren, Sir Charles, 151

MacNair, Mrs., 172, 173

Madame Tussaud's, a visit to, 54

Magisterial duties, preparation for, 154

"Maiden Tribute, The, of Modern Babylon" (Stead), results of, 145

Manchester, musical life of, 53

Manchester School of Thought, the revolt against, 104

Manie, the Spanish nurse, 3, 8

Manly, Kate, 205, 213

Manners of the masses, 258, 260

Marianne, Aunt, *see* Scobell, Mrs. Edwin

Marie, Queen of Roumania, 127

Marienbad, King Edward VII at, 100

Marjoribanks, E., books by, 102, 104; death of, 104

Market Drayton, 81

Markey, Aunt, *see* Hart Dyke, Mrs.

Marlowe, Thomas, 223, 227, 228, 229

Marne, Battle of the, 214

Marseilles, 145, 146

Marshall Hall, Sir Edward, *Life* of (Marjoribanks), 104

Mary, H. M. the Queen, 63, 187; Court dress worn by, 110

Maugham, W. Somerset, 104

Maurois, André, books by, 158

May, Lady, O.B.E., 184

May, Sir George, 184

Means, restricted, tiresomeness of, 11, 24, 59, 61, 85, 103, 147-8 *et alibi*

Meaux, 213

Melchett, Violet, Lady, 173

Men, accosting women, 105-6

Men and women, past and present social relations of, 265

Mental and spiritual equipment in childhood, 25

Mentone, in early 1914, 162

Menus, notes on, 101

Meredith, George, 105

Mérode, Cléo de, 120

Midwifery, Carli's experiences in, 83-4

Mill on the Floss, The (George Eliot), 39

Milliners' work-girls, life and wages of, 132 *sqq.*

Miners, outdoor baths of, 75

Mining accidents, 75

Ministry of Commerce, Paris, a call at, 207-8

Ministry of Food, work at, 182 *sqq.*; furnishing the Women's Service branch; 154; resignation from, 218, 219

Ministry of Information, Lord Northcliffe at, 218

Ministry of Pensions, some sample letters received at, 189

Ministry of Reconstruction, Committees of, 239; help of, 245

Ministry of Shipping, 204

"Mrs. Barnett, Robes" (author), 135

"Mrs. Jones, A" (author), 135

287

INDEX

Modesty, some considerations on, 25, 98-9

Mond, Lady (Violet, Lady Melchett), 173

Monmouth, 11

Monmouth Bridge, the shop by, 15-16

Monmouthshire Volunteers, the, 5, 15

Montagu of Beaulieu, Lady (*née* Crake), 63

Monte Carlo, past and present, 119 *sqq.*, visits to, and memories of, 121-2, 146, 160-1, 234, 273; Casino of, Cercle Privé of, 119; a little adventure at, 121-2

Monthly nurse, an inefficient, 111

Montpelier Place, 125

Moore, George, 66

Moratorium, the, 168

Morley of Blackburn, Viscount, resignation of, in 1914, 167

Morton, Thomas, and Mrs. Grundy, 99

Morning Post, 160th birthday of, "Pageant of Women" written for, by the author, 255

Mothers, intelligent, desirability of, 266

Motor car, the cheap, changes due to, 262

Motoring, excitements of, and attire for, 96-7

Mourning, store of, for the poor, 19

Mozart, W. A., 53

Murder, a, and a hanging, 55

Music halls, speaking in, 200; staple jokes at, 102

Music lessons, 32-3

Mussolini, Benito, rise of, 257

Myra's Journal, 64; author's position on, 129

NAINTRE, LUIGI, on post-War night life of Berlin, 118

Nakedness and naughtiness, 25, 98-9

Napoleon I, bust of, 223

Napoleon III at Ham, 216

National War Savings Association, speaking for, 173

"Naughty 'nineties," the, 104 *sqq.*

Navvy, a, in the soup kitchen, 28

Needlework panels, a "find" of, 124-5

Neilson, Julia, 272

Newcastle, an adverse Chairman at, 199

Newgate Fringe, the 5

Newlands, a garden party at, 271

Newnham College, 31

Newspaper knowledge of the masses, 257

New York World, the "Lusitania" cartoon in, 171

Night clubs, 181

Night life in Paris and Berlin, 118

"1920 Husband Hunt, The," a tactless article, 228-9

"Ninety-nine" as a spell, 22

"Nippies" at a Royal Garden Party, 110

Norland Nurses, 126

Norrie, Mrs., 248

Northcliffe, Viscount, the author's experiences with and his generosity, 218, 220, 221, 222-3, 224, 230, 234 *sqq.*; failing health of, 231; a last sight of, 231; a six weeks' holiday given by, to the author, 230, 234

Northcliffe, Viscountess, 203

Norton, Hon. Mrs. (*née* Caroline Sheridan), 153

Noses, powdering of, 46

Notting Dale, "life" in, 83-4

Novel-reading, supervision of, in girlhood, 39, 49

INDEX

Novels by the present author, 234, 253; obtaining local colour for, 135 *sqq.*

Noyon, 213, 216

Nurse and Paul, 8-9

Nurses, a foolish, 139, an inefficient, 111

Nussbaum, Professor, and Lister's technique, 140

"OBSERVER," the, help from, 254

Odhams, Messrs., the horrors at, in an air raid, 198

Old age, compensations of, 146; satisfaction with, 269-70

Old Age Pensions, 258

Old Bailey, the, disgraceful scenes outside, 103

Old furniture, collecting of, 123; a real find, 123-4

Omnibus tops, unused by good-class women, 95

Omnibuses non-existent in Twickenham, 62; use of by rich folk, 51

Orleans restaurant, a dinner at, 96

Ormiston Chant, Mrs., and the "Empire" promenade, 128

Orotava, 89

Orr Ewing, Mrs., 40

Outdoor speaking, 200

Oxford University, 33

PAGE, Walter Hines, and Mrs. Page, a tea with, 234, book by the former, *ib.*

"Pageant of Women" (author), occasion for which written, 255

Pall Mall Gazette, the, and the Age of Consent, 145

Pankhurst, Christabel, 152
  Mrs., 150, 152
  Sylvia, 152

Panshanger, balls at, 35

Paper currency, introduction of, 169

Parental beliefs, problem of, 46

Paris, a first visit to, 117; night life in, 118; the taxi-drivers of, 213; in War time, 205, 206, 207, a round tour from, into the devastated areas, 213, 217

Paris model houses, and small customers, 132

Parish Nurse, the, 38

Park, the, a drive in, 54-5, in the season, 95-6

Parkinson, Sir Thomas, 138, 139, 141

Parry, Squire, 35

Parties, enjoyment of, 271-2

Partridge, Sir Bernard, 272

Party-giving, informal, 262

Patten-wearing, 36

Patmore Fair, the end of, 37-8

Peckham Pioneer Health Centre, work of, 245 *sqq.*

Peel, Amelia (Emmie), 54, 56, 57, 58; marriage of, 59

Author's baby, death of, 129;

Aunts, the, and the author's reading, 39, 49

Captain William, 54, 55, 56, 123

Cecilia (Mrs. Harry Straker), 116, 117, 163, 237, 252; birth of, 111; marriage of, 233; presentation of, at the first post-War Royal Garden Party, 109; return of from Paris in 1914, 166; warwork and play of, and escapes during air raids, 169, 176, 197-8, 225, 272

Charles S., 43, 68, 72, 73, 80, 88, 92, 93, 94, 111, 118, 124, 141, 149, 160, 220, 225, 245; as a "best friend," 270; the author

INDEX

Peel, Charles S. *cont.*
  called back by, after an operation, 141; engagement to, 63, prospects of, 67; marriage of, 69, and the shoe-horn incident, 70, 254; an expert skier, 142; illness of, 80; an intuition of, 163; serious illness of, and change of occupation after, 254; as Special Constable, 171, 195, canteen work of, 191; and sport, 176-7; on never thinking of religion, 46
Charlotte (Aunt), 22, 43 *sqq.*, 72, 270; housekeeping by, 19; visits of, 17, 18; death of, 56
Denise (Mrs. P. D. P. Welman), 220, 237; Armistice Day memory of, 169; balls of, 272; birth of, 129, marriage of, 253; presentation of, 110
Marianne (Aunt), *see* Scobell, Mrs. Edwin
Mrs. F. W. (*née* Wake Walker), (mother-in-law), 68, 69, death of, 85
Rev. Francis William (father-in-law), 46, 69; death of, 85
Robert (grandfather), 12
Sir Robert, the second, 53
Susanna (Aunt), 53, 56, 57, 58-9; legacy from, 123; romance of, 54-5
Penny Readings, 38
People under 25, physical and mental conditions of, 246
Pernicious anæmia, liver for, 28
Peroxide beauty, a, 81-2
Perquisites, 113, 115
Personal appearance, dawn of interest in, 46-7
Phillips, Dr. Marion, 225

Phillpotts, Eden, 66
Phyllis, the pony, 24, 81
Physical union and mental congruity, two views on, 263, 264
Pig-killing, horrors of, 37, 72-3, 80
Pigeon shooting, at Hurlingham, 98, at Monte Carlo, 121
Plague, Dick's scare of, 12
Pless, Princess (*née* Cornwallis West), 271
Pneumonia, after an operation, 142; post-influenzal, 224
Poetry, learning of by heart, 40-1
Poker playing, 159
Police, the, and the unfortunates, 106, 107
Politics, lack of interest in, 73
Poor, the respectable, relieving and visiting of, 19-20
"Poor Teddy" (author), 62
Porridge, a recipe for, a French request for, 211
Portsmouth, an anxious mayor at, 194
Pougy, Liane de, 120
Poultry food, an order *re*, 188
Precedent, the lag in improvement due to, 266, 267
Presentations at Court, 107 *sqq.*
Price-fixing of the Cabinet Committee on Food Supplies, 178
Prison Reform, interest in, 153
Prison treatment of Suffragettes, 152, 154
Private Concerts, 100
Private Hansoms, and their Jehus, 95
Profiteering, 189
Prostitution, 264
Public amenities, present-day, 258
Public Baths, 258
Public Libraries, 258

Punch, on imported meat, 29; on the new poor and the new rich, 177

Queen Newspaper The, author's writing for, 63, and Household Editorship of, 113, 160, 221, 234; articles in, on War-time responsibilities of Women, 177, and on War Housekeeping, economical, 178, Carli's illustrations in, 62; letters received at, on Household allowances, 115; prestige of, 64

Questions, elder folks' dislike of, 26

RANELAGH, 97, 98

Rationing, 202, compulsory, 218

"Red" party, a, in Soho, 273

Reeves, Mrs. Pember, 183, 201, 228; book by, 184; loss of her only son, 203

Reform, preventive, interest in, 155

Reiss, Captain Richard, 239-40

Religious beliefs and ideas at various ages, 7, 25-6, 45-6, 74

Religious teaching, 25

Renault, Messrs., works of, and restaurant at, 210 *sqq.*

Respectability, Victorian, the two sides of, 99

Restlessness, present-day, causes of, 262, 264

Rew, Sir Henry, 182

Rhondda, Viscount, as Food Controller, 201, 218, 219

Rich folk, domestic extravagance of and its bad effects, 113 *sqq.*, economies of, 60-1 luxurious equipment of their houses, 77-8

Ridge, W. Pett, 104

"Right people," the, 101

Ritz, the, balls at, 272

Riviera, the, a first visit to, 119

Roberts, Arthur, classification by, of women, 81

Roberts, Mrs. Llewellyn, 225

Robeson, Paul, 273

Romanticist period, the, 104

Room, a, of one's own, joys and terrors of, 23-4

"Rose and the Ring, The" (Thackeray), 40

"Round About a Pound a Week" (Reeves), 184

Row, the, in the morning, 95

Roxburgh, J. F., headmaster of Stowe, 248

Royal Academy, the, 61; a learned gathering at, 272

Royal Garden Parties, memories of, 273

Royal York Terrace, Clifton, 2

Running away, 14 *sqq.*

Russia, 257; as a cheering topic, 139

ST. COLUMBA'S, Pont Street, canteen at, for Scottish soldiers, 191

St. James's Square, Lady Astor's parties in, 272

St. Michael's Grove, reputation of, 125

St. Paul's, Knightsbridge, author's marriage at, 69

St. Raphael, visited, 234

Salisbury, 3rd Marquess of, and divorced men, 101; villa of, 119

Sally, presence of mind of, 108

Samuel, Sir Herbert, as Chairman, 200

"Sandford and Merton," 40

Santa Cruz, Teneriffe, 89; a stay at, 91-2

Sarajevo, the assassination at, of the Archduke Francis Ferdinand, 163

Savoy Hotel, dinners at, 272

School epidemics, and dormitory accommodation, 248

Schools for Girls, a search for, 157, a good modern one in London, 157-8

Scobell, Mrs. Edwin (Aunt Marianne), and her husband, 18, 19, 20, 21, 22, 43 *sqq.*, 56, 81

Scott, Benjamin, and the Age of Consent, 145

Sea serpent, the, 12

Seal, a, lost and found, 12-13

Seaman, thrice torpedoed, a, 202

Second helpings, 31

Self-control, preferable to self-repression, 270

Senlis, 213, 214

Senn, Herman, 205

Serbia, Austrian declaration of war on, 164

Servants, at Clifton, 28; at Doward House, 28; at the Vicarage, 36, 37; at Wyesham, 8-9, *see also* Domestic Service

Sexual morality, breakdown of, 181; changed standard of, 263-4

Sexual perversion, 102

Shaw, G. B., 105

Shepherd, Rev. "Dick" on the horrible things at which people laugh, 102

Shoes, replacing boots for women, 177

Shooting, the author menaced with, 250

Shorncliffe Camp, coming-out ball at, 57-8

Shyness, manner resulting from, 276

Sickness and neighbourly assistance, 38

Sickness Insurance, 258

Silk stocking craze, the, 177

Silver-gilt plate, drawbacks of, 59, 60

Simon, Rt. Hon. Sir John, resignation of, in 1914, 167

Sitting-room, a, in the '80's, 49

Sleeveless dresses, sensation caused by, 98

Slimming, 100

Smartness, aspiration to, 95

Smith, Mr., as dance partner and after, 44, 45

Snow, Mrs., the cook, 28

Social duties in the '90's, 101

Social services and the working classes, 258

Society in the '90's, 94 *sqq.*

Society for the Prevention of Cruelty to Animals, the, 267

Society for the Protection of Children (N.S.P.C.C.), 267

Soho dress shops, 177

Soldiers' and Sailors' wives, a club for, in Lambeth, 170 *sqq.*

Soup, at midday, not liked by the French, 211

Soup kitchen, running a, 28

Southampton Dockyard, wretched conditions in, 204

Speaker's House, a party at, 272

Speaking on Food Economy, 190 *sqq.*, summary of work thus done, 202-3

"Speed the Plough" (Morton), source of Mrs. Grundy, 99

Sport and cruelty, 76

Sporting Club, Monte Carlo, 119

Stag and Mantle, Messrs., 109

Stanley, Miss Alma, 92

Stays, stiff, 47; a new style in, 67

INDEX

Stead, W. T., and "The Maiden Tribute of Modern Babylon," 145

Steevens, G. W., War Correspondent, widow of, the Beardsley group gathered together by, 105

"Story, The, of a Short Life" (Orr Ewing), 40

Stewart, Sir Charles, 173

Storm at sea, a, 89

Stowe Palace, a garden party at, 271; turning of into a public school, author's membership of the Ladies' Committee on, 247, 248

Strachey, Lytton, books by, 158

Strachey, Ray, book by, 31, 154

Straker, Major Harry, 237; marriage of, to Cecilia Peel, 233

"Stream, The, of Time" (author and her husband), 254; illness during proof-correction, 255

"Struwelpeter," 40

Submarine menace, the, 189, 202

Suffragettes the, and their doings, 150 *sqq.*, 163

Sunday book, a hated, 7, 40

Sunday entertaining, 95

Sunday suppers, 96

Sunday School class of boys, a, 51-2

Sunday Times, the, help from, 254

Surgeon's Hall, Edinburgh, riot at, against medical women, 153

Switzerland, winter holidays in, 142-3, 162, 250

Symons, Arthur, 104

TABLE CENTRES, 60

Tamworth, Viscount, 225

Tandem-driving, 21

Tea, country house, 78; at Dewsbury, 79-80

Tea-visiting, 98

Teachers, Socialist, 201

Teasing, ill-borne, 29

Teck, H.R.H. the Duchess of, 63

Teck, Princess May of, 63, 100, *see also* Mary, H.M. the Queen

Telephones, in the '90's, 98; once rare, 125

Temperance Meetings, 50

Temple, Hope, 66

Temporary sexual unions, the newer attitude to, 263-4

"10s. a week for House books," articles on, 111-12

Teneriffe, a voyage to and life in, 88 *sqq.*

Terry, Dame Ellen, 131

Theatres, speaking in, 200

Thomas, Rt. Hon. J. H., rise of, 257

"Three Figures of Mourning" (author), 62

Threlfall, Miss (Mrs. Harold Smith), 234

Tiara, the, 77

Times, The, fashion drawings in, Lord Northcliffe on, 226; offices of, Lord Northcliffe's room at, 222, 226; restricted to elders in the '80's, 35

Tipping the housemaid, 60

Tommy Atkins in France, 207

"Tony Sant" (author), 135, 234

Torquay, 56; a large meeting at, 199

Trade, attitude to, of the squirearchy, 76

Trafalgar Square on Armistice night, 224

Transport facilities, effects of, on the masses, 257, 258

Trevor, Lady, a tip from, 60

ul

INDEX

Trotter, a, 131

Trousseau, the author's, "undies" in, 68

Tube Stations, sheltering in, from air raids, 195, 198-9

Tuckers, 36

Tulips, an atrocity concerning, 8

Turtles, costly, 114-15

"Twelve Miles from a Shop" as a ready-made subject, 66

12s. a week *per* head for food and chance guests, 126

Twickenham, a move to, 61

Tyneside munition works and public houses, speaking in, 199-200

Tzigane band a, and its leader's elopement, 117-18

UNEMPLOYMENT in the '70's, 28; the post-War blight of, 258

Unemployment Benefit, 258

Underworld the, ignoring of, and ignorance of, 101-2

"Undies," diaphanous and other, 67, 68; in the '80's, 46

"Unfortunates," 264, 265; contempt felt for, and danger from, 106-7; display grounds of, 105; a rescue Sister on, 135-6

United Workers, the, speaking for, 173

University, the ladder to, 257

Unmarried mothers, 9, 263

"Unpleasantness," 101, 106

VAUGHAN, Father Bernard, S.J., 16

Vauxhall, Furze's Studio at, 61

Venereal disease, 102

Venice, beauty of, 250, 271

Verses, remembered, 40-1

Vigo Bay, 88, 89

Victoria, Queen, 99; and divorce, 101; at a Drawing-room, 109; death of, 150; on her girlhood, 58; on the "truly respectable Court" of Prussia, 119

Victoria Square, a visit to, 53, 54, 55, 56

Victorian convention, unmasking of, 105

Villa Miramar, Teneriffe, 88

Vincent, Lady Helen (Lady D'Abernon), beauty of, 271

"Virtue," modesty, and the nude, 25, 98-9

"Visiting," and "taking things" to the poor, 35

"Visits of Elizabeth, The" (Elinor Glyn), 67

Voluntary Economy Campaign, a suggested, 190

WAGE-EARNERS, physical disabilities of, 246

Wages, average pre-War, of a working man, 186; of servants in author's childhood, 8

Waists, position of, in 1914, 177; small, 68, 95

Wales, Prince of (*see also* Edward VII), 55, 96

Wales, Princess of (Queen Alexandra), pigeon-shooting at Hurlingham stopped by, 98; waiting to see, in the Park, 55, 95

Wake Walker, Vice-Admiral Sir Baldwin, Bart., R.N., 68, 69, 125

Walworth Public Library, and the L.C.C. travelling kitchen, 186

War, the, premonitions of, and preliminaries to, 162 *sqq.*;

INDEX

War the, *cont.*
   declaration of, 167; rise in,
      of Food prices, 113, 164,
      165, 168, 178-9
War activities of the author, 167,
   170 *sqq.*
"War baby," the, 263
War cookery recipes, demand
   for, 186
War marriages, 181
War office, the, 204
War Taxation and the great Land-
   owners, 114
Wartime entertaining, 177
War years, life during, book on,
   by the author, 253-4
"Wares of Autolicus" (Roy
   Devereux), 66
Warwick, Frances, Countess of,
   beauty of, 271-2; on ducal,
   domestic extravagance,
   114-15
Waste, attempts to check, 185;
   pre-War, of Bread, 187
Wedding outfit, collecting of,
   67-8
Week-ending, luggage formerly
   needed for, 96; spread
   of, 149
Weigall, Sir Archibald, 218
Wells, H. G., 105
Welman, Patrick D. Pole, mar-
   riage of, to Denise
   Peel, 253
Welsh pony, the, 19, 81
Welwyn Garden City, 239
West, Miss Cornwallis, later Prin-
   cess Pless, 271
Westminster, Constance, Duchess
   of, 271
Westminster Abbey, a visit to, 54
Westminster Aquarium, a visit
   to, 55
Westminster Gazette, The, 66
Wethered, Colonel and Mrs.
   Owen (Alice), 88

Wheeler, Mrs. Luke, 272
"White Cargo," cruel laughter
   at, 102
Widow's Pensions, 258
Wijey, Mrs. Mabel, 221
Wilberforce, William, 267
Wild oats, sowing of, 106
Wilde, Oscar, downfall of, how
   brought about, 103; trial
   of, and last days of,
   102 *sqq.*
Wilkie, Sir David, R.A., 69
William II, ex-Kaiser, 171, 215;
   at Cowes, 271
Wilson, Muriel, 121
Wilson, F.-M. Sir Henry, the
   murder of, 251-2
Wilton Place, marriage from, 69
Window-boxes, 98
Wintour, Ulick, 205, 225
Wireless, 258
Wives and Daughters (Gaskell), 39
Wollstonecroft, Mary, 153
Woman, a prize offered by, won
   by the author, and the
   results, 62, 64-5, author's
   editorship of, 129
Women in coal-mining work, 75;
   as "irresponsible persons,"
   265-6; political status of
   rise of, 265, 266; type of,
   understood by the *Daily
   Mail* staff, 227; the Vic-
   torian Englishman's cate-
   gories of, 265; working
   with, 184
Women Doctors, the pioneers,
   153
Women Police, 228
Women prisoners in Holloway
   Gaol, 152, 154, 155
Women workers for Higher
   Education and for the
   Franchise, unknown to the
   present generation of
   girls, 153

INDEX

Women's Pioneer Housing, Ltd., *raison d'être* of, and success, 244-5

Women's Service, at the Food Ministry, 183 *sqq.*

Women's Social and Political Union, the, 150

Women's Suffrage, author's interest in, 128, 143; basis of the objection to, 267; deputation on, to the Prime Minister, 151; last debate on, in the Lord's, 265; resolution on, in the Commons, fracas over, 150-1; strong feeling roused by, 128; struggle for, at last successful, 266; women pioneers of, 150 *sqq.*

Women's War Associations catering for, in the *Daily Mail*, 227-8; represented at a Royal Garden Party, 109; uniforms of, 177

Woodroffe, Mr. and Mrs., 63

Work as anodyne, 235

Working classes, anxieties of, 85, improved position of, 258, increased earnings of those in work, 190; the term "working class" now a misnomer, 260-1

Working women, the, difficulties of, 229

Writing for the Press, 62, 94, *see also Daily Mail*, etc.

Wye, river, 3, in flood, 12

Wyesham, 4, 24, 273; the babies at, 3, 4, 10, 11, 14; the bears' caverns in, 6-7; an "earthquake" at, 4-5; the garden at, 8; interior of and life at, 6 *sqq.*

YELLOW BOOK period, the, 104, 105

Yonge, C. M., books by, 39-40

York House, Twickenham, 63

Young, G. M., as editor, 254

Young people, post-War morals of, 263-4, and hardness of, 268

Zoo, the, visit to, 54

Lightning Source UK Ltd.
Milton Keynes UK
UKOW051823170613

212391UK00001B/195/P